RED

RED

A BIOGRAPHY OF RED SMITH

IRA BERKOW

McGraw-Hill Book Company

New York   St. Louis   San Francisco
Toronto   Hamburg   Mexico

For Dolly

Reprinted by arrangement with Times Books, a division of Random
House, Inc.

First McGraw-Hill Paperback edition, 1987.

1 2 3 4 5 6 7 8 9 A R G A R G 8 7

ISBN 0-07-004852-5

LIBRARY OF CONGRESS CATALOGING-IN-PUBLICATION DATA

Berkow, Ira.
  Red: a biography of Red Smith.
  Bibliography: p.
  Includes index.
  1. Smith, Red, 1905-1982. 2. Sportwriters—
  United States—Biography. I. Title.
[GV742.42.S54B46 1987]   070.4′49796′0924 [B]   87-38
ISBN 0-07-004852-5 (pbk.)

PERMISSIONS ACKNOWLEDGMENTS

ACKNOWLEDGMENTS

To draw up a complete list and credit the hundreds of people who were helpful in the making of this book would be a formidable if not fruitless task. Somewhere along the line some who shouldn't be left out might accidentally be left out, and though they would probably understand, it would make the author unhappy. Regardless, forthwith is the list, as incomplete as it may be:

In particular, I want to give heartfelt thanks to Red Smith's immediate family: his wife, Phyllis, his daughter, Kit Halloran, and his son, Terry Smith. They gave me as much cooperation—and it was considerable—as I needed. Besides interviews, they were also generous with memorabilia and letters.

I am also indebted in this regard to Red Smith's niece Georgia Dullea and his nephew Pat Smith, as well as to his stepchildren, Jenifer Weiss, Karen Weiss, Kim Weiss, Peter Weiss, and Robin Weiss.

I want to thank Jonathan Segal, the editor of this book and the source of the idea for it. His guidance and insights were invaluable. And I want to extend my appreciation to his talented associate Ruth Fecych.

At *The New York Times,* those who allowed me much-needed time and provided much-needed support include Abe Rosenthal, Arthur Gelb, James Greenfield, and of course, the man with whom I work most closely, Joe Vecchione.

For help well beyond the call of any conceivable duty, for his reading of the manuscript in its various stages, and for his suggestions for its improvement, I want to offer deep appreciation to Larry Klein.

For their careful reading and astute comments on the final manuscript, I extend special thank-yous to Bill Brink, Richard Close, David Fox, George Kaplan, Jim Kaplan, and Jay Lovinger.

For extensive interviews, sometimes repeated, I want to offer gratitude to Dave Anderson, Tom Callahan, Harold Claassen, John Dell, Norbert Engels, Joe Goldstein, W. C. Heinz, Lawrence Hennessey, Jerry Izenberg, Roger Kahn, Al Laney, Robert Lipsyte, Sam Muchnick, Barney Nagler, Arthur Pincus, Shirley Povich, Marion Roach, Harold Rosenthal, Irving Rudd, Fred Russell, Dick Schaap, Le Anne Schreiber, Fern Turkowitz, and Larry Servais.

I want to thank Samantha Stevenson, who was kind enough to share with me the transcriptions of her lengthy taped interviews with Red Smith.

I also want to thank others who were important in providing background information and various leads on Red Smith: Seth Abraham, Dorothy Abramson, Wayne Ambler, Roger Angell, Ray Arcel, Pete Axthelm, Bob Balfe, Red Barber, Sylvan Barnett, Phil Berger, Jacques Barzun, Burton Benjamin, Stu Black, Jim Brady, Bill Brashler, Jimmy Breslin, Sam Brightman, Bob Broeg, Bob Burnes, Dave Camerer, Bob Cooke, Howard Cosell, Cliff Cristl, Jim Crowley, Betty Daley, Robert Daley, Paul Derringer, Joe DiMaggio, Roger Donoghue, John Duxbury, Vincent Engels, Joe Falls, Edward Fischer, Goodrich Gamble, Ike Gellis, Bob Goldsholl, Frank Graham, Jr., Rocky Graziano, Jane Gross, Colleen Halloran, David Halloran, Mary Catherine Halloran, Michael Halloran, Margaret Halloran, Betty Heinz, Porter Henry, Ed Hogan, John Horn, Jerome Holtzman, Donald Honig, George F. Howlett, Jim Kaplan, Isaac Kleinerman, Richard Kluger, Margaret Kohler, Jim Kohn, Leonard Koppett, Alfred Knopf, Jr., Seymour Krim, Lloyd Larson, Bud Leavitt, Allen Lewis, Wilda Lewis, Skipper Lofting, Melissa Ludtke, Mike Lupica, Pat Lynch, Harry Markson, Mike Marshall, William J. Marshall, Morris McLemore, Curtis MacDougall, Lawrie Mifflin, Marvin Miller, David Moore, Art Morrow, Wally Moses, Pat Murphy, Bill Nack, Skeeter Newsome, Mark Nevils, Shad Northshield, Murray Olderman, Inar T. (Ollie) Olson, Sandy Padwe, Ernest Paolino, Muzz Patrick, Ted Ravinett, James Reston, Arthur Riback, Margaret Roach, Pat Ryan, Bus Saidt, Robert Schmuhl, John G. Scott, Tom Seaver, Herbert L. Shultz, Jim Schwartz, Wilfrid Sheed, Morrie Siegel, Seymour Siwoff, Chris Smith, Daisy Smith, Harold Smith, Elizabeth Smith, George Steinbrenner, John Stravinsky, Tom Stritch, Anne Tedman, Vernon Tietjen, Jim Toomey, Bill Veeck, George Vecsey, Joe Wershba, Harvey Wertz, Ted Williams, Dick Young, and Vic Ziegel.

For technical assistance, I want to thank Howard Angione, the electronic sage of *The New York Times*. I also offer gratitude to Leslie Chambliss, Esther Fein, Michael Jensen, Jr., Steve Jesselli, Marc Myers, and Sheila Yablon.

I also received extensive help from the main libraries of Chicago, Green Bay, Milwaukee, New York City, Philadelphia, and St. Louis, from the newspaper annex of the New York City Public Library and the Queens Borough Public Library. I want to thank for their help the Baseball Hall of Fame, the Pro Football Hall of Fame, and the Famous Writers School. Also of considerable aid were the morgue libraries of the *Chicago Sun-Times, The New York Times,* and the *St. Louis Post-Dispatch.*

FOREWORD

On Friday afternoon, January 15, 1982, I was home in Manhattan in front of my typewriter having just completed my sports column for *The New York Times* when the phone rang. The caller was Joe Vecchione, sports editor of *The Times*.

"Got bad news," Joe said. "Red died. . . . Can you come in and write the obit?"

"Yes," I said. "Of course."

It was about three-thirty and I would have to complete the obituary no later than 6:30 P.M., the deadline for copy. I usually write at home, but Vecchione thought that since all of Red's columns for *The Times* were in the morgue there, I could make use of them.

I gathered some of Smith's clips that I had saved over the years, and a couple of his books, which were bound collections of his best columns, and left my apartment. I searched for a cab, found one, and, as it jounced over potholes across town on that cold but sunny winter day, I thought of Smith.

His death at age seventy-six, due to kidney complications and congestive heart failure, came as a shock to me, though not a surprise. He had become increasingly ill over the previous two years. In the previous six months, *The Times* had more and more frequently been delivered without the 900-word column headed "Sports of the Times/Red Smith" brightening a corner of the sports section. Though he tried desperately, Red was often physically unable to write his assigned four columns a week.

When he died, he was in his fifty-fifth year as a newspaperman. He began with the *Milwaukee Sentinel* in 1927, a month or so after Lindbergh made his solo flight across the Atlantic. Smith became as distinctive in his profession as Lindbergh had in his. Just as Lindbergh proved more than just a stunt pilot, Smith proved more than just a sportswriter. He was one of the best writers in the country, newspaper or otherwise. His sports column invariably reflected his graceful use of language, his deft insights, and his humor—sometimes dry, sometimes ironical, sometimes even a bit slapstick—and there was always, too, his sense of humanity. He was syndicated with the *New York Herald Tribune* from 1945 through 1966 when the paper folded, then was carried by the Publishers-Hall Newspaper Syndicate to 100 newspapers across the country and abroad, with a circulation of some twenty million, and from 1971 until his death was with *The Times.* He was the most widely read sports columnist of his time. And one of the most influential.

Respected sportswriters of today, among them Pete Axthelm, Frank Deford and David Kindred, credit Smith with being an important role model for them. And Smith certainly made a major difference in my life.

I remember a column he wrote when I was a freshman at the University of Illinois in Chicago in 1958. I read the piece in the *Chicago Sun-Times,* which carried him regularly. Smith described the middleweight championship fight between Carmen Basilio, the title holder, and Sugar Ray Robinson, who succeeded in regaining the title. Basilio's eye had closed from the repeated pounding by Robinson, and late in the fight Smith described Basilio: "It was an odd and unforgettable picture—a gaunt, hatchet-faced fighting man wading everlastingly forward to meet a fate which he accepted with a curiously fixed expression of sleepiness. Seen from the left side with the eye more tightly closed than a dreamer's, he looked like a somnambulist fighting with some primeval instinct. . . ."

I was moved by Basilio's pluck, as portrayed by Smith. I had not read much of Smith before this—I hadn't read much of anything in high school before this—and I didn't know anything about him, but I began looking regularly for his column. I delighted in his wide range of subject and approach.

He placed people and events into perspective. He noted, with his typical irreverence toward sports, that the Yale Bowl "was just a mite squalid for a shrine." The brushback pitch in baseball, coming after two strikes, was, Smith wrote, in "the classic pattern, as rigidly formalized as the minuet." When Everett Case, a head basketball coach at North Carolina State, blamed players from the North for the college basketball scandals, Smith reminded that Southern colleges, too, had been giving players illegal financial help and allowing them to attend phony classes. Case, wrote Smith, "got integrity confused with geography."

He saw through pomposity and pricked it. He felt for the underdogs or underclass in sports, and wrote about their plight with concern: the stable swipes, the blacks, the ball players bound by the pernicious reserve clause.

There were great characters to be met in the world of Red Smith, such as the horse trainer Max Hirsch: "At lunch Hirsch said no, thank you, to the waiter with a tray of martinis. 'I'm running a horse this afternoon,' he said. 'If I drank one of them I'd probably bet on him.' "

Smith's descriptions were a joy: the Olympics were "the BVD ballet"; an outfielder making a terrific catch "stayed aloft so long he looked like an empty uniform hanging in its locker"; the partnership between two fight managers, Blinky Palermo and Eddie Coco, "was dissolved when a judge, in a fit of pique, gave Coco life for murdering a parking lot attendant."

Smith made the reader see and feel and think. He could set a scene and place the reader in it, but with the advantage of Smith as a guide. His language was fresh and witty and original. He strove to say things in new ways, and in doing so, saw things from a fresh angle. And it was people he was most interested in. Games came second.

All this from a man writing in an area—sports journalism—which for a long time had been set on a low rung of the literary ladder.

Smith himself wrote about numerous writers, and two of them are especially pertinent, John Lardner and James Thurber. About Lardner, Smith wrote: "The true humorist has a mind that functions differently from most and eyes that see past the horizon to discover wondrous things." And on Thurber, Smith said: "He recognized and appreciated his enormous talent but resented the fact that in many minds the definition of humorist was 'unserious.' Mentioning this rather angrily on a television program recently, he said, 'I except Great Britain and Continental Europe,' where, apparently, he was acccepted as the thoughtful and perceptive critic of humankind that all great humorists are."

Smith, too, was a humorist and a thoughtful and perceptive critic of humankind, and may or may not have consciously been thinking of himself when writing of Lardner and Thurber. But he wrote on another occasion, "I flinch whenever I see the word literature used in the same sentence with my name. I'm just a bum trying to make a living running a typewriter." He didn't diminish the importance of his work, however. He said: "It's no accident that of all the monuments left of the Greco-Roman culture, the biggest is the ball park, the Colosseum, the Shea Stadium of ancient times. The man who reports on these games contributes his small bit to the record of his time. It's one aspect of the culture we live in."

In later years I read something that William Zinsser, author of the highly respected guide *On Writing Well,* noted, and which, I believe,

I responded to when first coming across Smith. Zinsser said: "The writing that we most admire over the years—the King James Bible, Abraham Lincoln, E. B. White, Red Smith—is writing that has the strength of simplicity."

Later, too, I would read the poet and critic Donald Hall, who drew a comparison between Smith's lively use of metaphors and that of Shakespeare's.

And, I'd learn, Smith's fans also included people from housewives to truck drivers to Hemingway.

I wasn't crazy about all of Smith's columns, though. There were pieces I simply wasn't interested in, such as those on harness racing and, as a city kid, those about the outdoors and his one and only participation sport, fishing.

And yet even in some of them I found delightful reading. "A good deal of richly purple prose," he once wrote, "has been perpetrated in recent years on the subject of the bonefish in the Florida keys, a villainous little beast of inexhaustible malevolence. Pound for pound, the authors declare, he can outfight a maddened bull elephant, outrun a virtuous blonde, and outdive a British heavyweight. It is now possible to report that he can also outsmart a sportswriter, an anticlimax as ever was."

When I transferred from Chicago to Miami University in Oxford, Ohio, I continued to read Smith in the *Dayton Daily News* and the *Cincinnati Enquirer*. I also discovered his books—the first of several. They were both collections of his columns, *Out of the Red* and *Views of Sports*. I had entered college with the idea of becoming a lawyer for want of something better to become. I majored in English for want of something better to major in. Never, though, had I thought of sportswriting or even journalism as an occupation.

In Brandon Hall, I lived across the hallway from Dave Burgin, a student from Dayton. Dave was an assistant sports editor for the school paper, the *Miami Student*. We became friendly and discovered that we had a mutual interest in sports and in Red Smith. Burgin had dreams of becoming a sportswriter or sports editor. (He became sports editor of the *Washington Star* and the *San Francisco Examiner*, then assumed a series of general editorial positions and later became the editor-in-chief of the *Examiner*.) His hero was Red Smith. The pinup on his wall was the *Newsweek* cover of April 21, 1958, from which a baldish man with glasses peered out, with several sporting events going on in the background. The cover read: "Red Smith/Star of the Press Box."

Burgin suggested I try a story for him. I did, and a few months later, when he became sports editor, he gave me the sports column.

The longer I wrote the column, the less I thought of law as a profession.

I loved writing that column. I also loved rewriting it, lying in bed at night, changing words and paragraphs around, mortified when I realized I had left out an important fact, pleased to think I had created a felicitous phrase—what I considered felicitous, anyway. I wanted to get better at the column. That led me, in the late fall of 1960 when I was a junior, to send Smith two of my columns from the school paper. Just like that. I mean, we were both sports columnists, weren't we? I mailed the pieces to the *Herald Tribune* and asked him for comments. As if he had nothing better to do with his time or brain. I received nothing for two weeks. A month. Two months. Then when I returned from Christmas vacation to my apartment on High Street in Oxford, a letter was waiting for me, postmarked December 22, 1960. The return address on it was "W. W. Smith, 4 Cedar Tree Lane, Wire Mill Road, Stamford, Connecticut."

Here is what he had typed:

Dear Ira Berkow,

When I was a cub in Milwaukee I had a city editor who'd stroll over and read across a guy's shoulder when he was writing a lead. Sometimes he would approve, sometimes he'd say gently, "Try again," and walk away.

My advice is, try again. And then again. If you're for this racket, and not many really are, then you've got an eternity of sweat and tears ahead. I don't mean just you; I mean anybody.

My first impulse was to paste up your stories and write in marginal criticisms. They wouldn't have made you happy. Just keep trying to do it your way, never imitating.

I'd make two suggestions. Don't write "precocious phalanges." That's just a pretentious way of saying "educated toe," a cliché you were trying to avoid.

Be careful about the exact meaning of words: "crunched heads pungently." Pungently means sharp, keen, piercing, etc., usually with reference to taste or smell, not to physical combat.

Never mind about this. Keep trying to do it your way. Good luck and god bless. . . .

Yours,
Red Smith

I had hoped that he would like my stories more. But I was flattered that he had taken the time to read them—and to write. I pasted up those same two stories, sent them to him, and asked him to make me unhappy.

He wrote back with criticisms in the margins, and we kept up a modest correspondence that continued after I began my first newspaper job with the *Minneapolis Tribune* and lasted (with occasional brief notes) to nearly the end of his life.

A year after I first wrote to Smith, I met him in Cincinnati when he was covering the 1961 World Series between the Reds and the New York Yankees.

A college friend of mine named Jim Schwartz, who was from Cincinnati, got us jobs as runners for a UPI photographer. My post was in the mezzanine right above home plate in old Crosley Field. From there I could see the temporary press section just above me. There were long rows of makeshift wooden desktops set up in the stands. The photographer knew Smith and pointed him out to me.

Smith wore a dark fedora, and I could see that the rim of hair under the hat was nearly white, not what I expected of a man of fifty-six and certainly not what I expected of a man named Red. He wore wire-rim glasses, a nondescript sport jacket and loosened tie.

When the game ended, my friend and I walked upstairs and waited for Smith to finish working. His face was ruddy, and his brow was marked by a deep furrow. His nose looked slightly veiny and his mouth had a little twist to the right side. He was smoking a cigarette held deep in the V of two nicotine-stained fingers of his left hand. His hand trembled slightly. Then he began to type on a portable. A few moments later, he stopped, tore out the yellow copy paper, crumpled it, and tossed it to the floor. He rolled in another sheet and started typing again. When he rolled in the paper, I noticed that his right hand shook.

He crumpled several starts before he began to develop a rhythm. "Smith!" someone called. "Red Smith! Telephone, your office."

"What the hell do they want now?" Smith said. His voice had a slightly high, raspy quality to it, but it was firm. He made his way out of the narrow row of writers and walked up several concrete steps to the telephone. He looked slight—small-boned, about five feet eight, around 135 pounds.

Smith took the call, then returned to his seat and soon finished his piece. He packed up his typewriter, placed several sports reference books into a briefcase, and started down the steps. He was one of the last writers to leave the press area.

I met him at the bottom of the stairs and introduced myself. I felt shy. "I remember you, Ira," he said. I felt better.

Behind his rather thick glasses, his light blue eyes appeared large and slightly red around the edges. His look was direct, with a curious power of observation.

I introduced my friend, Jim, and the three of us chatted for about forty-five minutes as twilight descended and park attendants noisily swept up beer cans in the aisles. I don't remember anything I said to Smith or he said to me, but I remember a question Jim asked—and so did Smith, because he mentioned it in a foreword that he wrote years later for a collection of my columns. "Didn't writing about games every day grow dreadfully dull? the classmate asked," Smith wrote. "Only to dull minds, I told him, and I tried to explain that in newspaper work, unlike the wholesale hardware game, today was always different from yesterday and tomorrow refreshingly different from today."

When I began writing for newspapers, first in Minneapolis and then in New York, we'd see each other at various events—the Kentucky Derby, the U.S. Golf Open, the World Series, or at a press conference—and we'd chat. He was always approachable. We ran into each other in the restaurant of a Baltimore hotel, where we both were staying for the Preakness in 1969. He was having dinner alone, and I joined him. At one point, I wanted to write something down on a napkin, the name of a trainer or somebody Smith had said might make a good story for me. I remember feeling my pants pockets for a pen, and not finding one there, searching my jacket pockets. Nothing. I was embarrassed. What kind of a professional journalist was I that I didn't carry a writing instrument? Smith said, "That's okay," and felt in his pants pocket for a pen. Nothing. He tried his jacket pocket. Then he looked up and smiled. Red Smith wasn't carrying a pen either.

I continued reading Red Smith. His work endured, and so did his best lines: On an aging ball player named Willie Mays, for example, Smith wrote that "he's a folk hero who's future is behind him." When the Yankees were winning pennant after pennant with cold efficiency, Smith wrote that "rooting for the Yankees is like rooting for U.S. Steel." And when a Senate Investigating Committee called hearings about the reserve clause in baseball, Smith believed it was nothing more than a self-serving stunt. "In an effort to avoid publicity," he wrote, "the group started by interviewing that celebrated authority on constitutional law, Mr. Ty Cobb." Smith said that, though he disliked quoting himself, there is a line that's "been stolen so often that I feel I have to step up and take my share of the credit. I wrote that the year Lombardi came to Green Bay, the Packers were the most softbitten team in the league. And I said, 'They had overwhelmed one opponent, underwhelmed twelve, and whelmed one.'"

As I got older, and as he did, I came to learn of some of his flaws, as a man and writer, and some of his fears and vulnerabilities and excesses. But my high opinion of him was never diminished. Perhaps it was enhanced. He was a man, for all that. In his life, and in his writing, I saw him struggle as a man, and grow. He wrote about the deaths of close friends. And I learned of difficult changes in his life. The death of his wife of thirty-three years, the folding of his flagship newspaper the *Herald Tribune,* were followed by a period in which he seemed to be drifting, in his early sixties—his flagship paper in New York City was *Women's Wear Daily.* Then, at age sixty-seven, in 1971, Smith, with the support of his second wife and her five school-age children—a transition that wasn't always smooth, however—made a comeback no less dramatic than those of the athletes he wrote about. *The Times* hired him, and four years later, in 1976, Smith won the Pulitzer Prize for Distinguished Commentary.

In 1980, President Carter was influenced by—or at least gained support from—Smith's columns that called for a boycott of the Summer Olympics in Russia as a means of protesting the Soviet Union's invasion of Afghanistan. The United States did not send a team to the Olympics that year.

On March 15, 1981, the top-rated television show *60 Minutes* carried a profile of Red Smith. The reporter on the segment, Morley Safer, said that Smith was "America's foremost newspaperman" and "the keenest of all the observers of the games people play." Smith was then seventy-five years old.

I went to work at *The Times* in March of 1981. Smith, as far as I know, had not known *The Times* was interested in me until I joined the paper. During the period in which we regularly drew checks signed by the same person, I saw Smith only once—at the World Series at Yankee Stadium, and both of us were working. We talked briefly. I never saw him again. I had hoped to spend some time with him during Super Bowl week in Detroit. He died nine days before the game.

I wrote the obituary on Red Smith. It was longer than I had planned, and it just made the 6:30 P.M. deadline. *The Times* ran it on page one.

Ira Berkow
NEW YORK CITY
January 7, 1986

RED

CHAPTER
1

Green Bay, Wisconsin, September 25, 1905. It was a cool, fall Monday morning, a little past dawn, and the smell of rain was in the air. The small Midwestern town was just beginning to stir. The melancholy whistle of the Green Bay and Western railroad train with its broad cow-catcher was heard as it chugged along the tracks toward the Mason Street junction near the middle of town, and in the distance black smoke was seen tumbling out of the engine's tall chimney and into the overcast sky. It was not a train that ever seemed in a particular hurry, and many men who stood and waited on the wooden platform had impatiently pulled out watches from their trouser fobs to check the time and nod in agreement when someone invariably snorted that the railroad's initials, G. B. and W., stood for "Get Busy and Walk."

Over on Forest Street one might see Mr. Nachtwey, the mailman for Route 3 in Green Bay, wearing a bowler, high collar, and long mustache—or, as such facial additions were sometimes called, "soup strainers." He would hitch up his horse to his buggy to begin his rounds along the unpaved streets. He greeted Mr. Groessl, a neighbor and the brewmaster at the Rahr Brewery, one of three small breweries in this rather thirsty town. There were as many saloons— 122 for a town of about 20,000—as any other kind of business there, though the fastest-growing industry was paper manufacturing. In fact, the Green Bay Chamber of Commerce promotional leaflets would one day state that "the toilet tissue paper manufactured by Green Bay mills in one day could encircle the world at the equator and provide a surplus for a pretty enough bow knot to secure it."

On this morning, the three local mills on the outskirts of town had not yet rumbled awake. It was also quiet along Washington Street, the main thoroughfare paved with cobblestones, where the Bijou Theatre was located with its billboard that proclaimed "Continuous Refined Vaudeville" and starred this week "Frank Emerson—Old-time Minstrel and Champion Bone Soloist."

The *Green Bay Gazette,* a two-penny, eight-page newspaper, prepared in the ink-smelling offices, would soon come clanking off the heavy presses, carrying such news of the day in its staid seven-column measures as President Theodore Roosevelt calling off his trip to New Orleans because of the spread of Yellow Fever there, the thwarted lynching of a Negro in St. Louis, and locally, "Tombstone Smasher Seen By Several." In the two inches allotted for sports on the last page—the sports page as a journalistic concept was in its infancy—league standings showed the New York Giants of John McGraw and Christy Mathewson leading the National League and the Philadelphia Athletics of Connie Mack and Rube Waddell ahead in the American League.

In all of Green Bay, fewer than a dozen people owned automobiles. One was owned by the Smith Brothers' wholesale and retail grocery store on Main Street, on the east side of town. The three Smith brothers also had about ten horses stabled in the back, and nearby were truck gardens where they grew their own fruits and vegetables. The long, narrow store was opening at six o'clock as usual, and a few hired helpers and two of the Smith brothers, Edwin and Bert, were stocking the shelves. A third brother, Walter Philip Smith, was not there. Nor was he, as was often the case, behind the wheel of the Ford, driving within the accustomed twenty-five-mile radius of the store to seek grocery orders from farmers. (He listed his occupation as "commercial traveler.") Walter was home about a block from the store, at 1535 Morrow Street, a pale red-brick and white-shingled house.

One could imagine Walter Philip Smith—a young man, twenty-eight years old, six feet tall—on the first floor pacing about in shirt-sleeves with elastic bands above the elbows, wearing suspenders and high-button shoes. He moved between the parlor, with the foot-pump organ in the corner, and the living room, with frilly antimacassars on the Victorian couch, his oak Morris chair, and a box telephone on the wall with its number displayed, 73. He was waiting for word, or sounds from the bedroom. Finally, at 6:15 A.M., he heard what he had been hoping for—the squeal of a baby. The doctor had delivered Walter's small, light-haired wife, Ida Richardson Smith, of her second child in fifteen months.

Ida and Walter Smith named the boy Walter Wellesley. Their first child was named Arthur Richardson. Both boys were named after the Duke of Wellington, whose Christian name was Arthur Welles-ley. Ida Smith, a woman of literary and historical interests and active in the local library and the Shakespeare Club, claimed proudly to be a descendant of the fabled "Iron Duke," the military hero who defeated Napoleon at Waterloo. The name always bothered the boy. "Walter Wellesley" would always sound too stuffy for him. In school he was called "Wells." He would be pleased as he grew up to be nicknamed "Brick," because of the color of his hair. After college, he would begin to be called "Red," and remained "Red" long after his hair had receded from his high forehead and turned white.

Brick Smith learned to read well early on, at least from the age of five, and enjoyed the numerous books in the glass-enclosed case in the parlor, including, as he would recall many years later, the "corny" turn-of-the-century romances entitled *Long Straight Road* and *When Knighthood Was in Flower.* He said he "devoured" Jack London's adventure stories, the poetry of Robert Service and "all of Mark Twain." In the Green Bay library, he once looked up his namesake and came across an intriguing historical item. He discovered that as relatives of the Duke of Wellington they would have had to be descended by bar sinister, "from the wrong side of the blanket," as Smith would recall, for the benighted Duke had no direct legiti-mate descendants. Smith would take puckish delight in the fact. When he mentioned it to his mother, she stiffened, and though she never disputed his finding, she never recognized its validity, either.

His mother represented the Richardson side of the family, which was predominantly Irish, with a strain of English and German. The Smiths were English, but the family had been in this country so long they referred to themselves as American. A genealogy of the Smith family could be traced back to the Virginia colony. And even on this side of the family, and as far back as the 1600's, there was a breath of scandal. A John Smith, Red Smith would enjoy recalling, had left Virginia "under a considerable cloud—possibly as a horse thief, which was no small crime."

The Smiths next appeared around Morristown, New Jersey, where a few in the family served as wagoners for Washington's troops during the Revolutionary War. In the early 1800's John Mills Smith, who was Walter Wellesley Smith's great-grandfather, left to seek his fortune "out West." That turned out to be the lush virgin-forest area of northern Wisconsin, with its crystal clear waters, particularly around Green Bay. John Mills Smith was a timber scanner who could look at a forest and tell how many board feet it contained. Taken by the beauty of the area, he decided to stay. He cleared a cedar swamp in the northeast corner of town, found a wife, and started a wholesale vegetable business. He didn't make much money at it, but it fed his family.

When the Civil War broke out, John and his son Henry fought side by side in 1861 with the 20th Illinois Infantry under Ulysses S. Grant. Later Henry marched with General Sherman through the Carolinas in the final campaign of the war. Henry also ran into some difficulties in combat, around Salisbury, North Carolina, and wound up in a Confederate stockade. Years later he wrote eloquent monographs on his experience, read them to the Rotary Club, and also spun those tales to his grandchildren. He recalled being captured by the Rebels. He said he had given his horse "the spur" as "a bullet zipped through the air so close" he could "fairly feel the wind of it." Then suddenly his horse "went down like a log, with a bullet through her head. She fell so suddenly that she came down on the rider's leg" and he could make no effort to escape.

Young Brick also listened with rapt attention to the stories his father told of growing up in Green Bay, roughing it in the woods, the friendliness of some of the Winnebago Indians he encountered. Brick also delighted in stories about other family members, like that concerning two of his father's brothers, Sile and Howard. When those two were young, and chopping wood on their farm one day, Red Smith would write years later, "Uncle Sile said, 'Howard, put your finger on that block and I'll chop it off.' Howard did and Sile did. A case of overdoing mutual respect. Howard didn't think Sile would chop, and Sile didn't think Howard would leave his finger there."

Brick, who wore glasses from the first grade on to correct nearsightedness, would sometimes accompany his father to the store and perform odd jobs, especially around the stable. He also helped deliver neighborhood groceries, for in a column years later he referred to himself as a "four-eyed, unfrocked horseman who formerly drove a grocery wagon for Smith Brothers in Green Bay, Wisconsin." This conceivably was the beginning of a lifelong love affair with horses— though not, to be sure, a lifelong love affair with manual labor— manifested by his joy in writing about the world of horse racing.

Brick and his family—a sister, Katherine, was born three years after him—often spent summer Sunday afternoons together at Hagermeister Park, about a half-mile away, listening to band concerts. They would climb into rowboats on the East River, which flowed directly behind the Smith Brothers store, and for five cents a local man would row them the hundred feet across to the other side. The women wore white dresses, the men suits and straw hats, the boys knickers and caps. The music consisted primarily of patriotic marches, and American flags rippled on the bandstand. The notion of America as a growing world power, triumphant after the Spanish-American War, was in the air—along with the smell of beer from nearby stands and the odor of cigar smoke.

Though Brick would never take an active interest in music, his father's ear was so acute that even from across the river he could tell when a band member struck a flat note. Walter Philip Smith sang in groups around Green Bay as well as in the choir at High Mass in Saint Patrick's Catholic Church, even though he was not Catholic. It was his wife's church; he was baptized in the Moravian Church but had no denominational faith. Smith was a casual man and, though hardworking, not particularly ambitious and not much concerned with convention. He sought leisure time and was hard to hurry, a trait inherited by his son Brick. Walter Smith played rummy at the Elks Club, which threw the best New Year's Eve parties in town. He had a ready sense of humor, and his droll remarks made Brick laugh. Once, he heard his father good-naturedly disagree with a friend, saying, "Aw, your grandmother's hind leg."

Ida Richardson, nearby, exclaimed, "Oh, daddy!" She protested that such language might corrupt the children.

For Brick, though, it was a lesson in the use of a deft and subtle needle, and the object went away pricked but hardly knowing why, or if he did, possibly even enjoying it.

Walter Smith called his son "Brick." Ida didn't. At suppertime, when the boys were playing in the backyard, they would hear their mother call, "Ah-thuh" and "Well-es-ley!" She maintained a greater formality than her husband, and her pronunciation retained her accent from New York, where she grew up. She was raised on East Forty-first Street in Manhattan, and as a teenager worked in a sweat-shop for a dollar a day. At the turn of the century, her sister Katherine planned a trip to Green Bay to marry a man whom she had met there. The only proper way for a woman to travel then was with a companion, so the sisters set out by rail. For some reason, Katherine didn't marry, but the trip wasn't wasted. Ida met Walter Smith. She returned to New York; he came after her, wooed and won her, and took her back to Green Bay as his wife. (They would live there for much of their lives.)

Ida Smith was an excellent speaker, quick and witty. A boyhood friend of Brick Smith's, Larry Servais, nicknamed "Babe," recalled Mrs. Smith: "They used to take up a collection at school for the Women's Relief Corps. She was one of the head members of it. They took containers to all the grade schools in town for the kids to drop in their pennies and nickels and maybe dimes. A fund every spring to decorate graves of the old soldiers, from the Civil War and the Spanish-American War. She'd give a talk to the kids in the assembly. They loved to listen to her. She had a very ingratiating way about her. I think after she retired the fund fell apart."

Like her husband, she had a sense of humor and was not above practical jokes. When their friends the O'Connors came to dinner, Ida Smith was aware that Mr. O'Connor did not like veal. She made a dish that she said was pork, and he cleaned the plate. Only after-ward did she tell him, with a gleam in her eye, that it was veal. With her children, though, she was the disciplinarian of the house. Larry Servais remembered having to wait for Brick to come out to play on Saturday morning when his mother, despite his long face, insisted that he first "crumb the breakfast table."

Brick developed an interest in sports, and would recall that as a small boy "rolled on the floor with laughter" at Ring Lardner's humorous stories about bumbling and boastful ballplayers, which his mother read to him from the *Saturday Evening Post.* The first book he borrowed from the North Side Branch of the Kellogg Public Library was *Pitching in a Pinch,* by Christy Mathewson. Years later he could still remember where the book stood on the shelves.

"As a small boy," Smith recalled, "I was always the littlest kid, the last one picked in games." But this never seemed to gnaw at his ego, and he played baseball, called "rounders," all day. He described himself as being "distinguished by flaming hair, milk-bottle glasses, and the two left feet of the nonathlete." Nonetheless he still "used to do wild daydreaming, imagining me as a pitcher with deliveries that nobody ever had before, as a boxer who was possessed with a knockout punch."

He would always think of baseball as "an evocation of childhood. It was a game played in a pasture lot on hot summer afternoons, leisurely afternoons, and it was wonderful fun," he wrote, "even for athletes like me. Still it was great fun and I lived it and as a boy never willingly missed seeing a game in the Wisconsin-Illinois League."

The Green Bay team that young Smith joyously watched wore small-billed caps and the large letters "G" and "B" sewn onto the fronts of their woolen, collared jerseys and without numbers on their backs—it would be several years before baseball players would wear numbers. The team played in small Hagermeister Park, which could seat about 5,000 in the wooden grandstand and bleachers. And even though the team played in Class C, then the lowest classification in organized baseball, Hagermeister Park was still the place where, Smith would write, "a kid went to worship people like Bobby Lynch, the third baseman and manager of the Green Bay team." A star player in the league whom Smith remembered was a bow-legged, left-handed outfielder for Aurora named Casey Stengel. Stengel had been a hold-out at the beginning of the 1911 season, threatening to quit baseball and return to dental school if the team didn't meet his salary demands. He bargained for and finally got $175 a month. He went on to lead the league in batting at .352, helping to furnish the "Bays" and Smith's hero, Lynch, with a number of trying afternoons.

As for football, Smith rarely got closer to the field than when, he wrote years later, "I toiled through a Thanksgiving morning helping clear snow off the field for the annual game between East High and West, to climax the conclusion of the football season." Later, in 1919, the professional team, the Green Bay Packers, made its first appearance. Smith went to their games at Hagermeister Park. Volunteers passed their hats for nickels and dimes to support the team founded by Curly Lambeau, a local high school hero who had returned home after attending Notre Dame on a football scholarship. The Packers caused a great deal of excitement in the local newspaper, the *Gazette,* whose staff was, for the most part, George Whitney Calhoun, sports editor and sports columnist. Calhoun also served as publicity and promotional director for the new team. He was probably the first sportswriter young Brick read regularly in a newspaper, since the *Gazette* was delivered daily to the Smith home. Calhoun, known as "Cal," had a withered arm and leg, a blustery personality, and a cigar stub invariably clenched between his teeth. He wrote football stories that carried such openly promotional headlines as "Why Not Reserve Your Seats Now?" And he wrote, "The famous Chicago Bears . . . will play at Green Bay provided the management can be positive of meeting their extreme guarantee. The game will be, without question, the greatest football exhibition ever witnessed in Wisconsin." Another time, Cal wrote that the Packers had been "robbed" by the referee.

Smith had a lively interest in all this. Babe Servais said that Smith as a boy "knew as much about sports and the players as any man." Smith's involvement in spectator sports was less than consuming, however. From a recreational standpoint, his greatest joy would be found, Smith recalled, in going with friends to the mudbottom "swimming hole in Hell Creek, just below the slaughter house. It was a sylvan spot, when the wind was right. . . ."

But, he would later say, if he had a sport it would be fishing. His family owned a little land and a cottage on Lily Lake, near Green Bay, where Walter Smith, an avid fisherman, introduced his sons to the pastime. Brick took to it immediately. "I was never a little toothless kid with a store string and the bent pin, putting the sportsmen to shame," wrote Smith, "but I was fishing in the warm water streams around home with a worm and a hook."

Sometimes he would fish alone, but more often he would be accompanied by Servais or Norbert Engels, another neighbor and friend, or Brick's brother Art. The boys also hiked, sometimes accompanied by Gyp, the Smith family's crooked-legged cocker spaniel. Gyp "was not fearless," Smith wrote years later, "but he didn't expect to die because in his youth he used up all the standard means of destruction without tangible results. Besides experimenting with all the normal sicknesses, he tried drowning, hanged himself, was shot (a flesh wound with a .22 rifle), run over by an automobile (he limped a few days but suffered no loss of appetite), and was outpointed by an express train. Having survived them all, he attained to a cocksure, dissolute, and thoroughly unreconstructed maturity. If he felt like killing a chicken, and he always did, he killed her and be damned to it. He knew my father would pay the damages."

As the boys grew older, they took overnight camping trips where, Smith wrote, "the mosquitoes enjoyed having guests."

Smith had a slow, deliberate way of speaking, thinking a split-second before talking, and, like his father, a leisurely approach to things in general. When he was hiking or riding a bicycle, his brother or his friends would usually have to wait up for him. "You couldn't hurry him," recalled Servais. "He wouldn't hurry if his pants were on fire." Smith would call it a "God-given laziness." But there was another reason. Writing many years later about fishing on Lake Muckasie in Green Bay in a boat with an outboard motor, he noted that "The bay sparkled. . . . The bluffs on the mainland towered cool and green. The Strawberry Islands were emeralds nestling in rumpled blue settings. The golden banks of Chambers Island shimmered on the horizon. It was beauty to be savored slowly. When the outboard quits every half-mile and the passenger cranks, you travel slowly. You savor everything."

Imperturbability was a Smith hallmark. Once, when he was about fourteen, he was out at a bog lake with several boys. The others had climbed into a big, flat-bottomed rowboat. There wasn't quite enough room for another body, and Smith, moving slowly, was the odd boy out. But he thought he could squeeze on as it pulled away from shore. He made an uncustomary dash for the boat, leaped for it, missed, and landed in some six inches of water and a base of oozy mud.

"He quickly started to sink as the boat pulled away, but made no effort to save himself," recalled Servais. Art Smith, Brick's brother, was in the boat and yelled for the oarsman to back up. "The water was almost up to Brick's neck when two of the boys grabbed him and started pulling him out. But his back was toward the boat, and Smith berated them for scraping his back on the side of the boat. One of the boys said, 'Here we are saving his life, and he's complaining.' Brick said, 'It was your fault I landed in the muck, and it was up to you to get me out.' "

One time Brick and Servais resolved to save their nickels, as Smith later wrote, "and go halvers on an Old Town canoe, which was easily the most desirable of the treasures advertised in *Boy's Life*. We calculated that about a year of self-denial would put the project over. Then would come a summer to fill any kid's dream." It was not to be. "The climate of capitalism breeds discord. The canoe fund hadn't reached $3 before we hated each other's guts. We divided the partnership and parted with bitter words. A day later we were the best of friends again, but in the meantime we had squandered our capital on loose living in the Palace of Sweets."

As a boy, Smith rarely got into fist fights. "He never was aggressive or looking for trouble," said Servais, "but he was quick to stand up for his rights. He and I had our squabbles, but we never came to physical combat. One time after a falling-out, we did not see each other for about three days when Smith came over to my house and said, 'Art's no company.'"

The Smith brothers were often contentious. Art was fifteen months older and they were, as Red later said, "totally different in temperament." Art was brasher and a great tease. And who better to tease than one's younger brother? Art usually beat him up, Smith would recall, "although if I really got my temper up, I could whip him, and did a few times." But Art was bigger, and his quick temper generally resulted in his landing the first—and most telling—blow.

There was one notable exception, a fight in their house when Brick chased Art into the bathroom and knocked him into the tub. It was an old-fashioned boat-shaped tub sitting on four white porcelain feet, with a rim about knee-high. "Every time Art clambered out, I'd hit him again," Smith would write. "The tub's rim would catch him behind the knees . . . and he'd fall back with a deep, hollow, wonderfully satisfying boom." Years after that fight Smith was talking to a Philadelphia A's pitcher named Chubby Dean, who recalled playing on a baseball field that had a right-field fence made of tin. "Dean," wrote Smith, "recalled that a line drive pulled against that fence made the loudest, most resoundingly beautiful music he'd ever heard. I understood perfectly."

As they got older, the boys wound down their fighting. Smith said that they had always basically liked each other and generally liked the same things, such as hiking, camping, and fishing. Art, though, was considerably more advanced in the area of girls. "I was afraid of girls," Smith said. "I admired my brother and his social ease. Art was so daring he even had dates with our high-school French teacher. I was shy. I don't think I ever had a date until I finished high school."

Art was the dapper older brother. "He always had a merry look about him," recalled Norbert Engels. "He had clean features and was thought of as good-looking, where Brick had fairly average looks." As they grew into their teens, Brick continued to spend his leisure time reading and tramping through the outdoors. Art spent more of his time at Van Schindel's poolroom, a place in which, Smith would write, "I don't suppose there was a more sophisticated crowd of cosmopolites anywhere. . . ."

Art Smith was not a good student, though he had, said Engels, "plenty of brains." He didn't apply himself in class, while his younger brother did. Brick skipped the third grade and, because the Woelz Grammar School had only one room for each grade, Brick and Art found themselves in the same classroom from then on. This made both brothers uncomfortable and may have been the cause of some of their fights. Art apparently resented seeing his younger brother in the same classroom and getting better grades.

The Smith brothers went to public school instead of parochial school despite their mother's Roman Catholicism. This represented a parental compromise. Walter Smith, a non-Catholic, kept his promise to his wife to bring up the children as Catholics—and the boys rarely missed Mass—but Smith firmly believed in what he considered the broader outlook of public education and that's what the boys received in their first twelve years.

The education was solid, and Brick did his homework. In his sophomore year at East High, though, he discovered that kids who had gone to other primary schools had learned the rules of grammar and he had not. He was supposed to have learned it in the eighth grade but, he said, "my eighth-grade teacher was lousy. I talked good enough English because good English was spoken at home. And I could recognize errors in English because they weren't what I was accustomed to hearing at home, but I couldn't tell why there's an adverb modifying a verb. I had no idea. So I got a book of English grammar and I studied it." He taught himself the rules by diagramming sentences.

In high school, Smith took the common core of subjects—English, literature, algebra and geometry, science, American and ancient history, commercial geography, and French. France was in the news, of course, when Smith began high school in 1918. France was where much of World War I was raging, and two Green Bay artillery batteries were called to duty in 1917 when the United States entered the war. Before the units left for battle, much of the town turned out to bid them farewell. There was a parade down Washington Street and townsfolk waved flags and cheered as the soldiers in round helmets came by on horse-drawn artillery wagons.

Smith was a B student overall, and his most prominent extracurricular activity was the French Club. Its modest admission requirement was an eighty average or above in French class. Though he was an excellent student in English—his grades were often in the nineties —Smith never had a great grasp of foreign languages, and never professed to. Years later, he occasionally used a French phrase in his column, thus perhaps giving some indication of his early learning process in the subject. Once, driving along a dangerous curving road in the French Alps, he stopped to dip into his Michelin guide and found this warning: *"Nous en déconseillons formellement le parcours aux automobilistes non entraînés à la conduite en montagne."* Smith translated this in his column: "We formally disrecommend the course to motorists not trained to the conduct of mountain."

Smith's interest in journalism was inspired by Vincent Engels, Norbert's older brother. It began when Smith was in grade school. Vincent was walking by the Smith house, he would recall, when several kids, including his brother and Brick and Art, "came tumbling out." It was the first time he had met the Smiths.

One of them asked, "Where you goin'?"

Vincent said, "I'm going to Baird's Creek."

"What're you goin' to do?"

"Well, I got a fly rod here and I'm going to practice fishing."

"Ain't no fish in Baird's Creek."

"Yes, there's chubs. Wanna come along?" They did.

They walked the two miles along the railroad tracks to Baird's Creek. Brick was very much interested in learning about fly casting, while Art was mischievous, throwing stones into the water. "I took off Art's cap and wouldn't give it back to him until he stole it back," recalled Vincent Engels. "But he stopped throwing the stones."

Brick Smith had never seen a fly rod before or anyone casting with a fly, that small, feathered or colored silk lure made to resemble an insect. He was anxious to plumb the secret of this intriguing artifice. "Vince taught me how to cut a willow branch and make a very poor fly rod out of it and cast for chubs and minnows in the stream. He became a hero of mine," Smith wrote. "He was going to Notre Dame, studying journalism, and therefore I felt it was necessary for me to do the same. That was great. I'd be like him. And of course, later I realized that sitting on my duff pounding a typewriter was a pretty easy way to make a living. It seemed attractive, exciting, and a lot better than lifting things."

In high school, there was little indication that Smith was a particularly gifted writer. However, in his senior year he did win the school's annual essay contest, with a humorous look at the school debating team. Smith won a free copy of the three-dollar school yearbook.

Smith graduated from East High in 1922. In the *Aeroplane,* the school yearbook, he is photographed in an oval-shaped frame, hair combed carefully back on his high forehead, wearing a tie, stiff collar, dark suit jacket, but no glasses—their removal may have been a call to teenage vanity since others were photographed with glasses. The inscription beside the photograph said: "Wellesly Smith—'Brick'— A kind-hearted, good-natured bit of humanity. Add to this a freckled face and some red hair and brains, and you have 'Brick.' "

Despite an "e" left out in Wellesley, the characterization seemed to have been on target. But it wasn't nearly so accurate as the "Senior Class Prophecy" in the *Aeroplane.* The anonymous writer prophesied that "Wellesley Smith is a journalist on the staff of *The New York Times,* while Erling Carlson is managing editor of the same great daily."

The soothsayer was dead wrong about Carlson—he became a businessman—but was absolutely correct about Smith, though it took the East High grad forty-nine and a half years to fulfill the prophecy.

The Smith family never was wealthy, and Brick had occasional difficulties with his brother and with friends, but overall, as he later said, "I had it as good as any kid could have it." Except for one tragedy in his life, which concerned his sister, Katherine Louise. She was three years younger, but mutual interests drew them close. They both liked words and would go through the dictionary together, looking up one word, finding another new one, then a third, relishing the exotic sounds and definitions. Both also had an eye for art. (Before he began to think seriously of journalism, Brick had considered becoming a caricaturist or commercial artist.) In summer, they walked through the woods; in winter, they would go skating together with their friends. Katherine was a bright, petite, lively girl who favored bright cotton dresses in summer and a huge bow to tie her blond hair in back. Her friends called her "Smitty." In the summer of 1923, just after Smitty had completed her first year at Saint Joseph's Academy, two of Mrs. Smith's maiden sisters came to Green Bay for a visit from New York City. One of them, Katherine, Smitty's namesake, was suffering from a mild case of tuberculosis, and it was decided that the clean Wisconsin air would be healthful. Tuberculosis was a dreaded disease then, claiming the lives of thousands yearly in America. Mrs. Smith's sisters stayed with the family on Morrow Street that summer. The ailing sister improved, and then both sisters returned home. The visit, though, would leave a terrible mark. Katherine Louise soon came down with tuberculosis.

It was a lingering illness, and she became bedridden. Her parents set up the parlor, which was next to their bedroom, as her bedroom, making sure that the stained glass doors of the parlor were never completely closed. It was a hard time for the family, and Brick was deeply saddened. He spent many hours with his sister, reading to her and playing the newly invented crossword puzzles. Babe Servais recalls talking with Mr. Smith in the living room, and that they could hear Katherine's laughter. Suddenly she began to cough, a racking cough. Mr. Smith let out an expletive under his breath. "It was the first time I ever heard him swear," recalled Servais. Mr. and Mrs. Smith, without hysterics, rushed to their daughter's side. Katherine Smith died on February 3, 1927, three years after she had contracted the illness. She was nineteen. Brick was then a senior in college and returned home from South Bend, Indiana. He told a friend years later that he felt guilty that he had been enjoying himself so much away at school and had given too little thought to his dying sister and to his family, who suffered with her.

"I was in grade school then," a neighbor, Bill Murray, would later write in a letter, "but I have a vivid memory of seeing her in her coffin in the living room in their little pink brick house, candles flickering, people crying, a great hushed sadness with her grieving family and friends." Even years afterward, Red's throat would catch with emotion when Katherine was mentioned.

CHAPTER
2

The world had changed dramatically by the time Walter Wellesley Smith graduated from high school in 1922, and the change was evident in Green Bay. The airplane, flown for the first time less than two years before Smith was born, was no longer a great novelty, and stunt fliers, risking life and limb, were common at county fairs, including one for local Brown County. Radios had just begun to enter homes, and the Smiths bought one. Automobiles were now seen everywhere after the advent of the assembly line and interchangeable parts, and there were some 20,000 cars in Brown County. The freedom offered by the automobile and the exuberance at the end of the Great War had helped create a more open society in America.

People were singing the popular song "Ain't We Got Fun," but a conservative movement was also growing. It culminated in the passage of the Eighteenth Amendment, Prohibition, which didn't stop the nation from drinking and had little impact in Green Bay and the rest of Wisconsin, a largely German population that relied on the medicinal and spiritual benefits of imbibing beer. The cuspidors in the saloons were never removed, and men continued to come in as though there were no law at all—authorities were often sympathetic to the citizenry. The most popular books in the local libraries were often those detailing how to make home whiskey.

In sports, radio and newspapers were bringing news of Babe Ruth, who was knocking the ball out of the park while putting people into it; the heavyweight champion, Jack Dempsey, was trying to overcome the shame of being labeled a "slacker" for not going to war. Notre Dame, a team Brick followed closely, had hired a new football coach in 1918, a man of Norwegian descent named Knute Rockne, who would lead the "Fighting Irish" to unprecedented football glory. They became the most popular college football team in the country.

Smith applied to Notre Dame after his high school graduation and was accepted. But he wasn't able to attend in the fall of 1922. The Smith Brothers business was having difficulties. Chain groceries had started up and were able to charge less with their "cash and carry" policies. The smaller grocery still had to rely on making deliveries —which boosted expenses—and it had to rely on credit, not all of which was paid. So Walter Smith simply didn't have the $1,000 it would cost for his son's freshman year at South Bend.

"I stayed out of school one year simply to scuffle up a few bucks," recalled Smith. He took a job as a clerk, filling orders for the Morley-Murphy-Olfell Hardware Company in Green Bay. "It wasn't a very responsible job," said Smith.

Art Smith would, with a smile, later say of his brother, "He was the slowest man God ever let live." To prove his point Art recalled Smith's boss at the hardware store: The day Brick was quitting, his boss watched him plod through the fishing tackle and exclaimed, "My God! That man is fast! When he quits I'm going to hire half a man to do his work."

Notre Dame cost $700 a year, including tuition, board, books, and laundry. Smith had saved enough money for college but not quite enough for train travel and incidentals. He persuaded his father's first cousin, Ethel Smith, who lived on a farm outside of Green Bay and who was fond of him, to lend him the rest.

When Walter Smith asked his son what he was planning to study, his son said he wanted to be a newspaperman.

"Whoever heard of a newspaperman with money?" asked the father.

"Whoever heard of a Smith with money?" replied the son.

Under the circumstances, it might have seemed an unfeeling remark to someone who was struggling in business. However, it might have been quite sensitive, discreetly telling his father that he believed a happy, fulfilling life—apparently the kind that his father had helped provide—was more important than money.

Arriving on campus at South Bend, Brick Smith saw a fairly small school set on the flat land of Indiana. The University of Notre Dame consisted of five classroom buildings and seven small dormitories. It was an all-male Catholic school with a student enrollment of about 1,500 and a growing reputation for scholarship as well as for football. Dominating the landscape was the Administration Building with its gold-leaf Golden Dome topped by the Golden Madonna, arms opened in greeting, shimmering brightly in the sunlight.

Smith headed for Brownson Hall, where he would live his freshman year. The dormitory was arranged barracks-style, with beds separated by hanging sheets. "That was," recalled Smith, "the cheapest place to live."

Smith is remembered as having very casual dress and study habits. "He wore sweaters and corduroy pants and hobnail shoes, which were the style then," recalled Howard Phalin, a classmate. "He dressed like he didn't have a nickel, as opposed to some others. That's because he didn't care how he dressed. It just didn't seem important to him, and he never complained about not having money."

In his first year Smith took journalism, English, history, biology, public speaking, religion, physical training, and Spanish. He received eighties and nineties in all but biology—a seventy—and Spanish. "I flunked one semester of Spanish and quit," recalled Smith. "I don't think I have any gift of tongues."

Of Smith's study habits, Howard Phalin recalls Smith lying in bed and reading. "There was always a light over his shoulder—and he wasn't always studying his school work. He'd be reading Shakespeare. He read Shakespeare all the time."

Every student at Notre Dame had to take part in some kind of athletic endeavor, a legacy of the ancient Greek notion—not necessarily correct in Smith's case—of "sound body, sound mind." Smith, quite slight at about five feet six, 130 pounds, bespectacled and still rather timid, signed up for a calisthenics class twice a week. "I hated my instructor," recalled Smith. "I think the man's name was Cox, a senior who ran on the track team. I don't know why I hated his guts, maybe because he had the bearing of a drill sergeant." During exercises, the instructor would bellow, "Up and down, up and down. C'mon there, Smith, get the lead out." In high school, Smith recalled, "I discovered that I couldn't run fast. So I decided to run long. To get away from Cox, I signed up as a miler."

The track coach was also the football coach, Knute Rockne. At the time, Rockne also administered all sports as athletic director, turned out a syndicated newspaper column two or three times a week, had several books published under his name (with the help of a ghostwriter) and toured the country as an after-dinner speaker. "He was a great man," Smith wrote, "who happened to choose football as a career. It is likely that he would have had exceptional success in almost any other field, for he had exceptional qualities— an agile and original and keenly analytical mind, a quick wit, one of those incredibly retentive memories, and a tremendous gift for influencing people. He could address an assembly of middle-aged, pot-bellied automobile salesmen—this is eyewitness testimony—and, pretending this was a football dressing room, lift them shouting out of their chairs with an old-style fight talk. He would soar to a screaming crescendo and break it off there without warning, looking on mischievously while abashed listeners discovered they were on their feet."

Rockne was short but well-built, prematurely bald, and, wrote Smith, had "small, sharp eyes and a bent and flattened nose. The nose had been remodeled by a baseball bat, and twelve-year-old Knute exhibited it triumphantly at home to parents who had forbidden him to play football. 'You think football is rough,' he told them. 'Look what I got in baseball.' This broke down parental objections to football. . . ."

To Rockne's freshman track team in 1923 came young Smith, refugee from the calisthenics class. For a few weeks he trained with the varsity team. They ran on the cinder track that encircled Cartier Field, which was then also the football field that could seat about 10,000 on its wooden benches. ". . . While the padded gladiators butted heads on the infield," wrote Smith, Rockne somehow "seemed able to watch a half-miler and a left end simultaneously. In those days his only assistant was Hunk Anderson, who would finish his job at the Edwards Iron Works in South Bend and hustle out to the campus to serve as unpaid line coach. Most practice sessions started with Rock giving preliminary instruction to the backs and ends while Hunk got the interior linemen warmed up. At length, Rock would call, 'Ah, Heartley, would you be good enough to bring the behemoths over here?' 'Hell,' Hunk would say, 'they ain't even bleeding yet.' "

Amid this atmosphere Smith trod the cinders, preparing for the freshman-varsity handicap meet that started the indoor season. In later years, Smith occasionally recalled that race in which "a four-eyed, rubber-legged freshman wobbled around the dirt track in the old Notre Dame gymnasium in anguished pursuit of a field of mile runners." He ran ten laps of the twelve-lap mile. "I contend I would have finished sooner or later, if Rock hadn't got me confused with a judge at one of the turns, who was also stationary. 'Hey, over there on the turn,' Rock shouted, 'step aside, will you? We want to start the quarter-mile.' "

Smith never ran track again. In later years he wrote that he was "a former footracer who was defeated only once in a career that extended over the bigger part of a mile."

"In those days at Notre Dame," he recalled, "I was a good specta-tor." Football, of course, was the most exalted sports activity on campus. There were pep rallies on Friday nights when a parade of students carrying red flares marched through the campus and roused others from dormitories, leading all to the gymnasium. There, team members would speak, and then would come the highlight—Coach Rockne. There'd be a burst of wild enthusiasm, and in a brief speech he'd bring down the house.

When the football team played away from home, Smith and hun-dreds of others watched the games on a grid-graph in a large audito-rium on campus. The graph was wall-size and made of canvas. It was painted with lines to resemble a football field. The game came over the radio, and as it did, a man with a flashlight behind the canvas simulated the action, stopping the light on the yard-line where the play had stopped.

The football teams at Notre Dame in Smith's four years there won 35 games, tied one and lost only four. The 1924 team would be the best-known. It was the undefeated, untied national champion; it beat Stanford in the Rose Bowl, and it inspired one of the most famous sports stories ever written.

Grantland Rice, the most popular sportswriter in the country, began his story of Notre Dame's victory over Army at the Polo Grounds in New York on October 18, 1924, with this lead: "Out-lined against a blue-gray October sky, the Four Horsemen rode again. In dramatic lore they are known as Famine, Pestilence, De-struction, and Death. These are only aliases. Their real names are Stuhldreher, Miller, Crowley and Layden. . . ."

Smith would recall coming across a copy of the *Brooklyn Eagle*—

someone at school was receiving the paper from home—and reading the story. "I remember being thrilled by it," recalled Smith. In later years Smith became close friends with Rice, respected him enormously and said his "gee whiz" approach was perfect for his fun-loving times. But Smith did question Rice's lead and wondered from what perspective Rice had seen the game. For to view the backfield outlined against the sky, the writer would have had to be lying on the field, perhaps in the middle of the field.

But, Smith wrote, "the magic of the catchwords transformed a gifted, exciting, wonderfully coordinated pony backfield into a quartet of immortals." That backfield would always be known as "The Four Horsemen of Notre Dame" and more than sixty years later still rode in dramatic lore through such unlikely places as *Bartlett's Familiar Quotations.*

It was in 1925, though, that Smith received "the biggest boot I ever got out of a football contest." Notre Dame was playing host to Northwestern and was losing 10–0 at the half. "During intermission," Smith would write, "Rockne told his players he was through with 'em, walked out and took a seat in the stands." The Irish responded with "indescribably vicious charges" and came back for two long scoring drives and won 13–10. "There wasn't a spectacular play in the entire advance. . . . But the fury of that comeback drive could be sensed in the farthest seat in the stands."

The following week Smith saw a strong Notre Dame team, in its last game of the season, lose to Nebraska. "It was a startling upset," recalled Smith, "and I was somewhat surprised to discover that I ate dinner with a hearty appetite that night. I got my usual eight or nine hours sleep that night. And from that time on, I think I have been able to accept the fact that when you go to an athletic contest, you're going to win or you're going to lose or maybe it will rain and you'll get a tie."

Smith was particularly interested in two of the "Horsemen." One, Jim Crowley, was from Smith's high school. Since Crowley was one of the best football players in East High history, Smith and many others followed his career closely. Crowley remembered Smith as a "guy well-liked on campus," and they were friendly though never especially close. (Crowley had been one year ahead of Smith at East High and two years ahead of him at Notre Dame.)

Smith also had an especially warm spot for Elmer Layden, and with good reason. To earn money, Smith waited on tables in the school dining hall. "The twenty-two [football] players on the first and second teams took their meals at two tables in the dining hall," Smith wrote years later. "One undergraduate waiter"—Smith—"worked both tables. He wheeled the vittles in on double-decked carts from the kitchen, which was in another building across the courtyard. Because he invariably had to make another round trip for seconds, he was no better than 7 to 2 to get his tables cleared and the dishes back to the kitchen in time to eat with the other waiters, and when he wasn't on time, he didn't eat.

"When the last mound of tapioca vanished, so did twenty-one athletes. One stayed to help tidy up so the kid could make the deadline. This one was Elmer Layden. . . . He wasn't asked to help and he didn't expect thanks. He was just that kind of gentleman."

Smith also found time, briefly, to try writing for the school newspaper, the *Notre Dame Daily*. "That was a misnomer," recalled Smith, "because it came out irregularly, and it finally folded at the end of my freshman year. I was a reporter for it but a lousy one. I had a miserable beat, and I didn't do any work."

Smith's easygoing manner and, recalled classmate Mark Nevils, "his droll, dry sort of wit" made him popular. Smith took part in the social activities of his place and time. One of these, in the Prohibition era, was drinking. Drinking, recalled Smith, "was de rigueur" in college.

"Having decided it was the thing to do and done it, I enjoyed a drink with the boys," he recalled. "I drank when I could from college days on. In college, we drank whiskey and gin and needled-beer, that is, near-beer needled with ether. We were taking what amounted to our lives—our college careers—in our hands by drinking." College officials meted out stiff penalties for breaking the liquor law. "If they caught you even a little bit inebriated, they kicked you out of school," recalled Larry Hennessey, a classmate. Nonetheless, Smith and his companions traveled to the west end of South Bend and drank in speak-easies there. "Or," said Smith, "if we were going to have, say, Easter Week in Chicago, one of us would go up to Detroit and go across the border and get a satchel or two satchels full of whiskey and bring it back and we'd all contribute our money and our hiding spaces and stash the bottles in our dorm rooms."

Going away to school had been important for Smith. He was growing out of his boyhood shyness. "Living informally with guys —no girls, of course—I think was good for me," he would say. "I think it gave me a feeling of comfort, mixing with my peers." He had been accepted, and he had done well in the classroom, too. "I was no star scholar," he said, "but I was all right." His freshman average was eighty-two—seventy was passing—and his was a good mark at a good academic school.

The summer after his freshman year, Smith and his boyhood friend, Larry Servais, went trout fishing for a week in the north woods. "He showed the results of a year of college," recalled Servais. "He was more open, more expressive, than he'd ever been."

That summer Smith got a job operating an elevator at the North-land Hotel. His brother, Art, landed a temporary job as Green Bay correspondent for the three Milwaukee newspapers. Art, who had been expelled from high school for a prank and never graduated, was nonetheless a graceful and natural writer. "Art was sweet on a pretty girl who played the Mighty Wurlitzer in the Strand movie house," wrote Smith. "She was from Illinois and lived in the Northland Hotel. My being the hotel elevator operator there was a social outrage that cut Art to the gizzard—that his brother, wearing a menial's uniform, should ferry this celestial creature between lobby and fourth floor."

Curiously enough, it was this romantic triangle that opened the door for Smith to make his debut as a professional journalist. "Art," Smith would write, "bribed me out of my shameful estate by giving me the Milwaukee correspondent's job."

At Notre Dame in the following years, Smith took politics, philosophy, metaphysics, world and American literature, Shakespeare, sociology, French (one year, a seventy-six grade average or B-minus) and several journalism courses, from feature writing to news editing.

The originator of the journalism department at Notre Dame—in fact the *only* journalism teacher—was the popular Dr. John Michael Cooney. His classes were held in the basement of the library. Cooney sat on a high, raised chair, like a judge's bench. He was a tall man who wore wire-rim glasses and a high starched collar. He had a high forehead and a halo of hair, and his eyebrows were dark and bushy. He usually appeared serious but had a sly humor, and began his class every semester the same way. He put his hands in a cathedral arch on his desk and said, "Let us pray for sense." Other times, he would open his red classbook and announce, "We will now have the litany of saints," and he called the roll. Each of the fledgling "saints" in class answered "Here."

Smith learned a lot from Cooney. And years later when the alumni association sent forms and asked, among other questions, which person on campus did they most admire during their student days,

Smith did not, as many others did, say "Rockne." Smith wrote, "Dr. John Michael Cooney."

"He was a rural editor from Kentucky, a kind of homespun philosopher," Smith would recall. "I listened . . . to Dr. Cooney trying to tell us what the truth was or how difficult it was to establish truth, or what is the truth."

Newspaper work is knowing, not writing, Cooney used to tell his journalism students. "In other words," Smith would recall, "the essential thing is to report the facts; if there is time for good writing as well, that's frosting on the cake."

Cooney was fierce about cutting out the flab in writing. He said that if at the Last Judgment we must account for every idle word, as the Scriptures warn, then most of us will be busy late into the night.

During an examination period, he announced, "Only ten minutes left. You can't write much in ten minutes, but you can cross out a great deal."

Edward Fischer, a student of Cooney's who became a journalism professor at Notre Dame, remembered Cooney's hard line about being specific. "No jargon, no gobbledygook," said Fischer. "He liked to see a sentence so definite that, he said, it would cast a shadow."

For Cooney, writing was something one didn't just dash off. "He said the greater the writing, the greater were the chances that you put more agony into it," said Fischer. "There's a price to pay for everything. And if something was done fast when it didn't have to be, then he felt it would probably be a sloppy job."

Cooney demanded that his students expand their interests. If one was a rabid sports fan, for example, Cooney rarely let that student write sports. There would be plenty of time to write about one's interests after he had discovered the rest of the world and added depth to his perceptions.

Fischer remembers Doc Cooney sending him to cover a wedding at a log chapel within view of the classroom. Then he had Fischer phone the information to the two South Bend papers, the *Tribune* and the *News-Times.* "You can imagine going up to a wedding and asking questions of the bride and groom," said Fischer. "Doc Cooney wasn't doing it for the wedding, he was doing it for me. He wanted me to learn how to face up to being embarrassed." Cooney initiated such object lessons with all his students, and one might imagine Brick Smith, especially as a diffident freshman, being forced to expand in this way, and the impact it would have on his personality.

Cooney, taking a page from the Greeks, instructed each of his students to try to know thyself. "Some people are sprinters and some are milers," he said. "The sprinter is capable of the brief, brilliant thing. The miler is good for the long grind. Learn which you are and live with it."

During Smith's college days, two of the most influential American writing figures were F. Scott Fitzgerald and H. L. Mencken—one a novelist, or literary miler, and the other a journalist, or sprinter. Smith appreciated the writing skills of both, but preferred Mencken to Fitzgerald. After Fitzgerald published *This Side of Paradise* in 1920, he was hailed by some as the spokesman for "The Jazz Age" and its glittering, bored, disillusioned generation. The self-pitying aspects of Fitzgerald's writing would later lead Smith to characterize Fitzgerald's as "the crybaby generation." Fitzgerald's effete, gaudy world was a long way from the flannel shirts, hobnail boots, and football world—a male's world—that Smith was finding comfortable at Notre Dame.

Mencken's approach was more to Smith's predilection. Mencken, a cigar-smoking iconoclast, was a tough newspaperman and later a magazine editor and essayist whose sharp criticisms of the middle class stung the country. Some of his most dazzling and critical reporting was of the landmark Scopes or "Monkey Trial," in 1925, when John Scopes, a high-school teacher in Dayton, Tennessee, was put on trial for teaching the Darwinian theory of evolution instead of the Biblical interpretation of man's origins. It was the same year that Fitzgerald published his masterpiece, *The Great Gatsby,* the tale of a man obsessed with money.

In the fall of 1925, Smith began his third year at Notre Dame, taking such courses as Poetry and Poets, Philosophy of Mind and Ethics, Metaphysics, and Shakespeare; attending football games at Cartier Field, where, because of the wildly popular football team, the seating capacity had been expanded from 10,000 to 25,000; he was also working as editor of the *Dome,* the Notre Dame annual. The theory that a junior should edit the annual, recalled Smith, stemmed "from the idea that seniors are too busy getting culture, getting graduated, or getting something." It was a prestigious appointment with fiscal advantages: it paid $500. Smith got the job for two reasons: He had backed the winning candidate for president of the student council, and since the editorship of the *Dome* was an appointive office, Smith was "rewarded" for his political activities. Also, he was qualified, as one of Doc Cooney's better students. He also sought the job because it paid. "That was most valuable," recalled Smith. A friend of Smith's, Leo McIntyre, said he thought the money helped keep Smith in school.

Smith endeavored to put out, as he called it, "a damned good annual." He arranged appointments to have photographs taken, assigned deans to write about their departments, and got his staff of students to cover the scope of the university. The book was typically uplifting and rather sanitized, as might be expected of a production overseen by a faculty adviser. Smith wrote the introduction and gave ample credit to the people who worked on the book, sometimes inserting personal notes. One concerned George Mead, who helped with the photography. "His peculiar facility for carrying a load of responsibility without allowing it to interfere the least with his peace of mind," Smith wrote, "fitted him perfectly for the position. Appointed late in the year, he proceeded about his work in a matter-of-fact manner that was an inspiration to those of a less stable temperament." (The editor seemed to be poking fun at himself—a typical Smith device, though not always an accurate one. Mark Nevils, business manager of the *Dome,* remembers Smith as being "unusually mild-mannered.") Smith added about Mead, "A sense of humor is a precious possession."

Smith concluded the two-page introduction with, "Regardless of its initial impression, the book will not reach its final test until time has worn away the rough edge of memory." The last phrase displayed some influences of the rhythm and figure of speech of Shakespeare. "Then," Smith continued, "if it brings to you the spirit of Notre Dame, if it renews old days and old dreams, it will have succeeded. If it fails in this purpose it will have failed in the end."

The *Dome* was a literate, good-looking, well-organized 430-page book. It was also a financial success. It made a profit of $3,400, which held the record for years.

It did this despite Smith's reputation, perhaps fostered by himself, of being less than hard-working. Walter Layne, a sophomore working on the *Dome,* recalled Smith and his classmate, Joe Brieg, another *Dome* worker. "Brick and Joe were good friends," said Layne, "and Joe always said that Brick was the only person on campus lazier than he was."

In his senior year, Smith had been in school about two weeks when he received a two-page letter from his father, written in a clean, legible hand with black ink on Smith Brothers Company stationery. The letter was dated September 25, 1926, Smith's twenty-first birthday:

Dear Brick,

Your birthday this time is a really important one to you. Wish I could send you a chk for a thousand for a starter, but guess I'll have to postpone that part of it for a time—and send just best wishes and hope that before many years have passed you will be able to sign your own name to checks for more than one thousand. After all, the mere ability to make money isn't such a much. There are lots of things that will seem a great deal more important to you as time goes on. I must confess that for the past few years I have felt that so far as I am concerned, I haven't been such a howling success as I would have liked to be. But on the whole there have been many hardships and perhaps some of them will be overcome before long.

There isn't much of anything I can say as it wouldn't have much weight coming from one who hadn't made much of a success of his life than I have of mine. But there's one thing of which I am convinced—that is (for a young man starting out as you will be now) make up your mind what you want. Don't do it in a haphazard way, but seriously study it out & decide what it's going to be & then go after it & allow nothing to interfere with the attainment of it. There is little any normal young man can't have if that plan is followed. It will mean a lot of sacrifice, but if you want what you are going after bad enough, the sacrifices won't seem so bad.

Well, enough of that—Dempsey got licked—the Packers beat Detroit—The Bears play here tomorrow. Aunt K & mother are going out to dinner tonight. I played bridge couple times lately & made the price of a ticket to the football game. The weather is rotten—Business is dead. Gene had his tonsils out today, and my pipe has gone out. Many happy returns—

Love Dad

When Red Smith died fifty-five years later, this poignant letter was by far the oldest item found among his personal papers. He treasured the letter and adored his father. In the long run he adopted many of his father's feelings about life.

Smith continued to be hard-pressed for money at college and went to Vincent Engels for help. Engels, Smith's boyhood hero who had studied journalism in South Bend and taught Brick how to fly-cast, began teaching English at Notre Dame in the fall of 1926.

"He came around and said 'I've got to have some money on the side because I'll be wanting to go to the Senior Ball this spring,'" recalled Engels. "He knew I had the right to have a secretary. He said, 'I'd like the job.' I said I'd like to have him, since Brick was always good company." Usually, the fifty dollars paid to each student-secretary for the year was applied to his tuition. But Smith had already paid up his tuition. "He told me," Engels said, " 'I'd like the fifty dollars in cash, if I can get it from personnel.' I said, 'It's all right with me if you can talk those people into that deal because they're pretty tight.' I don't know how, but he talked them into it. And he worked as my secretary for a year."

"It was a good job," Smith recalled. "I didn't do any work."

As the date for graduation neared, June 5, 1927, Smith began making plans for his future. It seemed bright, though uncertain. His grades had improved, and he would be graduating with a high eighties average, good enough to have *cum laude* inscribed on his diploma. His father's optimistic words in the letter on Brick's twenty-first birthday, that all things are possible to a young man who is willing to make sacrifices, seemed realistic. It was possible to look at what a young daredevil pilot—also a Midwesterner and just three years older than Smith—had accomplished just two weeks before Smith's graduation. Charles Lindbergh, piloting his small plane through great winds and heavy rains, astounded the world by making the first solo flight in history across the Atlantic. Flappers were dancing the Charleston. The stock market was booming. Ruth was slugging home runs on the way to his record sixty in one season. "The country," recalled Larry Hennessey, Smith's classmate, "was rocking along. Everything was grand."

Smith had determined to become a journalist. He envisioned romance and high adventure traveling the world. In the school library he went through the Ayers Directory, a listing of newspapers, and wrote to about twenty-five prominent ones. To each one he began, "Dear Sir: I have just been graduated from Notre Dame and . . ."

He waited for the responses so he could sift through the job offers. "I got back just one reply," he would recall. "It was from *The New York Times*. And it said, 'No.' "

CHAPTER
3

Brick Smith had been home in Green Bay for about a month, and he was becoming discouraged about getting a newspaper job. He applied for a public relations position with a local aluminum company. While he waited for the company to make a decision, he continued to try newspapers. Then one evening, while the Smith family was at dinner, their phone rang. Smith's father answered. "For you," he said to his son. "Long distance." There was a hushed tone of excitement in Walter Smith's voice. Long-distance calls were rare in 1927, generally made only in cases of urgency. The call was from Milwaukee, about 90 miles away, and the caller was Ed Hart, city editor of the *Milwaukee Sentinel*.

Hart's call was in response to a letter Smith had sent him a few weeks earlier. Smith had written at the suggestion of Vince Engels, who knew Hart. Hart had originally been from Green Bay, and Engels had worked for him one summer. Smith would describe the letter asking Hart for a job as one of "arrant flattery." "I wrote him some nonsense about how I had admired him from afar and so on," recalled Smith. "I told him that he was the best news editor I ever knew—a Doc Cooney fact, since I knew no other."

"I understand you're looking for work," said Hart.

"Yes," said Smith.

"I need a cub reporter to cover general assignment. I'm offering twenty-four dollars a week. That suit you?"

Smith didn't hesitate, and a few days later he was in Milwaukee ready to start life as a newspaperman.

Smith never expressed an interest in trying to write a novel or traveling to Europe to become an expatriate writer as many of the intellectuals and would-be writers did. His ambitions were limited to bringing the news to people—newspapers were still the way most people got their information in 1927. Reporting on radio was still in an embryonic stage. Smith did not have any burning desire to inform —it was simply a way of doing something interesting and enjoyable and earning a living at it.

A city of over half a million, Milwaukee was separated into several ethnic areas. The heaviest concentration was German, followed by Polish—the Polish churches on what seemed like every corner on the south side lent a distinctive sight to the skyline with their tall, narrow steeples. On the east side was the Third Ward, known as the Italian district. The *Sentinel* was located downtown on Mason and Broadway, right along the Milwaukee River, just downriver from some of the city's tanneries, such as the American Hide and Leather Company, which gave off a pungent odor. The river was sometimes as dirty as the air sometimes smelled. Smith, recalled Margaret Kohler, also a young reporter on the *Sentinel* then, told her that "one day he'd like to write a lead to a story about pulling somebody out of the dark, dank waters of the Milwaukee River." He didn't. "I became," Smith would later write, "W. R. Hearst's Milwaukee representative at fires, schoolboard meetings, and games of skill (low hole card wild) in police headquarters."

Hearst's *Sentinel,* like most of his papers across the country, specialized in the sensational. There seemed, recalled Margaret Kohler, to be standing headlines like "Lover Found Stabbed by Husband." But it was a good place to learn, and the reporters Smith moved with were a hardy breed not unlike their brothers and sisters ninety miles south in Chicago, which was the setting for the only somewhat exaggerated play *The Front Page,* first performed in 1928, about the roistering life of city reporters.

Smith shared an apartment near downtown, at 100 Prospect Avenue, with two other young men, but didn't spend much time there. "We didn't have any forty-hour week then," he recalled. He worked days and he worked nights. And when he wasn't working nights, he was staying out nights, anyway. Besides his routine assignments, he recalled that "every once in a while I'd be the ninth guy covering a murder investigation" and for now, that was just fine. He was learning, he said, how to write a story.

Because the *Sentinel* was a morning paper, Smith often did not get off work until past midnight. "The area [the Third Ward] was all speak-easies and nightclubs and three-piece combos and canaries," Smith recalled. One of the places he frequented was Alesantrapo's Bright Spot. He remembered the entertainers there and at other clubs smoking pot—"known in those days as 'muggles' and 'reefers.' They worked all night and smoked the stuff to keep up their spirits." Smith tried "a couple," which, he recalled, "had no effect on me whatsoever." He was also growing somewhat more comfortable in the social company of females; and there was one, he would recall years later, "who was kind to me." He added no details. As for life as a cub reporter, he said, "I loved it and thought it was the most exciting thing in the world."

He was discovering what it took to be a good reporter and that it was "tough." He didn't break into print until several weeks after he began. He was learning, he said, how to write a story, and "struggling to get a sentence right." He was trying to get the facts straight, to tell the truth as he saw it, and yet not be a snoop. He found, as he would say, that he wasn't "as good as some—I wasn't one of those who could go out and find the kidnapper and the child—but I got my facts straight and did a thorough job." And he would seek the exact word, the one, he said "that goes straight to the target," and he would work at "trying not to settle for the inexact." Or, as Mark Twain, one of Smith's favorite authors, had insisted, the difference between the nearly right word and the right word was the difference between the lightning bug and the lightning.

Smith covered no sports. The sports department was, as is traditional, a separate domain from general assignment. But Smith became friendly with the sports editor, Red Thisted, and went as Thisted's guest to a Milwaukee Brewer game. The Brewers were a minor-league team, then in the American Association. "The Brewers were trying for a pennant," said Smith, "and I remember that the game didn't excite me. It was just a free ticket to a ball game."

Smith, though, read the sports pages. He became a regular reader of Damon Runyon, whose syndicated columns—sports and general assignment—originated in New York and ran in the *Sentinel*. "Runyon could do things with the alphabet that made a fellow want to throw his typewriter away and go dig coal for a living," Smith would write. "He was one of the few men of our time with genuinely original ideas about what words were for. He created a new language and enough characters to people a fair-sized town."

Smith recalled reading with delight a Runyon column about an afternoon in which J. P. Morgan was called before a Senate Banking Committee. Everyone seemed to be playing the stock market, and no one played it better than Morgan, perhaps the richest man in the world. Runyon, Smith wrote, "sketched an unforgettable picture of the lawyers hanging breathlessly on the financier's words in the hope that he'd drop a tip." Another column described a deathbed scene in which an old gambler gave advice to his boy. Smith committed to memory Runyon's telling of the anecdote:

Son, the old man said, as you go around and about this world, some day you will come upon a man who will lay down in front of you a new deck of cards with the seal unbroken and offer to bet he can make the jack of spades jump out of the deck and squirt cider in your ear. Son, the old man continued, do not bet him because just as sure as you do, you are going to get an earful of cider.

Smith read and wrote, and never got a byline in ten months at the *Sentinel*. Which wasn't a disgrace. Only top reporters, or someone with a scoop, would get a byline. Margaret Kohler remembered Smith—who was then being called "Red" or "Walt"—always having a little unusual twist to everything he wrote. Lloyd Larson, who would become the sports editor of the *Sentinel*, also remembered Smith. "We started about the same time," said Larson. "But he didn't seem much different from the rest of the young reporters. He worked hard and was fun to be around. But he was no Damon Runyon."

It was unusual for a newspaper reporter to have a college degree, as Smith had; in fact, not many people in the 1920's had college degrees. High school was often considered enough formal education, and then one entered the job market. Yet, despite his academic advantages, Smith was not advancing at the paper. He was twenty-two years old and feeling frustrated. He had been promised raises, but ten months after he began work, he was still earning his original salary, and borrowing from newspaper friends in order to lay out more on living, drinking, and his poker education. "I was earning twenty-four dollars a week," Smith would recall, "and spending twenty-five dollars a week."

One spring night in 1928, Smith returned to the *Sentinel* office from police headquarters and found a party going on in the composing room. A linotype operator was getting a better job and he had bought some liquor. Smith began drinking and talking with one of his card-playing friends, a veteran newspaper makeup editor named Jack Copeland. The two then went around Milwaukee drinking in the speakies until daylight. At one point, Copeland pulled out a letter from a former *Sentinel* copyreader. He was a "boomer," someone who went from job to job, and had "boomed" on down to the *St. Louis Star*.

"He wrote Cope," recalled Smith, "and said, 'C'mon down, there are lots of jobs here for copyreaders.' I think he was just lonesome. But Copeland couldn't leave the state because he had a divorce trial coming up." But the letter appealed to Smith because it said that weekly salaries were forty and fifty dollars there.

Quickly, Smith wired the *Star*'s city editor, advertising himself as an all-round newspaperman with complete experience. "I was faking it," Smith recalled. "But they were paying forty a week." A wire came back saying he was hired as a copyreader. "I took it, even though I had never read copy before and I was terrified." And he was on the train heading for St. Louis.

Smith had never been to St. Louis before, knew no one there, had almost no money, and knew nothing about his new job. One can imagine him, on that day in late June 1928, wondering about his future as he peered out the window of the train that steamed through the mixture of green and golden grazing lands and corn fields of Illinois and crossed the Mississippi River into St. Louis. The train hissed to a stop in the cavernous Union Station, one of the busiest train stations in the world. By the time Smith had walked through the noisy concourse and outside to Market Street, he, like all first-time visitors to St. Louis, would be struck by the atmosphere—mid-afternoon in the city looked like dusk. Unless a strong wind was blowing from the plains, it looked like dusk any hour of the day in St. Louis. Smoke from the chemical plants across the Mississippi in East St. Louis and the local chimney smoke laid a dark blanket over the city and at once threatened the future of aviation in St. Louis and made it impossible to keep a shirt collar clean for long. "Presumably the sun rose, but whether it did nobody knows," rhapsodized a newspaper editorial of that period.

Smith found the Newstead Hotel at the corner of Oliver Street and Newstead Avenue and checked in. The hotel, once an old apartment building, housed a number of permanent guests, mostly elderly pensioners and transients. It seemed a suitable place for a young man of his means. "It was," Smith would recall, "a flea bag."

But he was not diminished by it. He was, as he said, "still open to the deep romance of journalism."

The afternoon *Star*, which published every day but Sunday, put out five editions daily in trying to compete with its two more profitable competitors, the *Post-Dispatch* and the *Times*. (The other paper in town, the *Globe-Democrat*, published in the morning.) The afternoon papers had special late editions for sports and used different colored paper for their eye-catching cover pages: the *Times* was pink, the *Post-Dispatch* orange, and the *Star* green. In the evening, newsboys hauled the papers with the new headlines. The *Star* was thinner than its competitors, and ranged from sixteen to twenty-four pages a day; the two others might have double or triple that number of pages. But the *Star* tried to compete by having livelier writing and quicker delivery onto the streets with late-breaking stories. The *Star*'s editorial department was on the fifth floor of the Star Building. It was a noisy, narrow office occupying about half the floor, where some seventy reporters and editors were jammed around the desks. In the *Star* office, clattering with upright typewriters and the ticker-tape machines, Smith sat at the horseshoe-shaped copy desk with a handful of other editors, some of whom wore the traditional green eyeshades.

One afternoon the new man, Smith, was writing headlines and sweating through two editions at a quick pace. He had just penciled a headline and tossed it on a nearby pile when the slot man, the head copyreader, picked it up. "Good God," Smith heard the man mutter, "can't that redhead write even a B-head?" (A B-head is a headline on a one-column, usually unimportant, story.) "It jarred me," Smith recalled. Not long afterward, the managing editor, a large, gruff man named Frank Taylor, who was from Green Bay, called Smith over to his desk.

Taylor had just fired three members of his six-man sports department. He had learned that they had been accepting gratuities from a wrestling promoter to ballyhoo his events in the paper. "Taylor came to me," recalled Smith, "because I was the most disposable body on the copy desk."

"Did you ever work in sports?" asked Taylor.

"No," said Smith.

"Do you know anything about sports?"

"Only what the average fan knows," said Smith.

"They tell me," said Taylor, "that you're very good on football."

"Well, if you say so," said Smith.

Taylor looked at him. "Are you honest? If a fight manager offered you ten dollars, would you take it?"

Smith thought for a moment. "Ten dollars is a lot of money," said Smith.

"Report to the sports editor on Monday," said Taylor.

Smith had no burning ambition to be a sportswriter, but it was a relief to be off the copy desk. He hated the routine of it, and some of the writing that he had to edit was, he thought, terrible, too often cliché-ridden with overblown prose—as was the general level of sportswriting in newspapers across the country. But Smith credited his several months on the copy desk with reverse inspiration. "The horrible examples that came over my desk daily," he recalled, "shocked me into trying to do better."

The only regular byline on the *Star* news pages was that of the mustachioed, star crime reporter, Harry T. Brundige. In sports, though, bylines were more common because the coverage had a more personal slant. The paper wanted the sportswriter to have fun with his subjects; after all, sports were entertainment and therefore should be written entertainingly, a concept Smith agreed with. Smith did not get a byline for a couple of months, while covering boxing, basketball, and track, but he was good enough to be assigned to cover the St. Louis Browns for the 1929 season, starting with spring training.

The Browns were the second baseball team in a two-team baseball town. The majority of fans favored the Cardinals, who had won two National League pennants in the previous three seasons. The Browns had never won a pennant in their twenty-seven years in the American League, and in the three previous seasons had finished 29, 50½, and 19 games out of first place. Still, the assignment was a plum for Smith, who was only twenty-three years old. He had never been to the South and, until he departed from Union Station, had never had a newspaper byline. His first, under the headline SCHANG IS MISSING AS BROWNIE TRAIN HEADS SOUTH, read "W. W. Smith":

"EN ROUTE TO THE BROWNS CAMP AT WEST PALM BEACH, FLA.

Feb. 25—The Browns' special coach, which carries everyone but Brownies, is heading for Florida and spring practice, while members of the party wonder what has happened to Wallie Schang."

Smith reported that the train carried an "advance guard" of Browns employees but only one player, Ed Grimes, a rookie. Many of the other players were already at camp, and no one was certain whether catcher Schang was holding out or had simply missed the train.

Smith's dispatch the next day, from West Palm Beach, noted that "smiling mid-summer" greeted the Browns and manager Dan Howley. "The trip" of the nine who had left St. Louis was "uneventful, except for the failure" of Schang to make the train "and the oversight of scout Otto Williams in neglecting to bring his guitar."

The prose was clean, breezy, and gave the impression that the writer, who sometimes signed his pieces "W. W. Smith," and other times "Walter W. Smith," was having a grand time. And they read as though young Smith was not at all intimidated by his first major writing assignment. In fact, the only person who scared him was the team owner, Phillip deCatesby Ball. "Phil Ball was a little bit of a guy but a crusty zillionaire and probably arrogant and I was just terrified of him," Smith would recall. "I don't know why, but when I had to ask him a question about something or other, I did it with fear and trembling."

It was, as Smith wrote later, his "great good fortune" that managing the Browns was the tall, dapper, kindly Dan Howley, who "was willing to double as wet nurse, friend, and teacher of a grass-green rookie writer."

"Were you stuck for a story, Dan was your man," Smith wrote years later. "Did you need someone to show you where first base was in a new park, Dan had the time and the patience to guide you to the bag.

"And to second base, too. Could you profit by evening-long lectures on the science of inside baseball (as who can't?), Dan's time and knowledge and eloquence were yours to command.

". . . The kid breaking in with Dan got the break of his life, and that went for the kid who broke in as a player as well as the one trying to be a newspaperman."

Howley was generous, but he could be moved "to fury." Smith observed Howley's reaction when he learned that a rookie outfielder welshed on a sixty-cent loss in a rummy game. "He never spoke to the player about it, since Dan considered that sort of thing outside a manager's province, but as long as the rookie traveled with the club, he slept in an upper berth." In those days, when the teams usually reserved two private cars with first-class accommodations for all, "assignment to an upper was a social disgrace."

The Browns had finished third the season before—though nineteen games out of first—and now in spring training this ball club, "bent on working up some pre-season perspiration," Smith wrote years later, had an eye toward winning its first pennant. Standouts on the team were the aging but still competent catcher Schang (he eventually materialized); Sam Gray and General Crowder, both pitchers; slugging Heinie Manush in left field; first baseman Lu Blue; third baseman Oscar Melillo, who won his colleagues' respect and admiration while living on brown bread and spinach ("a noxious weed," Smith said) as he doggedly fought to conquer Bright's disease and some of the American League's best pitchers; and the swift, strong-armed shortstop Red Kress.

Kress and Smith, who became friendly, had several things in common: Each was nicknamed Red, they were close to the same age —Kress twenty-two, Smith twenty-three—and each was in his second full year in his profession. "There was [in Kress]," Smith wrote then, "a happy ebullience one could sense from afar: a fan in the deepest bleachers somehow knew that that kid at shortstop was having the time of his life, that there was no place in the world that he would trade for this."

One sensed the same about the bouncy, warm-weather prose under the byline of W. W. Smith. Something else: "Both of us," Smith recalled, "were broke." Though Smith was making more than he ever had—which still wasn't a great deal—he spent liberally. And Kress was earning $2,000 a season, about the same as Smith though Kress worked only eight months of the year.

Ball, the Browns' owner, was a penny pincher. He kept a tight rein on players' salaries as well as on expenses. The team stayed in West Palm Beach at a second-rate hotel—Smith recalled it as "a cardboard palace." "The $1.50 table d'hôte," Smith wrote years later, "offered a choice of ice cream or pie for dessert. Players were warned in writing that anyone who ordered pie à la mode had to pay the additional dime himself."

Before a spring training game Smith carried his eighteen-pound Remington portable typewriter to the small pressbox at Wright Field. During the game he kept score in his scorebook, chatted with his confreres, turned back to the field to watch the ballplayers, and typed with a two-finger, hunt-and-peck style that he had picked up on his own in high school. When a few innings passed, he'd either hand the copy or dictate it to a Western Union teletype operator nearby, who tapped the information on a "bug" back to St. Louis. Smith would have already written one story—a feature—for the early editions, which would generally be replaced by his game story for the later editions. There usually wasn't room in the two-page sports section for both stories, and if there was room for a baseball feature, precedence would normally be given to the Cardinals.

Smith's stories were laced with unabashed if not boyish élan, with humor, and with an occasional cliché. He wrote:

Some of the rookies here are beginning to pound that old apple, pound it with an enthusiasm and earnestness that bodes no good for American League pitchers. Of course, such early season showings, when the pitchers put nothing on the ball but good wishes, mean little. Perhaps the lads who paste them will only punch holes in ether when they begin to face real pitching. But the odds are against it. The way some of the boys lean on the ball proves conclusively that they've seen a bat before.

After work, Smith and several of his writing cronies, and sometimes a ballplayer such as Red Kress, would take a bus to the beach and get soaped down at Gus's Baths. When possible, they also put on their swimming trunks with tank tops and swam in the ocean. Later that night, they would stop at a café, move on to a speak-easy, then possibly sit on the hotel porch with Howley and the coaches and, to the accompaniment of crickets, talk baseball late into the night.

One evening, Smith journeyed to Miami Beach to cover a heavyweight prizefight between Jack Sharkey and Young Stribling. He wrote for the following day's *Star:*
"Mrs. Stribling's boy, William Lawrence, danced into a hail of gloves at the Flamingo Park arena here last night and today Mrs. Cuckoshay's boy, John Paul, alias Jack Sharkey of Boston, is an 'outstanding contender for the heavyweight championship of the world'—if he can make anyone who saw the fight believe it. . . ." An example of the malfeasance of the fighters was Sharkey's wild swings and Stribling having to be warned three times by the referee "for jumping into the air as Sharkey swung, apparently trying to make the sailor's punches land foul. . . .

39

"As a fight, the exhibition on the beaches of Biscayne was a pitiful thing, but as a product of twelve-cylindered ballyhoo it was a revelation; and as a brilliant, glittering spectacle, as an occasion for America's Gold Coast residents to turn out in an array of gleaming shirt fronts, bare shoulders and flashing jewels, it was unequaled in the annals of the prize ring. . . ."

Despite his youthful cynicism in print, Smith was indeed impressed with the spectacle, if not with the fighters. Among the "Gold Coast residents," Smith recalled years later, "were Al Capone and his henchmen . . . sitting right next to me at ringside throughout the match. I took it all in with very wide eyes."

In early April the Browns broke camp to return north for the season, stopping for "hit-and-run exhibitions" in Rome, Georgia, Birmingham, Alabama, and Tulsa, Oklahoma. Smith was comfortable and happy with his beat, and the paper was happy with him. His stories were bright, and he met the deadlines. Once, though, he missed.

One night he went to the Western Union office to wire his story to St. Louis. When the sports editor didn't receive it, he wired Smith early the next morning. Smith responded that the story had been sent.

"Are you sure?" came the reply. Then Smith looked in his jacket pocket and found the story. On the way to Western Union he had, alas, stopped off for a drink.

Back in St. Louis, he became a regular at Sportsman's Park, dual home of the Browns and the Cardinals. It was an old, oddly shaped park on Grand Avenue. The designs of ballparks then were dictated by the neighborhood real estate. Smith said that it had "a garish, county-fair sort of layout." A low right field pavilion shaded a predominately wagering crowd out there. Large billboards on the outfield wall advertised such items as Ivory Soap and Philip Morris cigarettes, and between certain innings a recording from the billboard would play the familiar cry of Johnny the bellman, "Call for Phil-ip Mor-ris." Sportsman's Park was one of the many baseball parks still without a public address system. Instead, a deep-voiced, round-man named Jim Kelly stood at home plate, raised his megaphone and called out the lineups to the pressbox, which hung from the roof over the second deck of the stadium. Then Kelly waddled to left field and then to right field and called out only the batteries, the long walk to the outfield presumably sapping his enthusiasm for reading the entire lineups.

The park was not well-tended, and often the wooden seats were loose and wobbly as was the ladder that Smith and the other writers climbed to get to the pressbox. The water cooler in the pressbox was typical of the accommodations there: It seemed to work only during alternate innings.

Games started at three P.M., and at game's end Smith had to write quickly to make the *Star*'s late, green-covered editions for the street. There were "lots of times," he recalled, that his stomach churned nervously as his deadline approached, but he got his stories to the telegrapher as quickly as his more experienced colleagues. As time went on, he grew more comfortable and, like the others, would occasionally come to a game a few innings after it had started. Then he would place his scorebook on the narrow table at the open window in front of him and ask the writer beside him, "Fill me in, willya?"

In the pressbox, he met an assortment of writers from out of town, and none impressed him more than those from New York. To a young reporter in the Midwest just breaking in, the New York writers were, Smith later said, "god-like creatures." And to be accepted by them, he said, was "terribly important" to him. He said he never "ceased to be grateful to the two who first bothered to discover" his name and "treat him as an equal." They were Ken Smith of the *Mirror* and Tom Meany of the *World-Telegram*.

Smith found the vision of New York immensely appealing. He called it "the Capital," and it was certainly that in the newspaper business, as well as in finance, the arts, and communications in general. New York was the place where the best in his business went to make a name for themselves; Lardner went there from Chicago, Runyon from Denver, and Grantland Rice from Nashville. For the cub sportswriter in St. Louis, a dream was building. He wondered if one day there might be a spot for him on a daily in Manhattan.

He also met another Manhattan resident. On July 6, 1929, Smith wrote:

Society Note: Among distinguished visitors arriving last night at Union Station was Mr. George Herman Babe Ruth, large, very large New York clubman. . . .

Mr. G. H. B. brought some of his clubs with him, including the big black one with which he has made something of a name for himself among eastern club circles. He was accompanied by a large entourage, including one Mr. Lou Gehrig, Mr. Poosh-em-up Tony Lazzeri, Mr. Robert Meusel, Mr.

Waite Hoyt and a diminutive, parchment-faced egg named Mr. Miller Huggins. In short, those tough New York Yankees are in town.

"A very charming little city," Mr. G. H. B. Ruth remarked graciously as he eased his avoirdupois from the Pullman, "very charming indeed. St. Louis, if memory serves, is the home of short right-field fences and receptive right-field seats. I have business here."

(The slugger's language was also cleaned up considerably, just as in later years when Smith translated the Babe's racy diction into print this way: "He remembered how he'd really got his adjectival shoulders into a swing and had knocked the indelicacy ball against the Anglo-Saxon hotel out there.")

But before getting on with baseball business in St. Louis on that July travel day, Ruth had other concerns, such as a visit to some of the local speak-easies, followed by several reporters, including Smith. For Ruth, Smith would recall, "roistering" was a way of life. Yet Smith observed that Ruth was no drunk, though he could consume large amounts of beer. Smith also noted the prodigious portions of food Ruth ate and would recall that "his prowess with women was legendary." Smith learned that the Yankee trainer, Doc Woods, always had a bicarbonate of soda ready when the Babe walked into the clubhouse after a long, late night on the town. "The Babe," Smith later wrote, "would measure out a mound of bicarb smaller than the Pyramid of Cheops, mix and gulp it all down." Then, Smith said, quoting a friend named Jim Kahn, "he would belch and all the loose water in the showers would fall down."

Despite such personal peculiarities Ruth, Smith would say, "may have been the best baseball player I ever saw. . . . He may have been the greatest baseball player that ever lived. . . . He was a great left-handed pitcher before he was switched to the outfield. And he was an excellent fielder. He could run, with those pipe-stem legs. In his later years, he became fat, big fat Babe Ruth, but he was a big, strapping healthy athlete. A real athlete.

"And an animal. A likable animal. But an animal given to huge animal appetites and with no reason in the world why he should restrain those appetites. He'd never been taught any reason why he shouldn't drink or womanize or eat as he pleased. And so he did."

Meanwhile, the thirty-four-year-old Ruth, in 1929, was still a thunderous presence on the field, as well as off, having hit fifty-four home runs the year before and leading the Yankees to a four-game World Series sweep over the Cardinals. Now, as the Yankees split the four-game series with the Browns, Ruth had seven hits, including a homer, his eighteenth of the season (he finished with forty-six).

On the evening of July 9, when the Yankees pulled out of St. Louis, in a scene to be repeated many times, Smith recalled, Babe's friends delivered him to the station along with a laundry basket full of barbecued ribs and tubs of home brew. Then anybody—player, coach, or press—was welcome in the drawing room to munch on ribs, swill yeasty beer, and laugh at the Babe's favorite record on the Babe's portable phonograph. He would play Moran and Mack's talking record, "Two Black Crows," a hundred times and howl at the hundredth repetition of "How come the black horses ate more'n the white horses? / Search me, 'cept we had more black horses than white horses."

The major-league schedule generally called for a team to play two weeks at home and two weeks on the road. The longest train trip was from St. Louis—"which," Smith said, "seemed the end of the world then"—to Boston, a distance of 1,113 miles, and which took the train twenty-six hours to cover. He was in many respects living luxuriously. The baggage was picked up at the hotel by the porters and delivered to the train stations. The writers mingled with the players and slept in their own rooms on the train and in the hotel. One inconvenience was that the trains had no air-conditioning. Windows had to be kept open, which allowed the soot from the steam engine to waft in, along with dust from the side of the tracks. By the time a long trip ended, the men looked like they had visited a coal mine.

Another price to pay for the travel was missing home. And for Smith that sentiment included the city room. In Milwaukee and in his first several months in St. Louis, he had spent a great deal of time in the office around a crowd of companions. Though he was still traveling with lively cohorts, delighting in the train travel and seeing cities he had never seen before, Smith still felt pangs. One evening in Detroit, after covering the Browns against the Tigers, he went to a stage production of *The Front Page*.

"That crazy Charlie MacArthur and Ben Hecht play made me just homesick for the city room," recalled Smith. "Enough so that I went up to the *Free Press*." He made up an excuse to see some copy editor, a "boomer" he had known in Milwaukee. "Actually, I didn't know if he was there or not, but he might have been—he was everywhere.

"I didn't have any reason to be there. I just wanted to strike up a conversation. I wasn't very successful. I was a little shy to come in and say, 'Hell, I'm just homesick for the city room. I've just been to see the play and I want to sit around and talk.' They all had work to do and they went on about it. And pretty soon I just left."

In St. Louis, Smith had moved out of his hotel room and had begun to share an apartment, dominated by a long hall, with three other young men. One of them, Inar T. (Ollie) Olson, became one of his closest friends. The four men often threw parties, but always went through a ritual first. Two of them would drive down to a spot along the White River in Arkansas, some 200 miles from St. Louis, buy a five-gallon keg of moonshine, and bring it back to St. Louis. The liquor was considered to be at its best when aged, but since it was usually just a few weeks old, the aging process would have to be accelerated by stirring. So, for a few weeks before the party, whenever guests came into the apartment they were instructed to roll the keg the length of the hallway.

Some of the girls at the parties came from Webster College, in Webster Grove, a suburb of St. Louis. And one of them, a blue-eyed blonde whom Smith met on a June night in 1929, would make him more homesick than ever when he went on the road with the ball club.

Her name was Catherine Cody. Kay, as she was called, was five feet six, nearly as tall as Smith, who was introduced to her as "Red." Because she stood straight and poised, she gave the impression of being taller. She was, recalled a classmate, Anne Tedman, "a nice-looking girl. She never seemed nervous or jittery. She seemed to have a lot of confidence."

Though each also dated others in the group, Red and Kay were drawn to each other quickly. They shared and enjoyed each other's jokes and their mutual interest in books, from the current bestsellers to the classics. Kay majored in speech and drama—she was active in the theater group at school and starred in one of the Shakespeare plays—and studied Greek and Latin.

Smith took Kay to her senior prom, and Ann Tedman recalled, "I was surprised to see the man who was taking her. He didn't seem to be the macho kind of guy that Catherine Cody might be interested in. But I guess it was a good match."

CHAPTER
4

After Kay was graduated from Webster, she returned to Loretta Academy in St. Louis, where she had attended high school, and began teaching English and dramatics.

Kay Cody had known some hard realities. She was an only child whose mother had died when she was three and whose father apparently was an alcoholic. She was raised by her father and a widowed aunt, who had moved in with them.

As a child Kay found enjoyment in sports. She played tennis fairly well and later usually beat Red. But he seemed to have a good time and didn't let losing diminish his sense of masculinity. They would save photographs of themselves in conventional tennis apparel: she in a white dress and he in white flannel pants, wearing white canvas tennis shoes, both holding small wooden rackets. In one photo, Smith posed following through with a forehand swing; he looked as though he was about to strangle himself.

Smith considered Kay "refined," but open to the experiences of speak-easies on Third Avenue along the Mississippi riverfront and to the tales of characters along the sports beat. One evening, he would recall, he and Kay were leaving a movie house in St. Louis when they ran into George Zaharias, the wrestler who would marry the great athlete Babe Didrikson. "He asked how the 'pitcher' was," Smith later wrote, "and we said so-so and [then asked] what was he going to do to Pat O'Shocker the next night? Hideous malevolence warped his kisser.

" 'I'll moider 'im,' he said. Then he smiled like a white-robed choirboy and strutted into the theater.

"[Kay] was entranced. She'd never heard anybody say 'moider' him. It was some of those things you read about but never expect to experience, like winning the Irish Sweepstakes."

In 1930 Smith began covering the Cardinals, an assignment that indicated the newspaper was pleased with his work, since the Cardinals were the more popular of the two local big-league baseball teams. The assignment would last three seasons, and would fully acquaint Smith with the National League teams and convince him that not all owners watched their money as closely as Ball of the Browns did. After a game, the writers would often gather in the room of Clarence Lloyd, the Cardinals' traveling secretary. Sometimes the team owner, Sam Breadon, a sociable spirit, would make a trip and host the group in his room. "He poured booze and then started barbershop quartet stuff," Smith recalled. "And if you're young enough—and he wasn't so young—but I mean if the guests were, and you get enough Scotch in you, you're perfectly willing to sing, too. We had many a songfest in Sam's room on the road."

On a June night, Red wrote of one such trip (when Breadon wasn't there) from the Hotel Sinton in Cincinnati to his girl in St. Louis.

Kay, sweetheart . . . when I re-read your letter just now for the 'steenth time —honest—it seemed to me that my explanations for not having written in two days were awfully thin. I can't see now how anything would prevent me from writing. But here's why.

I guess I must have been more tired than I realized when I left St. Louis, for I've just slept, slept, slept, like a dead man since we came to Zinzinnati. First order of business here—write Catherine. Then the ball game, and it is an inviolable rule of the Cardinal organization that on returning from a game one must repair to Dr. Lloyd's room to have several highballs before dinner. But Tuesday afternoon must have been a salad day for me, for I was exceedingly green in judgment. By the time we went to dinner I was pretty well organized, as the saying goes, and when we finished eating at 8:30 I decided to lie down a couple of hours before doing my work. I woke at 2 A.M., took a walk to clear my head, and sat with a cold towel around the fine Smith brow, turban-fashion, until 4:30. And there I lay and dreamed of Catherine, unable to sleep, until daylight, when I suddenly popped off and slept till noon.

Time out: Today's game called off and must flash same to my office. [It had rained that day.]

So there was no time for writing before Wednesday's game, and after the game, the old Spanish custom was revived, dinner was followed by work, and I found myself too tired to do anything but flop in bed, determined to get up about 10 and write a nice long letter. Sam Muchnick [Muchnick was covering the Cardinals for the *St. Louis Times*] called me at 12:45 yesterday. Believe me, lady, I'd done spectacular sleeping. Never batted an eye before that.

So when I finished my work I said, "Smith, you'll write no letters this night. You'll go to bed to dream of the sweetest girl in the world and get up tomorrow morning to write." Which is what I did, and, my dear heart, please forgive two days of silence. I love you, darling, more than any letters or words can ever tell, and if I let a year go by without writing I'd still adore you with all my heart. Oh, believe me please, and know for sure that I'll always worship you.

You know how I love you, don't you? You know you're my girl, my life, dreams, hopes, work, play—everything. I know I can't get along at all without you, and I miss you so it's never possible for me to be really happy when I'm away. Oh, darling, know that I love you and need you and miss you so—and love me, just a little bit.

Yours,
Red

In 1931, when Smith received an offer from *The Sporting News,* the important nationally circulated baseball weekly that had its head-quarters in St. Louis, he discussed it with Kay.

At the end of a long letter to her, he wrote, "The good right arm is tiring, Sweetheart, but I want to tell you that Roy Stockton"—who covered the Cardinals for the *St. Louis Post-Dispatch*—"and Lloyd both emphatically advise me against going to *The Sporting News.* Both say they'll pay the money, but I wouldn't be happy. I'd be, they say, the property of the lice who run the paper and I wouldn't stand the treatment their men get for two weeks. Well, more of that anon, but please don't say anything about the offer . . . or especially about Lloyd's or Stockton's advice. It would be very bad if it were known that either Roy or Clarence speaks of Taylor Spink, the publisher, as a louse."

Taylor Spink was a volatile editor, with a caustic tongue and a reputation as an exceedingly demanding boss. He believed his employees should work, as he did, seven long days a week all year long. He telephoned writers at all hours and talked incessantly. Supposedly the only word in the English language he considered unspeakable was "vacation."

Taylor's father, Charles, also had a reputation for being abrasive. He had hired Ring Lardner in 1910 as editor of *The Sporting News.* Lardner left his position as sports columnist with the *Chicago Tribune* and soon regretted it. Recalling one particularly rocky moment at *The Sporting News,* Lardner wrote, "I fought all day to overcome a mad longing to spit in Mr. Spink's eye." Spink's side of the story sounded different. He said the paper was having financial problems in those days, and he paid the employees in scrip, temporary paper used for money. Spink figured that Ring, whom he called an alcoholic, was mad because the saloons wouldn't accept scrip. Whatever the reason, Lardner quit *The Sporting News* after three months.

Smith knew the Lardner story. He followed Lardner's career and read Lardner regularly. Lardner had left full-time newspaper work by the time Smith had begun his own career, but Lardner still wrote occasional sports pieces for newspapers and of course continued with his short stories.

Smith would lie in his Pullman berth while traveling with the Cardinals and read Lardner and, he recalled, "shiver with joy." One of the Lardner short stories in the *Saturday Evening Post* was written in letters by a rookie named "Danny":

. . . Stengels name aint Casey but that is just a nick name witch he says they call him because he come from Kansas City but that dont make sense but some of the boys has got nick names like wear they come from 1 of the pitchers Clyde Day but they call him Pea ridge Day because he come from a town name Pea ridge and he was the champion hog caller of Arkansaw and when he use to pitch in Brooklyn last yr he use to give a hog call after every ball he throwed but the club made him cut it out because the fans come down on the field every time he gives a call and the club had to hire the champion of iowa to set up in the stand and call them back. . . .

Although he didn't try to copy Lardner's antic grammar and deliberate misspellings, Smith did try to emulate the rhythm of the language and the way in which Lardner used words to keep the reader off balance. Smith said years later, "I could quote lines of his I wish I had written, and would have if I had been that good, like, ' "Shut up," he explained.' " Another Lardner line Smith quoted was one he read in Milwaukee during the 1927 World Series. Lardner wrote: "Then Koenig got a hit on a ground ball that would of been an easy out for any first baseman that was not quite so much of a recluse as Joe Harris."

One day in September 1930, when the Cardinals were making a late charge for the pennant, Smith was sitting in the narrow pressbox at Baker Bowl in Philadelphia. It was just before the start of a Cardinals-Phillies doubleheader, and Smith heard the voice of Stu Boggs, the Western Union chief, at the press-box entrance: "Well! It looks like old times."

Smith recalled: "Stu ushered in a tall, hollow-eyed man to a seat beside me. And I was filled with pleasure." It was Ring Lardner. Lardner had been in Philadelphia for the opening of a theatrical show and had wanted to see a chunky left-handed pitcher for the Cardinals named Bill Hallahan, who was having an excellent season.

Smith struck up a conversation with the famous writer. Lardner recalled the World Series of the previous fall. The Philadelphia Athletics had beaten the Cubs in four games to win, and the newspapers had made a great deal out of the strategy of Connie Mack, the A's manager. In the opening game he had passed over Lefty Grove and George Earnshaw, his star pitchers, to start the aged, seldom-used pitcher Howard Ehmke. Ehmke won the game and set a World Series record with thirteen strikeouts.

Did crafty old Mack catch the Cubs and their manager, Joe McCarthy, off guard, as the newspapers said?

"I talked with McCarthy about the World Series late last summer," Lardner said to Smith. "He told me, 'We're not worried about Grove and Earnshaw. We can hit speed. But there's one guy on the club. . . . He's a shit pitcher. That's Howard Ehmke, and he's the guy we're going to see in the Series.' "

Sitting with Smith, Lardner watched Hallahan pitch with a very difficult, strained delivery, and said, "He won't last very long." Lardner compared the motion with Walter Johnson's, which was free and easy, a three-quarter side motion.

Lardner chatted throughout the doubleheader, but Smith never could recall what else they talked about. "I may have been numb," Smith said.

Smith, as he had suggested to Kay, did not accept *The Sporting*

News offer. And he never seemed to tire of writing Kay about his deepest feelings. He wrote from Philadelphia on August 19, 1931:

... This having been an utterly uneventful day, I've nothing to add to the usual Congressional Report and there's nothing to interfere with my telling you right off the one thing I really want to say—that I love you and long for you with all my heart. . . . Oh, Kay dear, it's hard being away from you this long. Gee, it would be fun traveling with you along. Seeing new things with you, doing new things with you, watching the neckers along Riverside Drive with you, and joining them, instead of noticing them from a bus stop and wishing you and I were among them, playing with you, working with you, loving you, and then, when I'm tired, going to bed with you tight in my arms instead of lying alone in the dark and dreaming of you and aching for you. Or just being back in St. Louis and going to dumb movies or driving through the park or out in the country or driving straight as an arrow down the fairway three-hundred yards at Swat Ho, or eating punk sandwiches and mosquitos at Sala's, but looking into your eyes and adoring you.

Darling one, please write oftener and tell me you love me in every line. I've got to be told just as often as you do, you know. Oftener, because there's so little sense in your loving me that it's much harder to believe than that I love you. You know, it just occurred to me that my love for you is the most unreasoning, unpremeditated, irrational, unthinking and important thing in the world, and yet it's the most sensible, sane thing I've ever done. Is that a Chestertonian paradox or is it just a dumb crack? Anyway, it always seemed to me that my love for you and my two years with you have been fraught with contradiction as a kitchenette rickey. How's that for a simile? I stole it from the *World-Telegram.* But from that first night on Art Hill, when a golden moon spilled silver over everything, things have been all twisted. Here I am, one of the toughest, hardest-boiled newspapermen in the world, and as far as you're concerned I'm the softest softy I ever knew. Here's the very unselfish Smith and he doesn't give a whoop about anything but making his girl happy. I know a girl like you must have better sense than to love a guy like me, and I know you love me because you've told me so. But Sweetheart, write and tell me so again and again. I have to be reassured constantly. . . .

Smith also wrote Kay about what he had been reading, from novels by Willa Cather and Ernest Hemingway, both of whom he admired, to a popular history of the time, *The Mauve Decade* by Thomas Beer. Of the latter book, Smith wrote to Kay about coming across "the swellest line." The author "had spent a chapter telling of the depravity of the decade, and how Oscar Wilde became, in American sermons and American belief, second only to Nero as a sinner. He was damned from more than nine-hundred pulpits in five years. So Beer says:

" 'Wilde's art becomes dusty. But he has his standing as a great sinner, and polite Frenchmen working in the vast cemetery above Paris show the way patiently when rapt Americans pant: "Oo est le tombeau d' Oscar Wilde?" This might amuse him in the hell to which his adorers have condemned him with full benefit of Clergy.'

"Isn't that slick? It's a grand book."

Also during that summer of 1931, Smith's father and brother visited him in St. Louis. On his next road trip, Smith wrote Kay:

In a letter, my mother says, "I got a thrill out of the fact that your friends liked Dad and Arthur. Dad was quite taken with them all. The little dark-eyed one amused him very much. I am more anxious than ever to meet Kay. I wish she could come home with you at Christmas. How about it—could it be arranged?"

So you see, you have an invitation. . . . And at the end of the letter she says, "Love to Kay." Old lady, do you have a way with that family of mine! My mother's incurably sentimental and she's just straining at the leash, panting eagerness to love any girl who shows the slightest promise of marrying me off.

By the way, you're sorta planning on marrying me, aren't you, old girl? It'll upset my plans terribly if you don't. And think of the disappointment it would be to my mother.

Incidentally, if you don't go home with me at Christmas, I'm afraid I won't be able to get a date during the whole two weeks. Mary Lou Murray, my last bet (Bet, not Pet), has eloped with a professional football player. I guess you and I will be the last two people in the world to get married. There aren't many left.

I love you, Kay. I love you. Love me and keep improving your golf scores.

—Red

P.S. You gotta count the misses.

The 1931 baseball season provided Smith with the deepest pleasure of any in which he traveled with a ball club. The Cardinals had talent and characters. Managed by Gabby Street, the team included Frank Frisch at second base, whom Smith always considered one of the best players he'd ever seen, and the redoubtable Pepper Martin in center field. The leading pitchers were Hallahan, the veteran Burleigh Grimes, and a rookie named Paul Derringer, who won eighteen games. "I was wrapped up in the fortunes of that team," Smith recalled. "I was a devoted fan." The Cardinals had clinched the pennant by mid-September. He had come to know some of the players quite well, or thought he had. After one game he joked in print about the longest home run in history being the one that Frisch hit over and over again on the train as long as anyone was in earshot, "all the way from Sportsman's Park in St. Louis to Back Bay Station in Boston." Frisch didn't complain, but he wasn't so tolerant of Smith another time that season.

Frisch, Smith wrote years later, was "struggling through a brute of a batting slump [when] the Cardinals wangled a narrow victory over a pitcher who allowed only three or four hits, at most. They were rejoicing noisily when I encountered Frank in the clubhouse.

" 'Well, Dutchman,' I said tactfully, assuming he would be as jubilant as the rest, 'when are you going to hit one?'

"My ears still twang like twin guitars when I remember his reply. Not the words but the vehemence: even under today's relaxed standards, the words cannot be repeated here. The breath whooshed out of me. I made my way back to the press box and told my boss, Sid Keener, about the colloquy. Sid howled with laughter. 'That'll teach you,' he said, 'how to talk to a hitter when he's in a slump.'

"Two or three days later Frisch won a game with his bat. I did not seek him out but he saw me in the clubhouse.

" 'Hey,' he said, friendly as a puppy. 'I came out of my slump, eh?' "

Frisch was a college man out of Fordham, in New York City, but most of the players were farm boys, suspicious of big-city ways and big-city reporters. Smith was aware of this, and if he was to be successful in covering the team and making the players confident enough to talk to him, he had to break down barriers. That's what he did with the rookie Derringer.

"I was raised on a farm in Kentucky," recalled Derringer, "and Red and I ate together quite a bit on the trains. We talked baseball, but he was also interested in the folklore of Kentucky and about the farms and the stock and the hunting and fishing. I don't know how much he cared about that, but I felt good that he was interested enough to ask the questions.

"And I liked that he was honest. I remember one time I lost a sixteen-inning game and he asked me why. I said, 'Goddamit, Red, I don't know. You tell me.' He didn't beat around the bush."

Smith's particular favorite on the Cardinals was Pepper Martin, a hustling, hawk-nosed, ingenuous twenty-seven-year-old player from Oklahoma—nicknamed the Wild Horse of the Osage—who had little formal schooling. He hit .300 in 1931, his first full season in the major leagues, and starred in the World Series against the Athletics. After three Series games, during which he had seven hits in nine at-bats and stole three bases, a crowd gathered around Martin in a Philadelphia hotel.

"Pepper," someone asked, "how do you account for the way you're going?"

"I dunno," said Martin. "I'm just takin' my natural swing and the ball is hittin' the fat part of the bat."

"Mr. Martin, where did you learn to run the way you do?"

"Well, sir, I grew up in Oklahoma and once you start runnin' out there, there ain't nothing to stop you."

Smith deftly caught the flavor of Martin's speech. He didn't do quite as well with the story of the seventh and final game of the Series, in which his beloved Cardinals beat the A's:

"Black-jowled, swaggering, snarling, fighting against creeping age and an overwhelming weariness, Old Burleigh Grimes took fame by the throat today and claimed her for his own. . . ." He continued in this vein throughout the story, and so breathlessly did he proceed that he neglected to put in the score of the game.

Years later he would look back on his formative years at the *Star* and say that too often he was "awful cute." He said, "I tried every possible approach except to say the Cardinals yesterday defeated the Giants 7–3."

He was groping to be different, a trait common among young writers. He still wasn't the top baseball writer in town; Roy Stockton, the veteran writer for the *Post-Dispatch,* was the best known. Smith was trying to make his own mark. One early story, though, that drew favorable attention to Smith from readers was another "cute" one. It was an attempt to extend himself and experiment with dialogue, however unsophisticated, in a way he never had. In an advance piece about the first football game under the lights ever played at Washington University in St. Louis, on October 17, 1929, Smith portrayed glowworms talking jealously about how the arc lights upstaged them:

. . . Francis Field, customarily as black at that hour as a bootblack's fingernails, shone white under a blazing battery of twenty-four huge electric lamps, lights whose brilliance caused the glowworms to glance ruefully, almost apologetically, at the poor illumination they themselves shed. Under the floodlights half a hundred serious-faced young men were earnestly throwing one another down and jumping on the prostrate ones.

"Wal, I swan," ejaculated Mr. G. Worm, who despite his long abode in the gracious atmosphere of learning at the university, still clung to the bucolic idiom characteristic of those who live close to the soil. "Wal, I swan, Mommer, the world certainly do move."

Mommer smiled gently, her eyes gleaming as brightly as her tail. "It all goes to show," quoth Mommer, a pious soul, "that the forces of light eventually prevail."

Smith would continue to try things differently, but usually in a more restrained manner. Smith covered the Cardinals again in 1932, but this season wasn't nearly as thrilling as the previous one, as the Cardinals dropped to sixth place.

Smith was not so smitten with the team that he couldn't criticize it in a losing season. His readers, closely following the fortunes of the ball club, would not have tolerated anything less than an honest appraisal. "A wrestler who ignores his cues," Smith wrote after the 1932 season, "is pitched out of the trust." Smith sometimes criticized with a sledgehammer and sometimes with a needle. After one defeat, for example, he explained that the Cardinals "folded like a picnic chair." But he could be much less droll. In 1932, he wrote that Frank Frisch, at the "high salary" of $16,500 a year, "coasts through a season." Frisch's batting average had dropped from .311 to .292, and he had significantly lower totals in other categories, including having appeared in only 115 games, 16 fewer than the year before.

After the 1932 regular season Smith wrote that not only the Cards but "Herman Q. Fan" had also taken a beating. He said players disgruntled with salary disputes didn't always put out on the field, and baseball magnates stuck it to the fans, too. "Prices have fallen everywhere" in 1932, wrote Smith, referring to hard times caused by the Depression, "so general admission tickets no longer cost $1 at major-league parks. They cost $1.10." He also castigated the owners for lack of amplifiers to let fans know what was going on during a game.

In October, he covered the World Series matching the Cubs and the Yankees. He was in the Wrigley Field press box in Chicago on October 1 when Babe Ruth, as Smith said, either did or did not call his shot by pointing to the center-field bleachers in the third inning, and then hitting a home run to that spot off pitcher Charlie Root. That fifth game was played on a Saturday afternoon, and Smith did not write because the *Star* did not publish on Sunday. But he wrote a wrap-up story for Monday's paper, after the Yankees had won the Series in four straight games.

In his twenty-fourth paragraph—the byline now read "Walter W. Smith"—he wrote of Ruth and the star's ongoing clashes with the Chicago fans and players: The fans in left field before the game "pelted him with lemons. But at the plate he still clowned, signaling balls and strikes in mock gestures until he found a pitch that he liked. Twice he found what he wanted, and twice he smashed the longest drives ever seen in Wrigley Field."

Smith said later that no one in the press box made much of a stir about a "called shot," and it wasn't until the next day that some of the New York writers wrote that it had happened. "Ruth did make a deliberate set of gestures—not a quick, convulsive one—but it did not occur to me that he was calling his shot," Smith said years later. Smith said he recalled reading a quote from Ruth that said he didn't do it. "Some myths," said Smith, "won't die."

Smith returned to St. Louis after the Series and covered winter sports, a minor-league hockey team, boxing, and college basketball, all without much relish.

About new basketball rules, Smith wrote on December 8, 1932: "It will be remembered that the manly art of stalling, the slow break and the sleepy center-feed style of play which came into general use during the last few years so slowed up the game that last season the customers stayed away very briskly. There is no percentage in paying a dollar to sleep on a hard board seat behind a stanchion when you can sleep free on a soft bed at home. If you have a home these days.

"So the new rules were designed to make stalling a capital crime and to minimize the soporific effect of the center-feed game. . . . The two new rules introduced the half-court line which the offensive team must cross within ten seconds after gaining possession of the ball, and second, that a player holding the ball in the opponents' penalty lane (that is, the free-throw circle near the basket) must shoot, pass, or dribble within three seconds."

Neither rule, though, made Smith any more interested in the game than he had been. Nor did hockey hold any fascination for him, or wrestling, and many of the boxing matches he saw were tiresome. He was, he said, "bored with winter-time sports."

They were in stark contrast to the powerful dramas and tragedies prevailing in the rest of the world. "Empires," recalled Smith, "were falling all around me, and I was writing about some dumb basketball games."

The economies of many nations were collapsing. In America, businesses were folding, banks were closing, and sixteen million workers—one-third of the potential labor force—had lost their jobs.

At the turn of the new year, 1933, Smith made two important decisions: To leave sportswriting and to get married.

CHAPTER
5

On Saturday, February 11, 1933, in a small ceremony in a Catholic church on the south side of St. Louis, Catherine M. Cody and Walter Wellesley Smith were married. The couple moved into a one-bedroom apartment at 4141 Magnolia Avenue, across from Tower Grove Park. Kay was no longer working, having lost her teaching job as the Depression worsened. Smith had always hoped to make what he called "a decent living" in the newspaper business and dreamed of "getting $5,000 a year—$100 a week." A couple of raises in St. Louis had got him up to fifty dollars a week. Then he had to take a ten-percent cut in pay during the early days of the Depression. And now, "freshly married," he would recall that for "a wedding present" the paper cut his salary another ten percent. He had started in St. Louis at forty dollars a week and now, four and a half years later, was making $40.50 a week. "And all of a sudden," he said, "the banks closed with what few dollars we had, and we got down to nothing."

But he still had a job. Close to 100,000 St. Louisians, one-quarter of the work force, were unemployed. Smokeless factory chimneys were a common sight. Hungry people waited in long soup lines. Some people lived along the Mississippi in shanties in "Hooverville," named derisively for President Hoover. A refrain heard regularly in juke boxes and on the streets was "Brother, can you spare a dime?" At the same time, a certain ironic sense of humor existed, perhaps exemplified by the contemporary hit "Life Is Just a Bowl of Cherries."

On November 12, nine months and one day after they were married, Kay and Red Smith became the parents of a daughter, Catherine Wellesley. She was born at St. Louis Maternity Hospital, where her father was able to arrange an unconventional "two-week package deal" with the pediatrician and the hospital for various services, prenatal care, delivery, and postnatal care: Clinic fees were twenty-five cents, and a hospital bed three dollars a day. "We were getting along," Smith recalled. "After all, you could buy a loaf of bread for a nickel."

In June 1932, the *Star,* to save itself, merged with the *Times,* and became the *Star-Times,* with a circulation of around 160,000. When the papers merged, numerous people on each staff were fired. One of them was Sam Muchnick, Smith's friend who covered baseball for the *Times.* "We had two hours warning and were given two weeks pay—nothing more," recalled Muchnick.

Smith was fortunately one of those hired on with the new *Star-Times.* Profits were down for newspapers just as they were for almost everything else. At this time, too, the American Newspaper Guild was being organized, with its strength in New York and Washington, but finding support in other cities as well. Meetings of editorial staffs in St. Louis were held, and Smith took part. The *Star-Times* owner, Elzey Roberts, who had inherited his wealth from the family shoe business, seemed insensitive to the demands for, if not higher wages, then better working conditions for his employees. A reporter could be fired summarily and given no reason. Reporters and editors regularly worked twelve-hour shifts and more, sometimes starting in the dark and returning home in the dark. At the *Star-Times,* Roberts never gave his reporters money for incidentals, and Smith, who had no car, would hop into taxis with reporters from other papers who could put such travel on their expense accounts. Guild organizers asked Roberts if he were going to take a pay cut, too. And he said, according to John Scott, then a reporter on the *Star-Times,* "Certainly. I'm cutting ten percent off my salary as well."

Scott recalled, "He was going from $150,000 to $135,000. I remember Red turned to me and said, 'I think it's time for a change.' "

Red later recalled, "I was a busy little Guild organizer." Fifteen years before, there was an attempt at Guild organizing in St. Louis, but six employees at the *Post-Dispatch* were fired for it and that halted the movement. Now, though, under a National Labor Relations Board ruling, it was illegal for management to use such tactics, and the Guild was organized in St. Louis in early 1933.

Smith had another opportunity to supplement his income. Despite the firings that led to Smith's sportswriting job, a boxing or wrestling promoter might still approach a sports reporter and ask him, Smith recalled, "to help me out with the show comin' up. I'll take care of ya." One winter evening Smith was covering boxing at the St. Louis Auditorium when a fight promoter slipped him twenty dollars. Smith put it in his pocket and went home.

"That night," Smith would remember, "I tossed and turned and worried about what to do. The next morning I went in and gave it back."

Yet times were so tough that Smith even attempted manual labor, something that had always been abhorrent to him. In 1934, during a week off in wintertime, Smith took a job working construction on a government sewage project along the Mississippi. "It was bitter cold," Smith recalled, "and I lasted only a couple of days."

About that time he received an offer to leave the paper and write publicity for the Southwest Bell Telephone Company in St. Louis for "a king's ransom," as he termed it, of about ten dollars a week more than his newspaper salary. After considerable thought, he turned it down. "I only wanted to be a newspaperman," he would recall. "I was attached to the newspaper like an undernourished barnacle."

By then he was sitting "at a smoking typewriter," pounding out about ten thousand words for twelve hours a day as a rewrite man. "I was half of the staff of two rewrite men," Smith recalled, "and when the other guy—Carl Major—was on some kind of assignment, which was often, I literally had to write most of the paper." Smith had come to this job by, he would say, mutual consent of himself and Frank Taylor, the managing editor. Smith wanted to leave sports and Taylor needed a good rewrite man, one of the most important jobs on the editorial staff. It was the rewrite man who took sometimes formless information from reporters calling in off the street and turned it into readable—and sometimes exciting—prose.

Rewrite helped Smith's writing. He had to say a lot in a few words —the tighter the story, the more stories could be gotten into the paper—and Smith began to develop a firmer writing style than he had as a more leisurely sportswriter.

Sam Brightman was then a young reporter at the *Star-Times*. "The rewrite men were very highly respected," he recalled. "And Red was one of the best. A lot of them would have a bag of clichés, but Smith didn't, and he was as fast as the guys who wrote nothing but clichés. Whenever those guys would be handling a good murder story, 'the mystery woman' was always 'a svelte blonde.'

"Smith would take a phone call from a kid like me, and he'd stop and say, 'What did the building look like? What is there at the corner of thus and so?' When you'd be out on the street, you'd be grabbing things as quick as you could, running it in, and breezing it out over the phone. So I'd have to go back out and get the description better. But he would manage to get little touches of color in without slowing down the story. I remember I covered a big fire in an office building downtown. I called it in from a phone booth. I had talked to the fire chief. I had an estimate of damage. I had more goddamn stuff than you ever saw. And Smith asked, 'What color is the building?' I said, 'Yellow brick.' I was learning."

So was Smith. He still wrote occasional feature stories, sports and general assignment. He once was assigned to interview World War I flying ace Jimmy Doolittle, who was then causing a sensation by setting speed records in his airplane. Smith was nervous because he had never interviewed anyone so prominent. He found that Doolittle was very nervous, too. Smith would write about it years later:

It was fearfully tough sledding, although [Doolittle] was courteous and obviously trying to cooperate.

"I'm sorry," he apologized at last, "some people have the gift of narration and some haven't. I haven't."

Well, you don't go back and tell the boss that. After another half-hour of feeble questions and laconic replies, he explained, "When I started flying I was a test pilot. In those days that meant you took a new ship up to see if it would fly. If it didn't, the company built a new ship and got a new test pilot.

"If we had permitted ourselves to look for thrills then we would have been thrilled to death, literally. Instead, we had to grow a sort of armor against excitement. The result is I'm never aware of anything in the air except flying conditions, visibility, landing facilities—that sort of thing.

"The other day I flew a man from New York to Washington. A perfectly smooth hop without incident. That evening at dinner I heard him hold a group spellbound with a story of some plane trip he'd once made. When he finished, I realized he was talking of our ride that morning.

"He made it a fascinating story. I'd give a lot to be able to do that."

And with Smith's gentle persistence and guidance, he had.

Franklin Delano Roosevelt had been elected president in November 1932, and his first message to Congress, Smith would recall, was "Bring back beer." On Thursday night, April 6, 1933, Smith covered the end of Prohibition in St. Louis, a night of celebration in which thousands of people streamed to the two local breweries. Prohibition officially would end at midnight. The legal sale of beer would mean not only that one could drink without threat of arrest, but also that many jobs would be opened. Smith was at the Busch factory that night and for the next afternoon's paper he wrote:

. . . An endless stream of packed cases moved down a slide from the bottling machines on the upper floors to the loading platform where workmen stacked them ten high. . . .

At midnight, the clock in the brewhouse tower chimed. The sound was picked up and broadcast over a national chain of radio stations.

One minute later a blast from the brewery whistles signaled the end of the Volstead bone-dry era as far as beer is concerned.

The crowd set up a mighty cheer. . . .

Around this time Red's brother, Art, came to St. Louis. He had worked on several papers by now, including the *Detroit Mirror,* which had recently folded. Art tried to get a job on the *Star-Times.* "But nobody was hiring anybody," recalled Red. Art managed a deal with Frank Taylor. The paper was sending no one to spring training, and paying Clarence Lloyd, the Cardinals' traveling secretary and a former sportswriter, fifteen dollars a week to file pieces. Art told Taylor, "Give me the fifteen dollars a week." Taylor agreed, and "For the next six weeks or so," said Red, "Art was a sportswriter." At the time, the St. Louis papers, except for the *Post-Dispatch,* allowed the teams to pick up the expenses for writers traveling with them. Red recalled: "So food and lodging were free, and the fifteen dollars a week kept Art in cigarettes and toothpaste. Meanwhile, St. Louis owner Sam Breadon loved parties and poured with a heavy hand. Thus all the necessities of life were provided."

Art finally wangled a full-time job with the *Star-Times* in 1934.

"He was a feisty guy who got into trouble with bouncers," recalled Vern Tietjen, who worked on the paper then. "But he also stood up to editors." He was making eighteen dollars a week and thought this outrageous for a first-rate newspaperman. "Within a few weeks," Red later wrote, "Art was demanding a decent wage. Rebuffed, he quit on the spot."

Then Taylor called in Red and, Smith would write, "expressed the pious hope that I wouldn't be corrupted by my brother's false values."

Red stayed. He was married and had a family. Art was a bachelor. Besides, Red recalled, "I was the timid brother who clung to a job until a better one came up."

Art Smith moved on, this time to prospect for gold in the Yukon. Red helped stake him to it, though, to be sure, it wasn't very much. And if Art struck gold, they agreed, Red would share the riches. Art struck out.

Meanwhile, Red Smith continued typing. He got a taste of sports again in 1934 when he wrote periodic features on the Cardinals' pennant drive. In the deciding game for the National League championship, the Cardinals in Sportsman's Park beat Cincinnati behind the consummate pitching of the town's greatest hero and character, Jay Hanna (Dizzy) Dean.

. . . Packed in the aisles, standing on the ramps and clinging to the grandstand girders, the fans followed Dizzy with their eyes, cheered his every move.

They whooped when he rubbed resin on his hands. They yowled when he fired a strike past a batter. They stood and yelled when he lounged to the plate, trailing his bat in the dust. And when, in the seventh inning, with the game already won by eight runs, he hit a meaningless single, the roar that thundered from the stands was as though he had accomplished the twelve labors of Hercules. . . .

Two years earlier Smith, looking for extra money before his marriage, had proposed a story to the *Saturday Evening Post,* then the most popular and best-paying magazine in the country. The story concerned Dean, a little-known, brash rookie pitcher with great potential whom Smith covered on his Cardinals' beat. The *Post* told the little-known St. Louis sportswriter no. But after Dean won thirty games in the 1934 season and led the Cardinals to victory over Detroit in the World Series, the *Post* ran a Dean story. It was written not by Smith, but by the better-known St. Louis writer, J. Roy Stockton.

In August of 1935, Frank Taylor came to Smith with a brainstorm. "I want you to go out in the sticks and get some old broad, some old doll that's never been to a city, never seen an electric light, and bring her to town as a guest," said Taylor. "Get an old guy if you have to, but I prefer an old woman. Go find one."

Smith had recently read about a strike of tiff-miners* in a place called Old Mines, Missouri, in the foothills of the Ozarks. "This was an area settled by the French about the same time the fur traders were coming up from New Orleans and settling St. Louis, and you could still hear French spoken there," he would recall. "These tiff-miners were completely isolated—but I had read a travel piece about how the hard road had just come into Old Mines."

It was seventy-five miles from St. Louis, and since Smith was going on vacation, he would combine this work with what he would call "a vain quest for Ozark bass." So he and Kay and their daughter, whom they called Kit, piled into Smith's "flivver"—he had bought the old car for ten dollars when another sportswriter was about to junk it—and headed west.

When Smith reached Old Mines, he went to the tiff-miners' union headquarters and asked directions to the wilderness. He was directed to Calico Creek Hollow and advised to look up Mrs. Mary Susan Coleman Tigert. She turned out to be the incarnation of his dreams. His first piece in a five-part series—this piece bore the dateline "Fletcher, Mo."—began: "In the deep quiet of Calico Creek Hollow, at the end of a flinty Ozark Trail that meanders three miles through the woods from this quiet cross-roads post office, the writer of this article has discovered a woman 73 years old who in her entire life has never seen a railroad train, a gas stove, street car, movie, taxicab, sewing machine, airplane, hotel, vacuum sweeper, department store, lamp post, traffic cop, apartment house, boat or dentist; never has heard a radio; never ridden an elevator; never worn street clothes, chewed gum, eaten in a restaurant or talked over a telephone."

She smoked a corncob pipe, and lived in a two-room log cabin home with a rather new husband, John, who was about her age.

"Spry as a cricket for all her years," continued Smith, Mrs. Tigert "was chopping wood" when he came upon her. "A homemade sun-

---

*"Tiff" is a colloquialism for "barite," an unusually heavy, chalklike mineral.

bonnet covered her sparse gray hair, and tattered tennis shoes wrapped her feet. She wore an aged gray cotton dress. Her small brown eyes lighted with interest when she learned the visitor was from St. Louis.

" 'Then the big creek, you him?' she inquired eagerly.

" 'The big creek? Oh, you mean the Mississippi? Yes, that's in St. Louis. You have been there?'

"Her laugh echoed through the valley. 'But no! I do not leave this hollow. Seventy-t'ree years now I do not go.' "

Smith had difficulty getting her to St. Louis, but he said, "She fell in love with Kay, and besides, she could ride on a Mississippi River-boat."

Smith took her to the zoo and to the Statler Hotel Roof, where there was dancing and a show. "The city," she said, "he is all like gold." Smith recalled, "She was charming and colorful, smoking that corncob pipe and wearing that black sunbonnet. Everybody was daffy about her."

Smith's five-part series began on September 2, 1935, and was the second most prominent story on page one, below the story of Italy's rumored invasion of Ethiopia.

Readers and Smith's editors loved the stories of Old Lady Tigert. They were the talk of St. Louis. But one man remained unimpressed. He was O. K. Bovard, the flinty managing editor of the more conservative *Post-Dispatch*. He refused to give credit to many of the stories fueled by his audacious rival, Frank Taylor. In fact, very little impressed Bovard. "One time Bovard had fired a reporter and the guy came back the next day to cop a plea," recalled Bob Broeg, a sportswriter for the *Post-Dispatch*. "The guy begged Bovard to give him back his job, nearly got down on his knees. Bovard just kept on reading copy. In desperation, the guy blurted out, 'But Mr. Bovard, I've got to eat.' 'Not necessarily,' Bovard said."

Less than a year after Smith's series appeared, the *Post-Dispatch* sports editor Ed Wray suggested to Smith that he apply for a job there. Smith was very interested since "it was the only paper in town that paid real money," recalled Smith. But Bovard refused to entertain the notion of Smith being hired there. "He said the story of Old Lady Tigert was a movie scenario and that I was a faker and had faked the whole thing," said Smith. Wray and Roy Stockton, a favorite of Bovard's, appealed to the stern managing editor on Smith's behalf, and he seemed to be weakening. Smith, though, was realistic, as well as being indignant at Bovard's attitude. "I probably could have gone to work there," said Smith, "but I decided even if I could beat down Bovard's resistance, it would be unwise to be working for a managing editor who was convinced I was a faker."

Smith didn't arrive at that conclusion right away, though. While negotiating through Wray, Smith had received a cable from a former *Star* editor, Stanley Cryor, who was the news editor of the *Philadelphia Record* and wanted to hire Smith. Red turned down the offer, pretending he wanted more money. He thought he had a chance at the *Post-Dispatch* and reasoned that Kay was a St. Louis girl who would rather not leave town. But in the meantime, prospects with the *Post-Dispatch* had soured. Smith, covering a murder trial at the time, wrote to Cryor and asked if he was still interested. Cryor wired back, "Can renew offer."

The offer was for sixty dollars a week—five dollars a week more than Smith was earning at the *Star-Times.* Kay was hesitant. But Red told her that it meant going East and being close to New York, closer, that is, to the Big Time. "Stick with me, baby," he told her, with mock bravado, "and you'll be wearing diamonds and pearls."

Kay laughed. "Right," she said. "I've heard that line before." But she was willing. Her breadwinner—now thirty years old—would be coming home with an extra five dollars in his pay envelope. In mid-June of 1936, they packed their few belongings, and Red, Kay, and Kit piled into Smith's flivver and headed to, as Smith would write, "William Penn's green countrie towne."

C H A P T E R
6

"Walt Smith?" asked Kay Smith, looking up from the sports section of the *Philadelphia Record.* "That sounds like a hick. You can't use that name."

Whether this was Kay's sensitivity to becoming an Easterner, or simply repugnance for the name—maybe a bit of both—the fact is that the party of the second part did not dissent. Walter Wellesley Smith had never liked either of his two given names or any abbreviation thereof. Smith's first byline for the *Record* appeared on the second page of the Saturday, June 20, 1936, sports section. The story was about Pie Traynor, manager of the Pirates. When Smith handed it to the copy desk, the slot man noticed it had no byline. The slot man didn't know the new reporter and was aware only that the paper had hired a Walter Smith. So he penciled in the shorter version.

Philadelphia newspapers were informal about bylines in contrast to St. Louis, where it was J. Roy Stockton and R. J. Gillespie and W. W. or Walter W. Smith. In the *Record* the first names on bylines included Phil and Bill and Joe and Bud. Philadelphia was also freer with bylines. Smith didn't write his name onto his first piece for the

Record because, he said, he had "moral scruples against putting a byline on a story" if there was a possibility that he wasn't entitled to one. In St. Louis, the copy desk would strike the byline out.

Influenced by Kay, Smith asked the slot man not to use "Walt" again. Smith was embarrassed about this flight of ego, especially coming from a new hand, and made no other suggestion about the name. On Sunday, Smith covered the Phillies' 7–6 victory over the Pirates and sent in the story again without a byline. The next day the game account appeared with the slot man's new invention, the byline "Red Smith." Smith hadn't cared what name they used, and Kay didn't mind Red. Never again would it be anything else on a signed piece.

Smith had accepted the *Record* offer without even knowing if he would be in news or sports, nor did it matter to him. "I knew how many dollars a week I was going to get," Smith would recall. "That was the essential thing. I never asked what they wanted me to do." And as in the case of the byline, he didn't care. "I just wanted to be a newspaperman and earn a living at it."

When he got to Philadelphia, there happened to be a vacancy in the sports department, and Smith was assigned to fill it. By now, after having suffered through—and still trying to climb out of—the financial morass of the Depression, Smith was delighted simply to be working, and particularly pleased to be earning a living in his chosen profession. He had obviously resolved his conflict about covering sports while "empires" were collapsing. If he had to write sports, fine —it was an honest occupation, and could be a lot of fun. Five dollars more a week in pay could make it that much more pleasurable.

He went out to cover sports with enthusiasm.

"As early as the third inning yesterday," began the first game story by Red Smith, which was his second writing assignment at the *Record,* "Jimmy Wilson [the Phillies' manager] was casting longing glances toward a third-base box where gleamed the incredibly pink dome of James A. Farley, surrounded by deserving Democrats.

"A little earlier, posing with a baseball for news photographers, Big Jim had exhibited all the form of a top-flight pitcher, which was more than Mr. Fabian Kowalik was doing at the moment. . . ."

The Smith touch was evident in that lead—literate, descriptive, humorous, detached (with a view away from the field to the National Democratic Chairman), honest (in its portrayal of the bumbling home team), and concluding with the pleasing, unexpected twist involving the unfortunate Philly pitcher Kowalik. In the next paragraph, however, he described Kowalik's pitches as looking "as big as grapefruits" to the Pittsburgh hitters. The bromide suggested that Smith's stuff, though good, still needed polishing.

Between assignments, he and Kay looked for a place to live. After staying with the Cryors for a short period, the Smiths rented half of a modest two-family dwelling at 1463 Drayton Lane in Penn Wynne, a suburb just north of the Philadelphia city line and an easy drive to the *Record* office.

The *Record,* with a daily circulation of about 220,000, ranked third and last among Philadelphia's morning dailies in 1936. It followed the *Bulletin,* which had the largest daily circulation (more than 500,000), and the *Inquirer.* The two afternoon papers, the *Daily News* and the *Evening Ledger,* had lower circulations than the morning papers. The *Record* was one of the few liberal newspapers in the country, and Ed Hogan, then a *Record* sportswriter, recalled that it was "the Democratic mouthpiece for the entire Eastern seaboard." It was not uncommon for the *Record* to run front-page editorials such as the one castigating the local Republican administration as "a model of inefficiency, waste, and squalor."

"It was," recalled Smith, "a pretty decent paper." He respected it, but he could kid about it. Once when he and another *Record* sportswriter were about to leave town for a big fight and the World Series, city-side employees thrust "envious looks" at them when they handed in their expense vouchers. There was an allusion to sportswriting being cushy. "Colleagues," wrote Smith in the *Record*, "keep coming around and poking us slyly in the ribs with the lances which a crusading newspaper like this always keeps on hand for jousting with windmills."

Philadelphia, Smith would write, "has always been pictured as a blue-nosed dowager among cities, where life moves at a rheumatic crawl." Mencken called it "the most Pecksniffian of American cities, and thus probably leads the world," and W. C. Fields provided the most telling blow when he wrote for his epitaph, "On the whole, I'd rather be in Philadelphia."

On the whole Smith would rather have been in Philadelphia than St. Louis—even with the puritanical Sunday blue laws. In fact, Smith would write, it had only been since 1934 that "God-fearing Philadelphia left the gates of hell ajar by permitting baseball to be played at all on Sunday, and the law confined such profane activity to a few hours between morning devotions and vespers." The blue laws continued to prohibit on Sunday such activities as dancing, the conducting of general business, and the selling of liquor. The latter especially irked Smith. But he knew, of course, that there were ways to survive such strictures. Besides, his paycheck had improved and so had the variety of sports to cover. Philadelphia had two big-league baseball teams, a pro football team, many more college sports (including the annual Army-Navy football game) and more boxing than in St. Louis. Add to that the fact that New York was only ninety miles away and—well, he could dream, couldn't he?

Meanwhile, he would adjust to spending time in the Baker Bowl, where the Phillies played their home games. The small wooden ballpark had been built in 1887 and seated only 18,800. "Baker Bowl," Smith wrote years later, "had the charm of a city dump but not the size. If the right-fielder had beer on his breath, as he frequently did, the first baseman could smell it. For that matter, the whole team smelled most of the time, even though a sign covering the wall in right boasted, 'The Phillies Use Lifebuoy.' . . ."

The Phillies had not won a pennant in twenty-one years, had finished seventh out of eight teams in each of the previous three seasons, and were on their way to finishing last in 1936. Fans at games were few. And sometimes the reporters in the press box seemed to outnumber them.

In most ballparks the press was, as Smith noted, "segregated in a detention pen tucked away up under the roof." But in the Baker Bowl the press box was a section placed ten yards deep in the second deck of the grandstand directly behind home plate. "There," Smith would write about a particular day, "the flower of Philadelphia letters drowsed over scorebooks and whiled away the afternoon throwing peanuts at the head of Stan Baumgartner of the *Philadelphia Inquirer,* who sat in the front row. Running out of peanuts that day when the Cubs were in town, somebody started throwing paper cups of water. The water dripped into the box area below. Gerry Nugent (president of the club) hastened up to remonstrate.

" 'You must remember,' he said, 'we have patrons downstairs.'

" 'My God!' said Warren Brown, a Chicago sportswriter. 'What a story!' "

After the baseball season ended, Smith covered the winter sports that he had disdained in St. Louis. He accepted them now even during a "typical Philadelphia January" which was "cold as the smile of charity, wet as a drowned cat, slushily wretched." He wrote about the minor-league hockey team, the last-place Philadelphia Ramblers, and even about basketball. "And for a time," he would recall, he "fell in love" with the St. Joseph's College team, the Mighty Mites. They had no starter over six feet tall, with which the five-eight Smith could identify. They won, wrote Smith, "although built not quite so close to the ceiling" as their opponents. But overall Smith was no basketball aficionado. He wrote prior to one game: "My feeble brain reels at the thought that Dr. Naismith should have deemed it desirable to invent a new indoor sport when the distillers, the publishers, the chefs, and the Brothers Minsky already had provided adequate entertainment for the long winter evenings.

"However, this attitude is not necessarily shared by everyone. In some circles, a six-foot-six-inch center leaping about in a gaudy foundation garment inspires a more reverent respect than Whistler's Mother. For the benefit of citizens who feel this way about it, and also for readers with a sweet tooth for freak shows, some facts are presented herewith."

In February he got away from it all. He was assigned to the A's spring training camp, and, though he was sorry to leave Kay and three-year-old Kit, it was good to return to spring training after an absence of four years. The A's would train for the first time in Mexico City. Earle Mack, son of the A's manager, had been there several years earlier while barnstorming with an all-star team and had found the Mexicans wild about the games. He told his father that riches lay south of the border. It turned out, Smith would write, that with the ball park more than a mile above sea level "nobody could run without gasping for breath." And when someone did, he sometimes ran into sheep grazing in the outfield at Parque Delta. For training games the only opponents were a group of semi-pros. Soon, that paled. "Strictly for their own amusement," Smith wrote in the March 19, 1937, *Record,* "the Athletics played a ball game here today and beat the daylights out of themselves, 17–6."

The fans did not stream to the ball park, and the A's never again trained in Mexico.

Yet Smith's first trip out of the United States was an adventure, from the ball field to the cab rides. One taxi ride was especially memorable. Smith would write:

The cab driver wanted *un peso cinquenta* (one peso and fifty centavos), which was forty-two cents, but he was hammered down to one peso. He set off sullenly down Reforma Boulevard, scooting under the tail-board of a truck, cutting off another speeding cab by inches to prove that he was *muy hombre,* which means "very man," and if you're not that in Mexico, you're nothing.

One of his passengers was Cy Peterman [a sportswriter for the *Philadelphia Inquirer*]. Cy had learned one Spanish word, and now he employed it at the top of his voice.

"Despacio!" he screamed. *"Despacio!* Slow! Take it easy!"

The driver shoved the accelerator down to the boards to beat another car to an intersection. With life hanging in the balance, he swiveled to face the rear seat, one hand on the wheel and the other gesticulating indignantly.

"Despacio," he said firmly, *"un peso cinquenta."*

Besides the expatriates from Philadelphia in Mexico City, there was one from Moscow. Leon Trotsky, in exile, lived in Coyoacán, a suburb. The reporters covering the A's had endeavored to get an interview with Lenin's former war minister. In mid-afternoon, Thursday, March 18, "word came to the Athletics training camp that Trotsky would see the Philadelphia newspapermen," wrote Smith.

Smith's story carried a banner headline across the top of the first page of the *Record*'s second, or news feature, section:

RED TROTSKY TALKS TO RED SMITH

The red fire of revolution which forged the reputation of Leon Trotsky and was to become a worldwide conflagration is flickering out in the oldest, sleepiest village of the Western Hemisphere.

Today the arch-plotter of modern times sits in the study of a borrowed home . . . a mild and amiable and aimless old man pottering with old ideas.

The Great Revolutionist is somewhat bigger than a growler of beer and somewhat less fiery. Fumbling with the writing by which he earns a living, he exhibits all the wild-eyed revolutionary fervor, all the sinister aspect, all the mastery of men, all the compelling powers of oratory, all the irresistible ardor and magnetism of an elderly and not very successful delicatessen keeper in the Bronx. . . .

Leon Trotsky does not admit he is through

any more than he says in so many words that
he will return to the Soviet Union some day to
lead Russia and the workers of the world.

But the latter obviously is what he means
when he says:

"Stalin's biggest mistake was in exiling me.
He thought if he sent me out of the country,
he could ruin me by reviling and libeling me
in the press, in all the agencies of propaganda
which he controls.

"But outside of Russia, I have gathered a
new group around myself. I still do harm. My
writings, my books, what I say, they penetrate
Russia. I do harm."

Harm. He says it like a small boy insisting,
"I'm tough. I carry matches."

Smith pretended no expert knowledge of Soviet or Communist
affairs, and wrote the piece as description rather than analysis.
"Probably," wrote Smith, "it was the first time that any group of
interviewers met him on a completely equal footing of understanding; they knew precisely as much about Communism as he did about
baseball."

After six weeks in Mexico, Smith returned home with the A's to
start the 1937 season. On occasion, he also wrote a column, and in
one published upon his arrival in Philadelphia, he predicted that,
despite Connie Mack's guarded optimism, the A's would finish seventh or eighth. (They had been last the previous two seasons.) The
A's lost the season opener and continued losing "resolutely"
throughout the season—dropping ninety-seven games out of a hundred and fifty-four, in fact—and finished seventh, forty-six and a half
games behind the pennant-winning Yankees. (Only his old team, the
St. Louis Browns, were worse, finishing fifty-six games behind.)

"I found myself forming my warmest friendships in baseball not
with the top players," Smith would recall, "but with fellows who
were just making the grade." Two of those on the A's were a reserve
infielder, Wayne Ambler, and "the little shortstop Skeeter Newsome." "I used to wonder about this," recalled Smith. "Finally I
realized that these fellows lacked the natural attributes of [the stars],
that they would never have got to the big leagues at all if it weren't
for sheer bone effort—desire and effort. And it was these qualities in
them which one sensed and felt warmly about."

Ambler, a rookie in 1937 out of Duke University, broke in with a flash, but then "making a desperate try for a hit he never should have gone after," wrote Smith, "got his left thumb in the way of the ball," and jammed it. Later in the season Ambler fractured his jaw, sat out for a spell, taking his meals through a straw with his face wired, then returned to the field, "fighting the ball, fighting himself. . . ." He finished the season with a .216 batting average.

"Red," recalled Ambler, "was sort of like one of the guys. But unlike some of the hatchet writers, he usually wrote decent things or went into your personality or home life."

Some players confided in Smith, and he kept confidences. Some of it was off the record, which often is the bête noire of a reporter, having information he cannot report. But Smith would rather have been trusted with the information because, he said, the more he knew the better equipped he was to do his job. Though he wouldn't go out of his way to write something negative about a player, he could be wry. The A's briefly had a pitcher who threw junk balls, and could baffle hitters for a while with that slow stuff. Smith wrote that he "couldn't break out of a greenhouse with hand grenades." The following day, the A's were starting a road trip, and when Smith walked into the Broad Street station he was accosted by the pitcher who held the clipping in his hand. The player announced he was going to shove it down Smith's throat.

"What did you mean by this?" the player demanded.

"That means you don't throw hard," said Smith.

"I know I don't throw hard," said the pitcher. And then a look of doubt crossed his face.

"Any time that I'm going to knock you," said Smith, "you'll know it. There won't be any doubts."

The pitcher backed off.

The A's third baseman, Bill Werber, would become Smith's least favorite player. In Smith's view, Werber, who had a college education (from Duke) when few players did, "paraded" it. Sometimes he would take other players aside and lecture them. Once Skeeter Newsome at short had called for a pop-up, shouting, "I got it, I got it." Werber later corrected him. "Listen," he said, "you're using bad grammar. It's 'I have it, I have it.' "

At spring training, Smith had written a column that began, "They call Bill Werber a trouble maker" because Boston had traded him because of disagreements with the manager, Joe Cronin. Smith, though, gave Werber a chance when he first joined the A's. "He has poise and breeding and manners, and he got more out of his four years at Duke than a letter in baseball," wrote Smith. But as time went on Werber and Smith did not get along. Once, Werber, who stole many bases but also was thrown out many times, was caught trying to steal third with the score tied, two out in the ninth inning, and the A's best hitter at bat. Because a single would have scored him from second with the winning run, Smith raised doubts about "the wisdom of the strategy." On another steal attempt, Smith would write, he "made a leaping slide, spikes high. The . . . shortstop who had the ball was a quiet youngster just recovered from a serious injury. He was helped off the field, bleeding from long spike gashes on both arms and legs."

When Werber was traded to the Reds after the 1938 season, Smith wrote a "good riddance" column about him. The 1939 Reds won the National League pennant, and Smith, covering the World Series, went into the dugout to see an old friend from his Cardinal days, the pitcher Paul Derringer, now with the Reds. Werber saw Smith and hollered, "You son of a bitch! Get out of this dugout."

"No," said Smith.

Werber stood up from the bench and shouldered Smith. Derringer broke in between them. Smith had been carrying a portable type-writer and recalled, "I wanted desperately to hit him with it, but out there in front of a World Series crowd, no, I restrained myself. I couldn't punch an athlete. I could no more whip an athlete than I could whip Dempsey."

Smith left the dugout. Afterward, Charlie Dexter, a reporter, said to Smith, "What are you going to do? Are you going to protest?"

"No, Charlie," Smith said. "The player doesn't like me. I'll let it go."

In the fall of 1937, Smith, part of the small staff of the *Record,* was moving about swiftly. He would cover a football game at Villanova on Friday night, a football game at Penn on Saturday, and the Sunday pro game with the Eagles. "Then," he recalled, "I'd gallop out and write about the high-school championships because I didn't want the season to end." Smith, in Green Bay when the Packers were formed and at Notre Dame in its stirring football days of the Four Horsemen, had come to love football. "I loved it so much," he once said, that he stopped himself "just short of volunteering to rewrite the rulebook in English for nothing." Sometimes he loved the game perhaps a little too much as a writer. He once looked back at a football story of those days in which he had seen, he said, "a lot of shapeless troglodytes struggling in the primeval mud," and admitted that that was "awful."

Smith was writing seven days a week. And, despite the frantic pace, his reputation as a writer was growing in Philadelphia. Ed Hogan of the *Record* sports staff remembers watching Smith write. "He smoked too much and he knew it," said Hogan, "and he'd keep lighting cigarettes as he wrote. But he'd sit at the typewriter and paper would pile up. You know, false leads, crazy leads. He'd crumple 'em up and throw 'em away. Until finally he got what he wanted, and he'd bat it out in an hour or an hour and a half."

Art Morrow, who traveled with Smith when covering baseball for the *Inquirer,* said that sometimes a lead that Smith crumpled and threw away in the press box was picked up and used by another reporter.

"If there was a story Red felt was worth it, he'd spend a lot of time on it," recalled Morrow. "Maybe all night—if he could. But if the story was unimportant or not to his likes, he wouldn't devote much time to it. On the other hand, they had him doing so much you couldn't blame him for taking off once in a while. But that didn't happen too often."

On deadline, some telegraph operators could be a great help, while others produced frustration and anger among writers. Some of the operators would travel with the writers. Some were very good. There was a one-armed operator who knew as much as and sometimes more about the events than the reporters did. When he took dictation and found something wrong in the story, he simply changed it. Sometimes, though, an operator would get careless and drop a line or make an error and neglect to correct it. "Smith would complain," said Morrow. "Red was pretty particular about his stuff. Some of the wire-service workers grumbled that Red was a little too particular, but some of those old hands needed a little talking to."

Sometimes when Smith was in the office and the copy desk was overloaded and needed help, he pitched in. He didn't have to, being a hired writer. At the *Record,* stringers were paid twenty-five cents for every inch of their copy used in the newspaper. "The stringers would see Red," recalled Ed Hogan, then on the *Record* copy desk, "and they'd say, 'Ed, could you get Red to handle my copy?' He was like a diamond cutter. He had a way of changing a guy's paragraph or changing a word here that would brighten the story. And never cut any of their copy. He knew that would cost them money."

Smith liked going to the office, liked the camaraderie. Sometimes he wrote there. "I always courted interruptions," he said, "unless I was desperately on deadline."

"I was just starting out at the *Record*," recalled John Dell, "and I remember Red saying that you shouldn't be in awe of authority, of people in high places. Don't be afraid to question statements or actions."

On the beat, Art Morrow recalled that Smith "was not a guy to hold out. He'd swap stories." That is, he might share a scoop with the other writers. "He could get a lot of exclusives because people by and large liked him and told him things. But he never made other people look bad by scooping them. Actually, he didn't have to because with his writing ability it wasn't necessary." It was still the Depression, and Smith understood that men could be fired for having been beaten too often on stories. Smith appreciated the value of a job in those times. He also didn't believe that scoops in sports were very important. He didn't think it essential to be first, for example, to report a trade. He didn't believe it generally made a difference in the sale of newspapers.

Basically, Smith was a hard-core journalist, though, with few ambitions beyond the next deadline. It seemed true that, as he said, he had "no pressing need to express" himself. While traveling on trains and staying in hotels, he continued to read the best writers. One of his favorites was Hemingway; Smith appreciated the spare style and the concern for the exactness of words. He enjoyed John Galsworthy's storytelling and poetry, committing some to memory. Rereading Fitzgerald, Smith confirmed his beliefs, formed as an undergraduate, that Fitzgerald was a "self-conscious" writer and not always precise. He would recall a line in *The Great Gatsby:* "With a quick deft blow he broke her nose." Smith said this "didn't sound real to me. If a guy is mad he doesn't hit somebody deftly. He bangs her, he smashes her nose."

A few years before, in St. Louis, while trying to make money in the depths of the Depression, Smith bought a how-to-write-to-sell-fiction book and wrote some short stories. He sent them to *Collier's,* then one of the most popular magazines in the country. The stories were swiftly rejected. With neither time nor inclination nor energy, Smith never tried writing serious fiction again.

He had enough to do in daily journalism, and his interest in it remained keen. A Philadelphia high-school student named William West wrote Smith in 1937, asking several questions about journalism for a careers class. Smith replied:

Yours isn't an easy letter to answer, partly because I'm not sure of the answers to some of the questions, like, for example, the one about the qualifications of sportswriters.

But if you really are serious and not just sure you'd like the job because it would enable you to see a lot of games free, perhaps I can make a suggestion or so.

In the first place, all newspaper work is about 99^{44}/$_{100}$ percent hard, dull, routine work and only a part of the balance is glamor. It's a job which, like almost any other, can be fun at times, if often disappointing, insecure, and sometimes seems meaningless, but one in which the worker can find the satisfaction in doing his task well as in any other business. (That, incidentally, is a heck of a sentence for a newspaperman.)

Salaries, of course, depend on the employee, the paper, and the section of the country where it is published. In a large city the cub is likely to start somewhere around twenty-five dollars a week and I suppose the average for experienced men is forty or fifty dollars. Good ones may go up to a hundred dollars; only exceptional ones above that.

Good schools, like gold, are where you find 'em. Any recognized college or university can prepare the right man for newspaper work. . . . A product of journalism school myself, I have serious doubts that these schools do more to prepare a man for newspaper work than any general arts course in any good college. Still, I don't know any other course that improves on them.

Outside of journalism subjects, take all the English you can get, all the writing courses, languages, history, politics, economics. In short, a broad background is about the best educational equipment a newspaperman can have. And read, read, read. Everything good that ever was written.

About the only requisites I could name for a sportswriter are those of any ordinary reporter—intelligence, common sense, and an impersonal viewpoint. By the latter I mean the ability to stand a little apart, take no sides, and merely report what happens. The good sportswriter needs one thing more—a degree of writing ability, the capacity to put a little freshness and originality into his stories. This is so because in sports the important thing is the way a story is written, since the sports pages contain only a little real "spot" news in which the facts are the all-important things.

Lastly, the jobs in the newspaper business probably are no more plentiful, and no less so, than in most other fields. In sports, they are comparatively scarce because departments are much smaller than the local staffs.

But that shouldn't matter because a cub should by all means start on the local staff, not the sports page. Learn to recognize and present news first. Put in a long, stiff apprenticeship at it. Then, if your interest in sports hasn't faded by that time, it's comparatively easy to get a transfer to the sports side where you can spread your wings a little in a writing way.

In short, Smith was recommending the path he had taken: broad educational background, city-side newspaper experience, and continued reading. Smith's letter was a page and a half long and, except for a single strike-out of a single letter, was perfectly typed with no errors in punctuation, spelling, or grammar. His newspaper copy often was perfectly typed as well. Once he had thrown away the unused leads and was ready to set off on his writing journey, the thoughts in his head seemed to translate smoothly to his fingers on the typewriter keys.

Smith, though, was not as precise when itemizing his expense account. Once, a *Record* auditor handed back his statement and demanded that Smith make a more detailed accounting. Smith was offended. "He sat down," recalled Chick Elfont, a photographer with the *Record*, "and itemized everything he could think of. He said he got up at such-and-such an hour, had breakfast at such-and-such a restaurant with a waitress named Jane, was so impressed with her service that he left her an extra thirty-five-cent tip. He had who was there when he picked up his laundry in Cleveland, who the cab driver was who took him to the ball park in St. Louis.

"He pasted these sheets of paper together, and they stretched all the way across the newsroom to the auditor's desk. Smith dropped his expense sheets and walked away. The auditor ran after him and said, 'If you just give a general resume of your travels, that'll be sufficient.' "

At home, the Smiths were getting along financially and domestically, though it wasn't always easy. Smith traveled a lot, and Kay was not always thrilled to be home alone with a young daughter. Sometimes Smith stayed out late because he was covering an event, sometimes because he stopped off to have a drink and stayed long into the night.

After one baseball writers' dinner at a downtown Philadelphia hotel, a group sat around drinking into the early morning. "Everyone was having too much fun to go home," recalled Art Morrow, "so we began to just grab a place to sleep in the suite. Red was wadding up his jacket to make a pillow on the sofa, the only place left to sleep, but I beat him to it. He moaned about that the next morning at breakfast. He had tried to sleep on the floor and said he got no sleep at all."

On the day after one New Year's Eve, Smith wrote that

I opened one eye cautiously [upon] waking up this afternoon, and what do you suppose met my gaze? Good for little Johnny Wyrostek of Cedar Rapids, Iowa. Right on the first guess. "The bottom of the table," he says.

Well, sir! I was considering the feasibility of opening the other eye when I heard the sultry, musical tones which I recognized as belonging to the wife of my bosom, my favorite wife.

"Get it outta there, lout," she said in her sultry musical tones. "It's the next year already."

. . . I said, "Gawd, I wish it was over."

In 1938 Smith again went to spring training with the A's—this time in Lake Charles, Louisiana—and this time accompanied by Kay in the front seat and Kit in the back seat of their car.

"Wheeling lazily through the Virginia hills with the V-8 wolfing down oil," Smith wrote, "and with four-year-old Kit resolutely proving he travels fastest who travels alone. . . ." But they eventually made their destination.

At the ball park in Lake Charles, there was grass on the infield, in contrast to Parque Delta in Mexico City the spring before. Another important difference was that the A's were missing an outfielder. He was Wally Moses, who had batted .320 the year before and was holding out for more money. He did not show up in uniform at camp all spring. Though Smith tried to view sports as "fun and games," he also felt deeply that it was a livelihood for these ballplayers and thus serious business. But the reserve clause, which bound a player to one team for his career, or until the team saw fit to trade or release him, gave the owner virtually total control of a ballplayer's destiny.

Moses sought $12,500; Connie Mack, the angular, white-haired seventy-five-year-old owner and manager of the team, offered $10,000—the highest figure for any A's player. Smith dispassionately reported the case each side was making. Mack, who still wore stiff collars, said that he had paid higher salaries in the past and "it nearly ruined us." Moses said he was "only asking for what I'm worth" and threatened to sit out the year. In a column shortly after this, Smith presented the human side of the conflict, titled, "What Does a Holdout Think About?"

One afternoon, Smith sat with Moses and his wife on the veranda of the Majestic Hotel in Lake Charles. Smith, who himself had struggled to help form a guild to relieve reporters from autocratic rule, was sympathetic to the player, though he had a high personal regard for Mack.

"No use kidding myself about how long I'll be around, either," Moses told Smith. "I'm twenty-seven years old. I've been in professional baseball seven years; I'll have to be lucky to stay up eight more. Us little fellas, when our legs go, we're done.

"Now's the time I've got to get some money if I'm ever going to. . . ."

Smith concluded, "Wally is an honest young man, honest with himself. Too honest not to realize he faced a losing battle. He knew the other side had all the heavy artillery, all the ammunition.

"He knew the Athletics, if they chose, could let him quit baseball and could survive the loss. It might hurt them financially. It might arouse the wrath of the fans. But the crowd's memory is short, and a corporation has resources. Moses in flannels has arms and eyes and legs. In mufti he has only a lifelong habit of eating.

" 'It wouldn't be easy,' he said, 'but I could earn enough to live on outside of baseball'.

" 'Anyway,' his young wife said, 'we'd have a home. We could stay in one town for a change.'

" 'Yeh,' Wally said, 'but it'd be tough.' "

Mack wouldn't budge. Moses stormed out of their next meeting and returned home. In the end, Moses would sign. The ballplayers always did. And Moses accepted Mack's $10,000 just before the season opened.

By the end of six weeks of spring training, Smith wrote that "nothing" there "seems half so interesting as the old man [Mack]." Smith sat around and eagerly listened to Mack spin stories and listened to others spin stories of Mack. One had to do with the time an infielder misplayed a ball and several people on the bench had differing views of why he blew the play. Mack said he thought the ball wasn't hit as hard as the infielder thought it was. Mack was right. When the player came into the dugout, he said apologetically, "I grabbed at that ball before it got to me. It wasn't hit as hard as I thought."

"And Connie," wrote Smith another time, "up in his room, bobbing and ducking and stopping and weaving on his spindly shanks, his blue eyes bright and intent as he demonstrates for a writer's benefit the faults in a first baseman's defensive techniques."

Or another time, Smith wrote about Mack "posing for photographers after a camp game with his arm about the shoulders of a small tattered, barefoot and speechless boy whose face is black as doom and whose piano-tooth grin covers two full octaves. Connie is teaching the nipper how a slugger grips a bat, and as cameras click, a Negro in the crowd murmurs prayerfully, 'Lawdy, Lawdy, Lawdy, how I'd love to have one of them pictures of my boy. . . .' "

At Lake Charles, the reporters enjoyed barbecues and blackjack games, "unforgettable" pompano at Antoine's in New Orleans, and much social drinking. Smith drank, but only after he had filed his copy. Not so for one of his colleagues. "There was a writer who went on a drinking spree for about a week," recalls Art Morrow. "On the night the team was going to ship out, Smith and another reporter went up to the room of their inebriated friend. He was in no shape to move. So they were going to have to help him. The guy was lying in bed, and he looked up at these two guys and said, 'My paper has been getting stories from camp.' They said, 'Yes, we know.' He said, 'Who wrote these stories?' And Red said, 'Well, I did.' The guy in bed glared at Smith. 'You?' he said. 'Whose name did you sign?' Red said, 'Well, I signed your name.' And the guy shot him a look and said, 'You had the temerity to put my name on something *you* wrote? You're the first member of your family to speak English!'

"I'm not sure Red ever quite forgave him," recalled Morrow.

One of Smith's leads on a training camp game demonstrated his humor and the A's ineptness. "The Athletics," Smith wrote, "came within two runs and four hits of midseason form today.

"Up to the ninth inning of their exhibition with the New York Giants they regaled something under 5,000 observers with a splendid demonstration of how they go about being shut out in midsummer.

"However, not quite up to their peak of futility this early in the year, they slumped in the final frame, scored twice and wound up with only a 6 to 2 defeat."

Earle Mack, Connie's son, was not happy with such reporting. The *Philadelphia Record,* like most newspapers, allowed the ball clubs to pick up their reporters' traveling expenses, lodging, and food. The newspapers justified it by saying that they were doing the club a favor with free publicity. And among writers, there were always a certain amount of "homers," men who were rarely critical of the team. It came back to Smith that Earle Mack had considered him an ingrate. Mack said: "We take 'em around and feed 'em on the fat of the land and look what they do to us." Smith, though, viewed Earle Mack as "a moron" and would later say that such comments as Mack's "never influenced" his writing.

After a successful year of covering baseball, a wide range of other sports events, and writing a Sunday column, Smith, in September of 1939, was given a full-time column. He would join the *Record*'s other regular local sports columnist, Bill Dooly. Smith was becoming increasingly popular, and letters to the editor and to him demonstrated this. Though he would get some letters, he said, that began, "Dear Sir, you cur," the *Record* also printed such reader comments as "I want to say your Red Smith is the best sportswriter this town has been privileged to read in many a year. . . ." Kit Smith remembers a game that her father played with her as she got older. He'd come home and say, "Guess who thinks I'm wonderful today." One day, it was Bing Crosby, who had read a column of Smith's and had written him in praise. The game was Smith's way of bragging to his daughter with an attempt at humility. He would do similar things in print, poking fun at his "sweating, throbbing prose," calling himself "this errand boy for the Muses" and referring to "the columnist I love" and then recalling a particular failing, such as his "sedentary nature" or a pennant forecast gone awry.

He received a modest raise when he became a columnist, and this was helpful, since the Smiths had a fourth mouth to feed. Kay had given birth to a son, Terence Fitzgerald, on November 13, 1938.

One sportswriter who Smith was growing to like very much was Frank Graham, then columnist for the *New York Sun*. Graham, wrote Smith, "writes the way Carl Hubbell" pitched. "No rhetorical tricks, no showboating, but right down there through the strike zone with every pitch, and with something on every one." Smith also praised in print the hard-hitting, exposé-kind of writing of Dan Parker, particularly on boxing. When Parker, sports columnist for the *New York Mirror,* wrote about the forging of a boxer's record in order to fight in Philadelphia, Smith wrote that he owed a vote of thanks to Parker. The case, said Smith, "had escaped the notice of local fight writers, including—I must confess sheepishly—this reporter."

On occasion, Smith was hard-hitting, and caused a stir when he wondered acidly in print why the manager of Joe Louis was taking such a big cut of Louis's purses. Smith admired Louis. Smith wrote of the dignity, the professionalism, the humanity, and the radiant skills of the outstanding black heavyweight. "I am being careful not to use the stock line that he has been 'a credit to his race,' " wrote Smith in 1942. "There is an insulting condescension in that expression: it is tantamount to saying, 'He is a fine man, considering the color of his skin.' "

Despite this sensitivity Smith, in his eagerness to be lively, would not always put himself in the other fellow's skin. One wonders how blacks, reading the article on Connie Mack, viewed Smith's description of the small boy's face being "black as doom." Another time Smith wrote that he "particularly treasure[d]" this letter from a reader: "I and many others know you wisht you had some of Joe Louis cash. Dont be jelus. He is only a Negro but he never pick cotton. (Signed) A friend." Smith did not seem concerned that the writer was probably black, which may have been a reason for his semiliteracy in those days of racial segregation. Smith probably enjoyed so much the language and the irony of being called "friend" that the racial aspect was secondary.

There was, though, something else brewing on the world scene that would distract attention from almost everything else. That was war. Front-page headlines blared Hitler's military build-up, his take-over of Czechoslovakia and Austria, and then his invasion of Poland on September 1, 1939.

A week later, Smith began a column with

This is not the place for war talk and generally speaking there won't be much of it here. But today is the twenty-fifth anniversary of the first battle of the Marne and the guns are grumbling again along the Western Front and there's no use denying that day by day it becomes harder to concern oneself exclusively with games and who wins 'em.

Day by day it grows more difficult to support the pretty fiction that the future of civilization lies somewhere between Tony Galento's fist and Lou Nova's profile, or that the sun will be blotted out if Penn's football team fails to whip Yale.

Somehow these matters don't seem nearly so important as they did a year or even a month ago.

It cannot be so very long before it will become advisable and perhaps necessary to pay strict attention to the net yards gained from scrimmage by Villanova or the batting average of Joe DiMaggio.

So we'll go on whipping up our daily portion of froth and bubbles, remembering that as long as the battles we witness are fought with bats instead of bayonets, with headgears instead of gas masks, and with gloves instead of guns, some measure of sanity will be preserved in the land. . . .

And then Smith returned, for the most part, to lighter subjects. On an August morning in 1940, readers opened the *Record* and found

Smith's anniversary column—the anniversary being the appearance of his first column. "Threats of libel action have been few and far between . . . ," he wrote. "And our fearless and forthright predictions . . . exerted only a minor influence on the actual contesting of [sports] events." He told how, the previous evening, he had run into a "gentleman" in "a noted spa adjoining a parking lot." They talked about newspaper columns.

"I'll give you a tip," [the man] said. "No columnist ever amounted to anything unless he believed in something, with his whole heart and soul. What do you believe in?"

"The immortality of Connie Mack," we said. "Let's you and me drink to good old Connie."

"That won't do," the man said. "Everybody believes in Connie. You've got to believe in something controversial. Something you can write about and make people think about." And each time a name was suggested by the man, such as Heywood Broun and Eleanor Roosevelt, the columnist suggested they drink to that.

"Eleanor believes in young people," said the man. "All right," and they drank to young people. "But," the man continued, "you don't believe in anything."

At the time we had to confess this was so. But that was a long while ago. We have lived since then, and no longer are we the carefree, superficial wastrel of [last] night.

Now we believe, with passionate sincerity, in abstemiousness, clean living, regular hours, and a healthy, normal home life. With our whole heart and soul, we believe in national prohibition.

The column ended, but the serious question remained: What *did* Smith believe in? He believed in his family, though coming home at six-thirty in the morning would cause a problem with Kay. ("Where were you, up with a sick fight manager? Interviewing an insomniac batboy?" she was quoted as saying in the piece.) And he believed in hard work. Mostly, he believed in writing with integrity, writing that portrayed and sometimes interpreted his world without necessarily seeking to change it, though he would make specific recommendations.

He expressed the integrity in numerous ways, from the striving for purity in language to the self-examination of the sportswriter's role in wartime to the frank but comic chaffing at "Honest" Herman Taylor, as Smith referred to him, a local boxing promoter. Taylor one evening had stuffed people into his auditorium "at $5.75 apiece" to see the card, but because of "wretched mismanagement," Smith wrote, many customers stood in the aisles and "saw only a stranger's rear." Smith wrote this at a time when promoters were still paying some sportswriters ten dollars and up "to help with the promotion."

(Once, years later, when Kay was interviewed by a reporter and asked what Smith disliked most, she said, "Injustice." This came as a surprise to the interviewer, who was expecting an answer relating to sports. Then the interviewer, seeing the discussion had been elevated from his expectations, asked, "And what does your husband *like* the most?" And Kay replied, "My fried chicken.")

By now, Smith's excellent reputation was spreading beyond Philadelphia. Shirley Povich, the baseball writer and columnist for the *Washington Post,* recalled, "You couldn't ignore the things he was doing. They were so bright. He'd have a lead saying, 'Just as the A's were about to get the last out and retire to the clubhouse to admire themselves in the dressing-room mirror, the Senators came up with four runs.' "

Meanwhile, the war continued to expand overseas, and in America there were air-raid drills and grave concern. On the afternoon of December 7, 1941, Smith was on a train bound for Chicago, where the winter baseball meetings were being held, when he heard that bombs had fallen on Pearl Harbor. The next day President Roosevelt declared the United States to be at war against the Axis powers—Japan, Germany, and Italy.

On the agenda for the baseball owners in Chicago was the possibility of transferring the financially troubled St. Louis Browns to Los Angeles. Don Barnes, owner of the Browns, had commitments from Los Angeles interests for a move there. But the owners never got around to that. The meeting convened two days after Pearl Harbor. "Magnates kept slipping out of the conference rooms to listen to radio rumors that Jap bombers were over California," wrote Smith. "They experienced no prodding urge to send their million-dollar chattels junketing into that region. Barnes's plan went begging for an audience."

Six weeks later Smith was in Anaheim, California, covering the A's training when, one midnight, news reached camp that Japanese submarine gunners had shelled the Elwood oil fields at Santa Barbara. Smith was "fortunate" to rent a car and driver at that hour, left camp immediately and sped 110 miles up the California coast to cover the incident. His story, primarily a local reaction, ran the following day on the front page of the February 25, 1942, *Record.*

The oil fields suffered only slight damage because, Smith reported, the Japanese were "blundering" shots. Smith interviewed area residents and one man seemed to sum up their feelings: "Well, my gosh," he said slowly, "now that's getting right close to home, isn't it?"

Smith then returned to baseball and his light touch. The A's played an exhibition game against a squad at San Quentin state prison. Smith reported: "The Athletics, who have committed more crimes in their own line than many of the 4,000 residents of this snug stockade, were caught red-handed committing baseball here today.

"Because it was the first time a major-league team—or reasonably accurate facsimile thereof—ever played in this home for wayward boys, they made it quite a ceremonial affair. The captain of the yard himself threw out the first ball and chain."

Smith also went to Hollywood to look in on the making of *The Pride of the Yankees*. On the set, playing himself in the film, was Babe Ruth—who, at age forty-seven, had been retired from baseball for six years. Smith noted that when a letter was brought to Ruth to read, "the owner of baseball's sharpest eyes hesitated, then fished into a pocket and brought out a pair of glasses." Smith also spoke with the star of the film, Gary Cooper, who was apologetic about playing Gehrig. Smith wrote: "Says he always threw like a girl; anyhow, and it's worse trying to do it left-handed like Lou. Where he grew up in Montana, the kids didn't play ball, preferring to ride bucking horses."

In a notes column telling of these matters, Smith ended with this:

Then there were those Army nurses at an embarkation point. Just kids. Their eyes sparkled when we told them yarns about lunching with Gary Cooper and that sort of thing.

My, my, they said, newspaper men certainly did lead fascinating lives.

They were waiting for a transport to take them no one knew where, quite possibly through enemy-controlled waters into bomb-torn lands. We were going to lead our fascinating lives in Shibe Park.

I expect it'll be a while before we forget how that made us feel.

Millions of men, including of course numerous ball players, were being drafted into the armed services. Many more were enlisting; those men and women, particularly, had important personal decisions to make. What would Smith do? He was thirty-six when World War II broke out. The maximum age at which one could be drafted was thirty-seven, which he would reach on September 25, 1942.

Because of poor eyesight, he was classified 4-A and highly unlikely to be drafted.

Beyond that, he would say later, "I had a family"—Kit was eight and Terry three at the war's beginning—"and we didn't have any money and I didn't think I could afford to be a private in the Army." He said he didn't wish "to go looking for one of those phony public-relations commissions," and so he continued writing about sports.

The context, however, was changing dramatically. And he fought the sometimes "desperate feeling of being useless" during the war. He did that by keeping sports and the war effort in focus. He did write about "a preoccupied nation" and the travel restrictions on baseball—the A's would later train in Frederick, Maryland, and Wilmington, Delaware, to save on train fuel. And he discussed the "moral issue" of whether there should be sports at all during war-time. "If need be," Smith wrote, "we could get along without base-ball for a while. We can get along without cuffs on our pants, without pleasure cars, without plumbing or central heat. But we are not yet ready to admit that the Axis can make us give all these things up, even temporarily."

President Roosevelt insisted that sports were vital for morale. Smith found justification in the pursuit of sports activities. He re-ported on surveys made in war plants that showed increased produc-tivity "where there is an active interest in sports." He received a letter in 1943 from his Philadelphia colleague, Cy Peterman, then a war correspondent. "The men talk sports and they talk of home," Peterman wrote. "He said," Smith added, "the boys in Sicily and Italy were sore because the radio didn't give them enough details on the World Series. Even General Eisenhower kicked about it."

Smith occasionally received letters from the war front from men telling him they got his columns and looked forward to them. One foot soldier in Europe, Ernest Paolino of Philadelphia, recalled years later that his sister "regularly sent me batches of his columns. Next to an extra can of C-rations, they were what I looked forward to most."

Smith defended some of the wartime ball players, or "Four-effers." They weren't fighting, he explained, because they might have a de-fect, like a bad knee, that might "fold in a situation where one man's failure might cost a dozen lives."

Smith wrote, "It ought to be clear to everybody that the big lug is playing ball because the draft board hasn't seen fit to call him and because [the military] can't find any other earthly use for him. Same like you. Same like me." Smith's job, he said, was to allow the reader a respite from the "significant" news of the day. "What he wants, once he turns back to this page," wrote Smith, "is something of major inconsequence. . . ."

But he berated the city of Philadelphia for the sparse attendance —he had hyped the event—of an A's game in which all proceeds went to the war effort.

Yet Smith maintained his sense of humor. Covering a dull prizefight, he wrote, "In these times every man must play his part. Friday night I played the part of the aisle over which 18,870 people walked down toward ringside where they, at least, could have seen the fight if there'd been a fight."

Like thousands of other Americans at home during World War II, Smith planted a "victory garden." Smith said his tomatoes were a pleasant surprise, but that was all. "I never saw such faint-hearted cabbages," wrote Smith of his garden. He noted that the neighborhood rabbits, who were known to indulge in midnight snacks with other peoples' cabbage, left Smith's alone. "Chances are the rabbits didn't recognize the plants as cabbages," he wrote. "They're limp and stringy enough to pass for sauerkraut. . . ."

Meanwhile, he continued, "the carrots have been AWOL since induction. The potatoes are officially listed as missing. The radishes seem to be victims of amnesia, a common ailment in wartime. They can't tell themselves from the weeds. . . ."

Wartime sports sometimes didn't fare much better than Smith's garden. Most of the best players had gone off to war. By 1944, two-thirds of the men who were in the major leagues in 1941 were no longer on the diamond. Playing instead was, primarily, a collection of very young ballplayers and very old ballplayers who were classified 4-F for physical reasons.

The most unusual wartime player was Pete Gray, a one-armed outfielder who batted .218 in seventy-seven games for the Browns in 1945. Smith, like most others, was impressed with the courage of this "long-legged, gaunt" athlete. "He was a marvelous one-armed outfielder," recalled Smith, "but he was only a fair outfielder."

Smith wrote about a former Athletics catcher who operated a black-market butcher shop near the ball park. Meat, like other essential items, was rationed. "The catcher," Smith wrote, "was more valuable providing breakfast ham than he was catching." The catcher sued Smith for what Smith said "was my last $250,000." This at a time when, Kit Smith would recall, "I don't think my father had

$250 in the bank. He joked but he was worried." Smith hadn't used the catcher's name or his team, but the catcher believed he was easy to identify. Before the suit got very far along, the player died. Smith's lawyer—the lawyer for the *Record*—said that he thought he had the evil eye because that was the second time in a year that someone had sued the paper he was called on to defend and the plaintiff died. "Well, gee," Smith told him, "that's better than knowledge of the law."

Smith later recalled, "He was a Harvard lawyer and I don't think he was wild about that comment."

There was another side to the war that Smith reported. One such story concerned Jimmy Wilson, who had been a catcher and manager of the Phillies, and whom Smith respected and liked. Jimmy had a son named Bobby. Smith wrote:

Bobby had been a well-behaved kid around the training camps . . . and then he was a leggy, rangy boy growing up swiftly in prep school, and then he was getting ready to finish Princeton, a handsome youngster as fine and decent as any you ever met, an all-around athlete like his father. . . .

They were tremendously good friends, and Jimmy's pride in the boy was something to see. Jimmy insisted on the best of schools and the best of everything else that he himself hadn't had a chance for, but indulgence never spoiled Bobby. Jimmy was confident that a couple of years of seasoning and Bobby would be in the majors, but Jimmy's problem was not how to get the kid started in baseball but how to persuade him to finish his education before joining the Air Corps.

Next thing, there came the word that Bobby had volunteered to fly a special mission over enemy territory (in the China-Burma theater) and had flown out, and wouldn't be flying back. You couldn't say the news changed Jimmy outwardly. But . . . he seldom talked about the boy.

Then one night a trophy was presented in Bobby's honor at a baseball writers' banquet in Philadelphia. "Jimmy had to excuse himself," Smith wrote, "and ask an old friend to accept it for him."

On Wednesday, June 7, 1944, Smith's column bore the headline: NO GAME TODAY—INVASION!

It had been thirty months since Pearl Harbor, and the war lately had been turning decidedly in favor of the Allies. The world had waited anxiously for the day when American, British, and other allied troops would land in Europe. They did on D-Day—June 6, 1944—and the news was flashed around the world. "The train bringing the A's home was somewhere around Coatesville" when they heard the news, wrote Smith. "Most ball players talk baseball. These ball players didn't. There'll be time enough later to play games. And to write about 'em. Not today."

During the war, Smith tried to supplement his income by writing for the quality magazines known as "slicks." He had been trying for years. Finally, in 1944, he sold his first piece to the *Saturday Evening Post.* The story, a co-authored first-person account of a pro football player, Bill Hewitt, was a grim tale of working for George Halas, owner and coach of the Chicago Bears. It was called "Don't Send My Boy to Halas." Smith later wrote, "The *Post* paid us one thousand dollars, which we split down the middle. The piece kicked up a commotion in professional football circles, but one that hardly compared with the commotion in my breast. I had sold to the *Saturday Evening Post*—I was an immortal.

"I withheld the news from nobody and for at least a month ranked just a whisker beneath Hitler in the affections of my newspaper colleagues. But it was worth it."

This was the beginning of Smith's writing for many slicks, including *Collier's, Liberty,* and *Holiday.* With his first sale to a national magazine, at age thirty-eight, Smith understood that if he were to continue selling to the slicks, he must of course avoid the "sportswriter's occupational ailment of overwriting," as he put it, of straining "for the unusual angle," of "groping for the sprightly phrase and overreaching, [pitching] overboard into a purple waste of metaphors."Ailments that plagued him very little these days.

One early morning in late May of 1944, Al Laney of the *New York Herald Tribune* was at Pimlico Race Track in Baltimore to cover the Preakness. He was climbing the stairs to the press box at the top of the grandstand when he heard the click-click-click of a typewriter. When he drew closer, he saw Smith, alone in the outdoor press box, writing.

"What're you doing, Red?" Laney asked.

"A boy's book," said Smith.

"Why?" Laney asked.

"Because I have to feed my kids," said Smith, "and I can't do it on what the paper is paying me."

The juvenile book would be titled *Terry and Bunky Play Football.* It was based on Red's five-year-old son, Terry, and a pal of his. It was, Smith would say, "instruction sugar-coated with fiction." Smith would split the proceeds with Richard Fishel, a Philadelphia public-relations man who came to Smith with the idea.

Laney later said that he was embarrassed when Smith told him he couldn't earn enough to make a living as a journalist. "I was doing fairly well," recalled Laney, "making $140 a week. Red was making eighty dollars, and he was at least as good as I was."

Laney was a highly regarded sports feature writer and had been familiar with Smith since Red's St. Louis days. And as far back as the late 1930's, Laney had recommended Smith to Stanley Woodward, sports editor of the *Herald Tribune*. But Woodward took no action in regard to Smith.

During World War II, Woodward, who wore thick glasses, went overseas as a war correspondent with an airborne division at age forty-eight and parachuted from planes behind enemy lines, even though the loss of his glasses would have rendered him nearly blind. But he made it through the war.

After Woodward returned to the *Herald Tribune,* Laney gave him some of Smith's clippings one day and said, "Look, Stanley, you're always talking about building a great staff. Well, here's one of the best, maybe *the* best." Woodward just sulked and said nothing. Laney never found out why, and if he brought it up Woodward would "get mad and want to throw you out the window."

Laney wasn't sure if Woodward didn't like Smith's earlier work, or if Woodward felt Laney was pressuring him. Woodward's reaction to the suggestion to consider Smith was never explained.

Rufus Stanley Woodward was a gruff man who had been a lineman at Amherst, a student of Greek and Latin, and a literate, direct, no-frills writer. As an editor, he strove to produce the best sports section in the country, and competed fiercely, especially against *The New York Times,* which had a staff of about fifty compared to about twenty-five for the *Herald Tribune.* "Stanley," recalled Jerry Izenberg, who worked for Woodward, "used to look out the window of his office. He could see the Times Building a few blocks away. One time he shook his fist at the building. 'For Chrissakes, their biggest fucking problem is that they don't have enough chairs for the copy desk on Saturday. They've got a lot of people, so we can't outcrap 'em. But we sure as hell can outwrite 'em.'"

Laney had not said anything to Smith about his appeals to Woodward. Meanwhile, Smith was trying to get out of Philadelphia and into New York, where the money and prestige were substantially greater. *Look* magazine was seeking a sports editor, and Smith applied. "*Look* represented his ticket to get to New York," his daughter Kit Smith recalled years later. "I remember him saying, 'I'd leave the newspapers for that dumb magazine.' " But Frank Graham got the job in September of 1943. Smith was very disappointed. Another time, he received an offer from the *Brooklyn Eagle*. "But I decided," recalled Smith, "that Brooklyn was farther from New York than Philadelphia was."

Woodward, without Laney's knowledge, had begun to collect some of Smith's clippings.

Smith gained a little more attention when his piece "Gaelic Disaster," on the Army–Notre Dame game, was included in the *Best Sports Stories of 1944*, the first of what would be an annual anthology. Woodward had to take notice since Stanley was also included, along with Laney, who won the prize for the best story in the book.

Smith and Woodward had met on occasion in press boxes. Smith found Woodward to be, at times, "acerbic" and "impolitic." He wasn't sure how Woodward took him. "I guess I resented him a bit," recalled Smith. "He was an iconoclast. He was never one to accept the handout. He wanted to know for himself." During the war, "Stanley was dead set against sports. He felt games were nonessential and that we all should be fighting the war, that there shouldn't be a sports page, no baseball or horse racing, not even football—and he loved football. Well, of course, there shouldn't be necktie salesmen or florists or any of the nonessential industries, if you're fighting an all-out, 100 percent war. I disagreed with him. I felt there was some morale value to the games."

Besides their contrasting personalities and views, Woodward and Smith also had contrasting writing styles. Woodward, who wrote occasional columns, had an earnest and sometimes plodding style, as compared with Smith's generally droll approach. But Smith would repeat with delight some of Woodward's lines, like the time an Army coach blamed a one-sided defeat by Michigan on the West Point center's failure to give the football a quarter-turn on the snap to the quarterback. "That," wrote Woodward, "is like blaming the Johnstown flood on a leaky toilet in Altoona."

One day in June of 1945, Woodward phoned Smith, but Smith was out. Smith returned the call, but Woodward was out. Smith thought Woodward "wanted to know how old Connie Mack was, or something, you know, for a story." Smith's friend Garry Schumacher, a New York baseball writer, asked Smith one day, "Have you heard from Stanley Woodward?"

Smith told him of the two phone calls. "Well, get plenty [of money]," said Schumacher. "He's coming after you."

Smith would recall, "I waited all summer and I never heard a sound out of Stanley, and I was dying."

On the day after V-J Day, August 15, 1945, Smith finally received a phone call from Woodward. He said he wanted to talk to Smith about a job on the *Tribune*. Would Smith come up to New York? "Yes," said Smith. "Yes, I would."

With guarded excitement he and Kay drove to New York. Smith figured that if the discussion with Woodward didn't lead to a job, he would still enjoy an evening on Broadway—Red and Kay loved the theater. Perhaps they'd go to a show with his brother, Art, and Art's wife, Patti, which they had done several times in the past few years. Art had been in New York since 1942, working as a copy editor on the *Daily News*.

Kay and Red decided that if the *Herald Tribune* made an offer, and if it was even close to what he was making at the *Record*, he'd take it. The lure was not just the *Herald Tribune*, one of the best-written and best-edited newspapers in the country; it was New York. He would, he said, "be playing the Palace." Smith was nearly forty years old and knew he might never get another chance at New York. It was the city that meant success and wonder. It was the city of Jimmy Walker, the flamboyant mayor from 1926 to 1932, whom Smith first saw while covering the second Sharkey-Schemling heavyweight championship fight in New York in 1932. Smith would recall what Walker and New York meant to him, and to his dreams and vision of the city:

To . . . we hicks out in the Middle West . . . Walker was New York. He was the New York we had come to know, or to think we knew, through the columns of Winchell and O. O. McIntyre. He was the Broadway of George M. Cohan and Texas Guinan, the Polo Grounds of John McGraw, the Madison Square Garden of Tex Rickard and Jimmy Johnston. He was the New York of Babe Ruth and Tammany Hall and Tin Pan Alley.

He was the fiddler who called the turns in a dance which we pictured as never-ending. He was the debonair prophet of gaiety and extravagance and glitter. He was the embodiment of all the qualities which hicks like us resented and admired about New York.

Red and Kay met Woodward and Laney at Bleeck's, a wood-paneled restaurant and bar just downstairs from the *Herald Tribune*. Laney recalled the conversation with Woodward shortly before the Smiths arrived.

"How much do you think we ought to give this fella?" Woodward asked.

"Well," said Laney, "not less than me."

"Oh, no!" said Woodward.

"If you don't give it to him now, you'll be giving it to him within six months after he arrives."

The Smiths arrived, the four had lunch, then Laney sat with Kay while Woodward took Smith to his office upstairs. Woodward offered Smith one hundred dollars a week, twenty more than Smith was earning. The job was to write features and cover general sports stories. There was no mention of a column. (But Laney had told Smith earlier that he, Laney, wasn't going to write the column for long, and he was sure Stanley would have to pick Smith to succeed him.)

Smith needed nothing else, and he and Woodward shook hands on the deal.

Albert Gillis Laney, small, thoughtful, neatly dressed, and sporting a black brush mustache, wrote the *Herald Tribune* column five days a week and Woodward wrote it the other two days. The previous *Herald Tribune* columnist, Richards Vidmer, had left to become a war correspondent. "During the war," recalled Laney, "anyone who had an idea for a column could usually write it." Because space was limited due to the shortage of paper, the column would often be merely a digest, or wrap-up, of the sports news. But when the column was given over to an opinion or essay, the staff writers would contribute. Laney began doing two or three columns a week, and that gradually increased. Shortly after the war in Europe ended and Vidmer decided to remain in England, Woodward gave the full-time column to Laney. Woodward then needed another writer to replace Laney's features and general sports reporting.

"When the war was over," Woodward later wrote, "it was necessary for me to get a first-class man at once, and I knew the man I wanted. I had wanted him for approximately seven years. . . ." It was Smith. Woodward didn't say why he hadn't hired him earlier, though during the war there had been a freeze on hiring. "He was a glutton for punishment," Woodward continued. "He wrote a column seven days a week year in and year out and covered most of the top [sports] stories. . . . He was obviously writing too much, probably 500,000 words a year, but he made it all good and much of it excellent. Some of his columns were afterthoughts, conjured up out of thin air, written perhaps between innings of a ball game or between races. However, they were never dull, and it was easy to see what a man like this could do if relieved of the heavy burden he was carrying."

Woodward said he would never hire anyone who couldn't outwrite him. He obviously felt that Smith could. Unknown to Smith, Woodward had lied to the *Tribune* executives about him. They wanted to hire younger men, so Woodward told them Smith was in his early thirties.

In fact, Smith would write his first piece for the *Herald Tribune* of September 24, 1945, one day before his fortieth birthday. The word quickly circulated in New York that the *Herald Tribune* had hired a new sportswriter from Philadelphia. Barney Nagler, then a sportswriter for the *Bronx Home News* and later a columnist with the *Racing Form,* recalled walking along Broadway with Herman Taylor, the Philadelphia boxing promoter.

"Herman," Nagler said, "what kind of guy is this Red Smith?"

"He's not a good guy," said Taylor. "You can't trust him. He won't take."

CHAPTER
7

The Smiths prepared to move from their home in Penn Wynne to a small stucco house in Malverne, Long Island. The Smiths also needed a car. Smith had sold his car to help pay for the Penn Wynne house. For two years he had used public transportation around Philadelphia, or rented cars on the road to cover assignments. In the fall of 1945, cars were hard to get since automobile production had been cut to produce weapons and vehicles for defense. Smith went to a man he had known who he thought could help him, one Blinky Palermo, a mob-connected boxing manager who also owned an automobile dealership. Through him, Smith purchased a bottle-green Mercury convertible ("a dream car for Pop," recalled Kit Smith). Palermo was the only auto dealer, Smith would note, who, alongside his dealer's license, proudly hung his pardon from the state penitentiary.

Smith wrote his first piece for the *Herald Tribune* while still in Philadelphia. The Senators, who had an outside chance of catching the Tigers in the 1945 American League pennant race, were playing the A's there in late September of 1945. On September 24, Smith's first story said that the Senators lost the game 4–3 in twelve innings, on a rash of "boners and errors." One such play involved Bingo Binks, an outfielder who had failed to get his sunglasses from the dugout when the sun came out on an overcast day. "The sun-blinded Binks," wrote Smith, "never did see a fly ball which Ernie Kish drove into center with two out. Binks ran perhaps twenty feet off the path of the ball, shading his eyes with upraised hand, converting the third put-out into a two-base hit."

Smith set up the unexpected with his last verb, the ironic "converting."

The following day, he wrote that the Senators, who had finished their season nearly a week before the Tigers, would be "playing by ear from here out. They'll tune in [on radio] the Tigers' games against Cleveland."

Smith also clarified a claim by Clark Griffith, the Senators' owner, who protested a recent 4–3 loss because of an umpire's judgment call. The American League president, Will Harridge, turned down the protest, and Smith wrote: " 'They've taken the pennant away from us on a technicality,' lamented the man whose team never owned either pennant or first place."

These pieces swiftly proved that a fresh, funny new writer had joined the *Herald Tribune* sports department. Smith had pledged to himself that since he would now be writing less, he would take more time when he could and make every word the best word he could write. In the following months he covered a wide range of events and constantly met people who wondered where he had come from and who congratulated him on his work. He also reciprocated.

In the fall of 1945, Smith traveled to Annapolis to write a football story before the upcoming Army-Navy game. W. C. Heinz, back from his tour as a war correspondent and then a sports columnist for the *New York Sun,* was there, too. Someone said, "Red, do you know Bill Heinz?"

"No," Smith said. They were introduced and Smith, who admired Heinz's clean style and dedicated professionalism, asked, "Is that the typewriter that you write your stuff on?"

"Why yes," replied Heinz.

"It's a very good typewriter," said Smith.

Red's work immediately impressed the *Herald Tribune* sports staff and particularly pleased Al Laney, who had pushed to have Smith hired. Laney, a gentle, quiet man (trying to converse with him once, Woodward shouted, "Dammit! I'm going to have you wired for sound!"), now felt that Smith should replace him in writing the column. Laney never liked the pressure of producing a regular column and trying to be funny and clever five or six times a week. He preferred the more leisurely feature-writing assignments. Besides, he wanted to finish a book he was writing.

When Laney asked for a month off, Woodward gave it to him and gave the column to Smith. "Keep the column entertaining and write anything you want short of libel," Woodward told Smith.

Shortly after that, several *Herald Tribune* men were covering the same series, and Woodward gave all except Smith a specific assignment. Smith felt there was nothing left to cover.

"What do you want me to write about?" he asked.

"Write about the smell of cabbage in the hallway," replied Woodward.

Smith would quote that advice the rest of his life.

Smith's first column—on December 5, 1945, two and a half months after he had joined the paper—appeared under the heading "Another Viewpoint." It seemed a tentative heading, as a temporary replacement for Laney. Despite Smith's column-writing in Philadelphia and his zesty stories for the *Herald Tribune,* he still had to prove himself before the heading above his name would read "Views of Sports," the traditional head on the *Herald Tribune* column.

In the middle of the second sports page Smith broke into New York column-writing with a piece about the end of strange happenings in college football. During the war, many football players had to leave their colleges and take military training at another school, which they then played for. Smith dealt with this in the column titled "Liberty with Chaucer, Milton, and Guest." It began:

> As Chaucer or John Milton or Edgar A. Guest might have viewed wartime football:
>
> Far above Cayuga's waters,
> Brawn and strategem
> Pledged to other alma maters
> Served Cornell pro tem.
>
> Sons of Penn and North Dakota
> Furthered Dartmouth's fame;
> Celtic Swedes from Minnesota
> Played for Notre Dame.

Rochester and Hampden-Sydney
Drafted Temple's stars;
Tufts had men of every kidney
Learning to be tars.

In the view of General Sherman
War was merely hell.
In his day no lad from Furman
Scored for Citadel.

Leopards wont to run or pass or
Kick for Lafayette
Changed their spots for stripes au Nassau,
Informal Tigers yet!

Harvard men across the nation
Shuddered and turned pale.
Doomed to watch, for the duration,
Harvard men at Yale.

The verse ended and Smith picked up with the prose about the situation that was, he said, happily ended.

"From now on," he concluded, "it is devoutly to be hoped the coaches can dig up, and keep for a while, a few eager scholars who fan their coffee with their hats and never heard of West Point."

His column was set in two-column measure, as it often was at the *Record*. This may have made him feel at home. So at home, in fact, that he resurrected that verse from a column of his in Philadelphia the year before. It had proved effective then, and he probably reasoned that it would work again.

In his second column the next day, he described himself, as he had in Philadelphia, with the self-deprecating phrase "the tenant in this literary flophouse," and he related a tale about a fight manager in Philadelphia. "Mr. Hahn," wrote Smith, "had got back into action in the fistfight industry after a long, arid stretch at slightly honest work."

From this point forward, Red Smith was the lead sports columnist of the *Herald Tribune*. It would never have another.

Smith was an immediate success. He won the National Headliners Club Award for excellence in newspaper writing in 1946, and one of his columns was judged best feature story of the year in the following *Best Sports Stories* anthology. That column, oddly enough, was about the sport he liked least, basketball. It focused on Ernie Calverly, a guard who starred in Rhode Island State's overtime victory over Bowling Green in the National Invitation Tournament at Madison Square Garden. Smith was caught up in the excitement. "[Ernie] Calverly is a gaunt, pale young case of malnutrition . . . ," wrote Smith. "But when he lays hand on that ball and starts moving, he is a whole troop of Calverly, including the pretty white horses. The guy is terrific, colossal, and also very good."

What distinguished Smith as a columnist in New York, and, for that matter, the rest of the country, was not just his masterful use of the English language, nor his uncommon erudition in sports journalism, nor even his originality, but his sense of humor, stemming from the humorist's unusual way of looking at scenes and subjects.

Smith covered the major events, certainly, but he immensely enjoyed the province of the off-beat, the little-explored areas that were filled with comic possibilities.

He entered the world of the Westminster Kennel Club show at Madison Square Garden, and noted that a judge, Dr. M. Ross Taylor, "proved himself a champion among champions. He was imperious; he was painstakingly studious; he was profoundly authoritative of mien. He had splendid conformation—broad shoulders, white hair, and an erect carriage—and he was beautifully turned out in an ensemble of rich brown.

"One was inclined to hope that he would, in the end, award first prize to himself. . . ."

Another time, Smith set out to prove, somewhat beyond the shadow of doubt, after plowing through the "canon," that "Mr. Sherlock Holmes, the detective, was a horse player of degenerate principles who thought nothing of fixing a race and probably had his syringe in the veins of more than one thoroughbred saddled by his mysterious acquaintance, 'Wilson, the notorious canary trainer.'"

Smith also won the hearts of some housewives who knew little about sports. He once described a Bendix washing party in the suburbs in which the women, getting increasingly serious about their afternoon libation, eventually threw the wash in the sink and mixed their martinis in the washing machine.

In *P.M.*, a New York City newspaper, Frank Sullivan, the noted humorist, borrowing from Thomas Gray, wrote that Smith was "a humorist of purest ray serene."

Smith sent Sullivan a note expressing gratitude.

"Thank you for thanking me," responded Sullivan in a note, "but credit where credit is due, I say. If you knew how many people go around saying, 'Did you see Red Smith this morning?' as though they went somewhere and looked at you, when what they mean is, did you read Red Smith? I guess the cliché is about the most gratifying compliment a writer can get, but the trouble is he himself hardly ever hears it. It is always said in his absence. So you take it from me that it is said, constantly, about you."

When the *Herald Tribune* began syndicating Smith's column, one of the first newspapers to buy the column was the *Philadelphia Record*. Early in 1946, the *Record*'s editorial staff was on strike, but management continued to publish. The *Record* billed the syndicated column as "Red Smith Is Back Again." Some of Smith's former colleagues on the *Record* protested to him. (He continued to be a member of the Newspaper Guild.) Smith couldn't stop any paper from buying a syndicated column, but he insisted that the *Record* mark his column with the *Herald Tribune* copyright, which it hadn't done. And Smith promised to turn any of his proceeds from the Philadelphia sale—Smith split such proceeds with the *Herald Tribune*—to the Philadelphia chapter's strike fund.

"We were walking the picket line one bitter, bitter cold night," recalled Ed Hogan, then assistant sports editor of the *Record*, "and somebody passed the word that Red Smith had turned his money back to the Guild. Everybody sent up a cheer."

The *Herald Tribune*, unlike the liberal *Record*, represented top-hat Republicanism in editorial policy. Its circulation in 1945 was 306,000, compared with 449,000 for its rival, *The Times*. But the *Herald Tribune* often outsold *The Times* in the suburbs. "It had a class circulation," said Smith. But he, like most reporters, often retained antiestablishment sympathies. He continued—as he would all of his life—to refer to himself as "a working stiff."

Certainly, he felt affection for some members of sports management and called such baseball owners as Sam Breadon and Connie Mack friends. And sometimes a new conservatism seemed to creep into Smith's writing. In February of 1946, for example, he wrote about outfielder Danny Gardella, "one of the wartime accidents that happened to baseball." Gardella wanted more money than the Giants were willing to pay him, and manager Mel Ott threw him out of training camp. "[Gardella] didn't do anything that a better ball-player couldn't do with impunity," wrote Smith. "He merely held out and acted like a fresh kid about it, which was strictly in character. Dumpy, lumpy little coot that he is, he always has looked and acted like a small boy with a man's muscles."

Smith was displeased with Gardella's style, though Smith didn't mention specifically what Gardella was so "fresh" about. But Smith obviously felt that a player of minimal ability should be grateful to kiss the spats of those who employ him and not seek to make the best deal he can. Or, at minimum, not make a pretension at competence he did not have.

On the other hand, Smith could puncture the pomposity of establishment figures that he considered wrong-headed or stuffed shirts, such as Happy Chandler, then commissioner of baseball. Smith criticized several of Chandler's actions, including the suspension of Leo Durocher for a year. Chandler, who would refer to his adversary as "Whiskeyhead Smith," also had publicly stated that "an unholy alliance" existed among several writers, including Smith, to run Chandler out of baseball. Chandler added that he wouldn't be surprised "if there's a lot of money behind it."

Smith countered in his column: "I wish to state, using the first person, that if I can get paid for thinking Happy Chandler has performed like a clown and a mountebank, then I want all that kind of money I can get. Ordinarily I have to work for mine."

Smith, however, also championed the underclass of sports. In his column and in an *Elks* magazine story he campaigned for higher wages for major-league umpires, who were making $6,000 a year (". . . the head man in a game . . . shouldn't have to save string and used tinfoil to get along"). He also supported the grooms, exercise boys, and other stable help who were threatening to strike the tracks' management because of low pay and poor working conditions ("The experienced groom . . . forgets more about horses in a day than most racing commissioners learn in a lifetime. . . .").

Another time, Smith came to the defense of Rocky Graziano after an overzealous boxing commission had suspended Graziano for, Smith wrote, "not taking a hundred-thousand-dollar bribe before not throwing a fight that was not held." Smith liked Graziano, delighting in his zest in the ring and his unusual carpentry of the English language. ("They trut me good," Smith quoted Graziano on the hospitality the fighter received in Chicago.) And Graziano liked Smith. "Sometimes Red and me and my manager, a nice little guy named Irving Cohen, we'd go to a steak house or somethin' and we would bullshit and talk," recalled Graziano. "And Red would wanna pay the damn bill. He really would. And sometimes he did. He was a helluva guy. He wasn't cheap."

In mid-February 1946 Smith went south to spring training for the first time since 1943, when the A's had trained in the cold north ("and you could tell a ballplayer by the cut of his coat," wrote Smith). Smith had agreed to drive to Florida with Frank Graham, then a columnist for the New York *Journal-American.* He and Graham had been friendly since Smith was a rookie baseball writer with the Browns in 1929. Graham, like Smith, was short and wore glasses. Graham had lost an eye as a youth and now had a glass eye. Despite only a sixth-grade education, he possessed a facile mind and worked hard to become a highly literate writer. His juvenile, *Lou Gehrig: A Quiet Hero,* was one of the best-selling sports books for young readers.

Graham and Smith met to travel south one bitterly cold morning in front of Toots Shor's restaurant on Fifty-first Street. Graham got into Smith's new postwar car, and they drove to the *Herald Tribune* at Forty-first Street, where Smith had to drop off his column.

"Would you hold the wheel a minute," said Smith, "while I pop in and leave this copy with the elevator man?"

"No," said Graham. And that, recalled Smith, "was when I learned the bum couldn't drive."

Smith had no choice but to do all the driving to Florida. But he didn't mind. He loved being with Graham and enjoyed his idiosyncrasies. He called him "the little bastard who can't drive." He learned that Graham was dangerous with electric appliances. Graham once tried to replace a burned-out bulb on a ceiling fixture in his home. "I forget what the rewiring and replastering cost," wrote Smith. On the trip, Smith also sought "a hotel staff aggressive enough to get Frank Graham out of bed before noon."

In a press box one day, Graham rolled a sheet of copy paper into his typewriter, pecked out, "By Frank Graham," and sat back to consider his lead. Smith walked by and looked over Graham's shoulder at the words on the page. "It drags," Smith said, and walked away.

Another day, a cop stopped Smith's car on a highway between Richmond and Petersburg, Virginia, where large signs warned of a speed limit of 50 miles an hour. "Mr. Smith," the cop said, inspecting the license, "can't you read?"

"The son of a bitch can't even write," said Graham from the passenger seat.

Naturally, Graham and Smith became the closest of friends, on the road as well as at home with their families.

Graham had become the sports columnist of the *Sun* in 1934 when

Joe Vila died. Vila had written a long, rambling kind of column, which was definitely not Graham's style. Smith wrote of his friend:

At the time, sports columns in America were cut to a pattern: they were highly personal essays of opinion and comment expressing the writer's own view of the passing scene.

For almost twenty years, Frank Graham had been a newspaperman in the purest sense, a digger for truth, a reporter of facts.

He rejected the notion that having his stuff published in two-column measure must change him from reporter to pundit. . . . He was congenitally unable to preach or pontificate or force his own judgments on others; one quality of his greatness was what his friend Bob Kelley once described as "psychopathic modesty."

"My job," he told himself, "is to take the reader behind the scene where his ticket doesn't admit him—into the dugout and clubhouse, the football locker rooms, the jockeys' quarters, the fighter's dressing room—and let him see what goes on there and hear what is said."

If anybody had said in Frank's hearing that he invented the "conversation piece" column, he would have hooted. He only did it incomparably better than it ever was done before, or has been done since.

Smith cited Graham's "accurate ear" and "retentive memory" (he rarely took notes) and "purity of prose." It added up, Smith believed, "to the finest sports column of all time."

What Graham sometimes lacked in his columns, though, was a critical edge. His columns were more like photographs than paintings, unlike Smith's. Yet it was Graham who wrote the classic line on the ephemeral quality of the arrogant sports star. When Bob Meusel, the dour outfielder, was near the end of his career with the Yankees, Graham wrote, "He's learning to say hello when it's time to say good-bye."

From Graham, Smith learned the technique of not taking notes when interviewing someone in person. (He wrote notes after the interview; he also took notes in telephone interviews.) Smith, who had generally taken notes in the nineteen years he had been in journalism up to now, agreed with Graham that note-taking hampered the flow of conversation. (Though many reporters find that once a subject warms to his topic—especially one who has been frequently interviewed—note-taking is not an impediment and is virtually forgotten about.) "The trick," said Smith, "is to listen for the key phrase, or the favorite turn of expression of someone. It's not hard to remember, and you can recreate the conversation and have it sound nearly word-for-word, when it isn't."

Smith and Graham drove to Miami and took in the Flamingo Stakes at Hialeah. Then they motored across Florida to St. Petersburg where they pulled up to the Vinoy Park Hotel. On the porch sat a man in a white summer hat and white summer suit. "Where've you two little bastards been?" he asked. He was Grantland Rice. He and Graham had traveled together for years on the spring-training and spring-racing circuit. Now they were including Smith. "He was thrilled," recalls Smith's daughter, Kit. Rice and Graham were heroes to him, and he felt honored to be accepted by them. He called traveling with them "a treasured privilege." When the threesome began, Rice was fifty-six years old, Graham fifty-three, and Smith only forty.

Smith had seen Rice occasionally at a major golf tournament or at a World Series, but, Smith recalled, "I don't really think it's possible we got to know each other by name, or I should say he got to know my name" until Smith got to New York.

Rice had been the star of the sports firmament for nearly three decades, the most widely syndicated sport columnist in the country and famous as well for his movie newsreel segments called "Sportlight." Yet he was exceedingly modest—a prototypical Southern gentleman from Nashville and Vanderbilt University—warm, fun, and brimming with integrity. The ingredients Smith found irresistible.

"Perhaps it's not literally true that Grantland Rice put a white collar on the men of his profession because not all sportswriters before him were cap-and-sweater guys," Smith would write. "He was, however, the sportswriter whose company was sought by presidents and kings."

Rice was the most notable practitioner of the "Gee Whiz" school of sports journalism. Unlike some of his "Aw Nuts" sportswriting contemporaries, such as Westbrook Pegler and W. O. McGeehan, Rice hardly ever attacked anyone and seemed to accept sports virtually without qualm or criticism. He once said that "when a sportswriter stops making heroes out of athletes, it's time to get out of the business." Rice was the superstar sportswriter of the Golden Age of Sports ("the Golden Age of Nonsense," wrote Pegler). His accounts of games and personalities contained numerous Biblical allusions, references to Greek mythology, and comparisons to warfare. (When he traveled, he always carried two suitcases, one filled with clothes, the other filled with books.) He dubbed the four undergraduate running backs at Notre Dame in 1924 the "Four Horsemen"; Jack Dempsey's fists carried the "thunderbolts of Thor"; Walter Johnson was "The Big Train"; and a goal-line stand reminded Rice of "the Spartans at Thermopylae."

He was also a poet of sorts, his most lasting lines being an idealistic quatrain:

> When the One Great Scorer comes to
> write against your name
> He marks—not that you won or lost
> —but how you played the game.

Yet on occasion Rice could see a harder side of life. He wrote in "Two Sides of War":

> All wars are planned by old men
> In council rooms apart
> Who plan for greater armament
> And map the battle chart . . .
> I've noticed nearly all the dead
> Were hardly more than boys.

"I'm sure many people . . . consider him a boy scout writer, a boy scout poet," Smith would later say. "But then I've heard Kipling described as a boy scout poet and I think he was somewhat better than that. But Granny's jingles were catchy and, what shall I say, naive? Ingenuous? But Granny's greatest gift was, I think, that he was just right for his time."

In Florida in that spring of 1946, Smith captured the excitement of the servicemen returning to baseball. In the Red Sox camp, for example, he wrote of "the extraordinary Ted Williams, heavier and with the look of more power in his shoulders than before; Bobby Doerr, the great second baseman streamlined by many miles of marching under a full pack, who looks five years younger; . . . Johnny Pesky, a shortstop who can field an agitated horsefly. . . ." And Tommy Bridges, the Detroit pitcher, who "is probably the most esteemed character who ever hung his lingerie in a Briggs Stadium locker."

But Smith gave only slight mention to the most important social issue in sports history: the story of Jackie Robinson breaking into Organized Baseball.

On March 9, 1946, Smith wrote: "A baseball executive has been telling, with the warm, delighted chuckles of a man speaking of a very dear friend, how Branch Rickey came to take an apartment in Daytona Beach this spring instead of quarters in a swish beach club there. Seems Branch made reservations early in the beach club. Subsequently, he signed the Negroes, Jackie Robinson and John Wright, to train as Montreal farm hands in Daytona. Thereafter there came a brief, firm note from the beach club advising that the reservations for Rickey and party had been canceled. There was no explanation. . . ."

Later in the same column: "Earle Brucker, coach of the Athletics, has played with both of Montreal's colored rookies and considers Wright, a pitcher, the better prospect. . . . 'He's got nice form,' Clay Hopper, Royals' manager, says of Wright. The slender pitcher comes overhand smoothly, has good control."

In December of 1945, Branch Rickey, president and general manager of the Brooklyn Dodgers, had defied the other fifteen major-league owners and stunned not only the baseball world but the country in signing Jack Roosevelt Robinson to a Dodger contract.

No black—or known black—had played Organized Baseball since 1884, when Cap Anson, the star and manager of the Chicago White Stockings, refused to take the field against Toledo, which had a black player, Fleetwood Walker. "Get that nigger off the field," Anson is supposed to have demanded. Some players identified as "Indians" or "Cubans" probably were black, but no "known" Negroes had played in the major leagues or its farm teams in the twentieth century. Robinson would be the first, if he could make it.

At that time, racial prejudice in the United States was highly visible. Schools were segregated in the South; neighborhoods were segregated in the North. Ball parks were sometimes segregated in fact if not in writing. In Sportsman's Park in St. Louis, where Smith began covering baseball, black spectators were relegated to one area of the bleachers, or "the cheap seats," as they were called. When German prisoners of war were shipped by train across the American South, they sat in first-class seats while black soldiers on leave, wearing their uniforms, medals, and combat ribbons, were forced to sit in their customary second-class seats in the back of the train.

Rickey didn't sign Robinson solely for humanitarian reasons, though that was undeniably a consideration. He also did it for financial gain. He wanted a winning team in Brooklyn—winning teams traditionally make more money than losing ones—and he wanted to hire anyone who could help, he said, black or white. But he was also well aware of the growing pressure by government employment groups—particularly in New York State—to eliminate race prejudice in hiring practices; in this regard, he accurately foresaw a changing America.

The spring of 1946 was Robinson's first training camp with the Dodger organization, but except for his signing with the team, Robinson did not dominate the headlines. The excitement in the sports press concerned the first postwar season; besides, some considered Robinson a minor-league story. He was going to train with the Dodgers' farm club, the Montreal Royals, of the International League.

In the past, Smith had written sparingly about blacks in baseball. In January 1942, for example, he wrote a piece when a Philadelphia resident, once a legendary Negro League catcher named Louis Santop Loftin, died. Smith related how "Top" in an exhibition game threw out Ty Cobb, the finest base-stealer in the big leagues, five times. In June 1942 Smith did a piece on " 'Old' Satchel Paige, the top drawing card in baseball today," when Paige pitched in a Negro League all-star game in Philadelphia.

However, Smith didn't attack the color barrier in print. Unlike Hugh Bradley, for example, whose syndicated sports column appeared in Smith's paper, the *Record*. In a column on February 16, 1938, Bradley condemned the owners of the sixteen big-league teams for "not permitting a minority race" to earn a living out of their game. "Naturally," wrote Bradley, acerbic tongue in cheek, "they do it 'for the best interests of the nation.' " He added that there are "three or four amendments to the Constitution dealing with the subject."

Very few sportswriters came out so forthrightly as Bradley. Smith would recall talking with some A's who had played against such Negro League stars as Paige, Cannonball Redding, and Josh Gibson. "They told great tales about how good those players were, and I'd say, 'Then why can't they play in the major leagues?' And they'd say, 'They're still nigger ball players.' And I remember I was called a nigger-lover."

Smith said that at that time, "it never occurred to me that anyone was going to break the color line, and I wondered why they couldn't." But though his sympathies were, as they invariably had been, with the powerless, he still didn't imagine this was an issue to be challenged in print.

How did Smith feel in 1946 about a black trying to make it in Organized Baseball? He recalled years later: "I don't remember feeling any way except having a very lively interest in a good story. . . . I don't remember having any emotional reaction. But I would hope it was favorable, that I would be delighted."

In March 1946, he visited his old friend, Connie Mack, then eighty-three and still owner and manager of the A's. Smith and a few Philadelphia writers were in Mack's hotel room getting, as Smith said, "the usual spring training type interview." The Dodgers were coming to play the A's in an exhibition in West Palm Beach the following day, and a Philadelphia writer asked Mack, "Suppose they bring Robinson?"

Mack, recalled Smith, "just blew his stack. 'I have no respect for Rickey,' Connie said. 'I have no respect for him now.' He went into a tirade. Stan Baumgartner of the *Philadelphia Inquirer* said, 'You wouldn't want that in the paper, would you, Connie?' Mack said, 'I don't give a goddamn what you write. Yes, publish it.'

"Baumgartner wanted to run the story of Mack's racism, but Don Donaghey of the *Bulletin* recognized the furor that it would cause. He argued Mack into taking it off the record. At first he said no, then he agreed. Stan was furious at Don for killing a good story."

And Mack's reputation as a saintly institution, built in part through the years by Smith and other sportswriters, continued.

"I decided," Smith said later, "that I'd forgive old Connie for his ignorance."

Later that year Smith went to Jersey City to interview Robinson when he came in with Montreal. "I found him attractive," Smith would recall. "He told me he had made little of social difficulties that he had. I know that he couldn't always stay in certain hotels with the rest of the team." And then Smith asked if he was injury prone. He was injured at the time of the interview. "This made him indignant," recalled Smith. "He defended himself, angrily. But I had talked to his manager, Clay Hopper, who feared he was injury prone."

Smith was aware of the criticisms of blacks at the time. "One was," he said, "that they can't take it in the shins." Another was that they didn't have "ice water in their veins." Robinson was also aware of such whisperings and thus sensitive to the question of being "injury prone." Robinson would play 124 games (out of 156) for Montreal that season and lead the International League with a .349 batting average.

The following spring Robinson trained with the Dodgers, though he was still on the Montreal roster. The team trained in Havana to avoid racial tensions in segregated Florida. Leo Durocher, the Dodger manager, was in trouble with the commissioner's office over his associations with gamblers. Smith flew to Havana and interviewed Durocher about the gambling—calling him "Brother Leo . . . the monkish ascetic"—and about the ball club's prospects. When the Dodgers played exhibition games in Florida, Smith attended some and wrote humorous stories. On another occasion he mentioned the Dodgers, but all spring he did not touch the subject of Robinson trying to make it in the major leagues.

On his way back from spring training Smith stopped off at Aiken, South Carolina, where race horses are trained. "After three weeks among the murmuring palms and braying baseball dignitaries south of here," he wrote, "it was a relief to escape to this haven where a fellow can look at a complete horse for a change." He then went into a roundup of spring training and made no mention of Robinson.

Upon Smith's return to New York, he learned that Woodward had been upset with the generally sweet fare of columns from Florida. "Stanley," recalled Laney, "might have thought that Red was just monkeying around—and he wanted him to get some meat in his mouth and chew it up."

Stanley was about to send him a wire saying, "Will you stop Godding up those ball players?" Woodward, though, decided not to send it.

Smith hadn't realized what he had been doing. One wonders if he had fallen under Rice's dreamy spell. "I thought I had been writing pleasant little spring training columns about ballplayers," recalled Smith.

The major baseball story continued to be Durocher—a flamboyant national figure—and just before the 1947 season opened Durocher was suspended by Commissioner Chandler for one year. In an exhibition game with Montreal a few days before the season began, Smith was at Ebbets Field and began his column with a discussion of Durocher. As for Robinson, who was at first base for Montreal, Smith said he received applause when he took the field but "played an unexceptional game . . . and had no holiday at bat." He went 0-for-3 and didn't hit the ball out of the infield. In the fifth inning,

Smith reported, a release handed out in the press box announced that the Dodgers had purchased Robinson's contract from Montreal.

The other baseball writers and columnists dealt with Robinson in one way or another, but few made it a major issue. Arthur Daley of *The Times,* for example, relegated it to the eleventh paragraph of his column, and said that this was "the most delicate question of them all, Jackie Robinson. This subject is as easy to handle as a fistful of fish-hooks." That is, would Robinson make the team? Should he because he was black or because he was good? What were Rickey's motives? Daley thought them "sincere" in bringing up Robinson as a ballplayer and not a social paradigm.

"Smith," recalled Red Barber, then the Dodgers' radio broadcaster, "had a very simple outlook on Robinson and everybody else —give the fellow his fair chance. Smith hated bigotry and phoniness."

The day after Robinson had been placed on the Dodgers' roster, a Saturday, it was Stanley Woodward's turn to write the *Herald Tribune* column. He devoted the column to Robinson. In a strong, emotional piece, Woodward described Robinson as "carrying on his shoulders the impost of the negro race."

Less than a month later, on May 10, Woodward broke the sensational story that several players on the St. Louis Cardinals had planned to organize a boycott against the Dodgers because of Robinson's appearance. Smith wrote in his column:

Intolerance is an ugly word, unsightly in any company and particularly so on the sports page where, happily, it does not often appear. Without laboring the point, it is fair to say that on most playing fields a man is gauged by what he can do, and neither race nor creed nor color nor previous condition of servitude is a consideration. Which is one reason why American sports are as eloquent an expression as we have of the spirit of America.

That is why the disclosure of an abortive attempt to organize National League ballplayers into a bloc to deny Jackie Robinson, the Negro infielder, his chance with the Dodgers is at once shocking and heartening. It is shocking because the national game should have been the last place for the seeds of prejudice to grow. It is heartening because of the forthright and uncompromising action of the men who put the movement down.

Despite denials, it is completely true that an underground campaign instituted by one of Robinson's teammates and furthered by several members of the St. Louis Cardinals was begun to foment a player strike in protest against Jackie Robinson's admission to the league.

It was taken for granted in advance that publication of the story would bring denials. Indeed, one consideration was that if the facts were dragged into the open, the individuals involved would have to scurry and abandon their plan.

Almost certainly, this has come to pass. But before it did, two men took action which has added materially to their stature. Both men have been criticized in the past—Ford Frick on the occasions when, as president of the National League, he made decisions that displeased some persons, and Sam Breadon [owner of the Cardinals] whenever someone wanted a whipping boy to depict as the typical soulless club owner.

Smith said that Breadon rushed East when he "got wind of the plan," and he and Frick put a stop to it. Smith continued:

The inside story is a sorry lesson in how blind prejudice can warp otherwise estimable men. The ringleaders among the Cardinals are great athletes and, in ordinary circumstances, great guys. They are essentially decent fellows, and it is almost impossible to conceive of them being mixed up in this sort of thing.

Yet mixed up they were, and the only charitable explanation one can imagine is that somebody was using them. They couldn't have realized that the action they planned could have set off a major race riot, yet that was by no means impossible. They have Breadon and Frick to thank that they are well out of it now, that Robinson has not been damaged and nobody's throat has been cut.

In attempting to be fair-minded, Smith strained to give the benefit of the doubt to some of the Cardinal players he knew. Was he being naive? And though he always said that it was not the journalist's position to "plumb the psyche"—"I've always felt that if you're going to be a psychologist you should at least have a medical license" —he had to wonder what emotional trauma such an act would cause Robinson.

Another point Smith made was curious. He was shocked, he wrote, at the Cardinals' action because "the national game" should be the last place where prejudice should grow. But the national game had barred blacks for more than sixty years.

Not until the following year, on February 19, 1948, did Smith devote a full column to blacks in baseball.

He wrote a moving story of the motivation of Branch Rickey in bringing up the first black player. When Rickey coached baseball at the University of Michigan in 1903, he had a black catcher who was not allowed to register at the Oliver Hotel in South Bend when the team played Notre Dame. Rickey recalled Charley Thomas holding up his hands and, in tears, saying, "It's these. They're black. . . . If only they were white! . . . I wouldn't be different."

Rickey said, "Tommy, the day will come when they won't have to be white."

Smith continued:

That was forty-five years ago. It was forty-three years before Rickey found the right time and the right place and the right guy in Jackie Robinson. In those years Rickey has gone a lot of places and done a lot of things and been pictured in many lights. He may be all the things they have called him—a rush of wind in an empty room, a glib horse trader, a specious orator, a coon-shouting revivalist. He has been described, in purest Brooklynese and with a faithful accuracy, as "a man of many facets—all turned on."

It remains a simple matter of fact that he has not forgotten Charley Thomas. He has kept up with Charley Thomas, knows where he is today and what he is doing and how he is doing. Charley's doing all right, by the way.

In the circumstances, it was not hard to believe Rickey yesterday when he described his feelings at the major-league meeting [two years before] where fifteen club owners approved a report stating that the employment of a Negro in professional baseball was jeopardizing their investment.

"I was," he said, "deeply disturbed."

In 1956 Smith would write that Robinson's "arrival in Brooklyn was a turning point in the history and the character of the game; it may not be stretching things to say it was a turning point in the history of this country." Smith added, "I think I failed to understand, to appreciate really, the burden Robinson was carrying on his shoulders." As years went on, Smith would carry a mental image of Robinson. On the final day of the 1951 season, the Dodgers needed a win to tie for the National League pennant. It was the bottom of the twelfth inning at Shibe Park and it was getting dark. The Phillies had the bases loaded and two out. Eddie Waitkus smashed a drive toward center field. Robinson at second base, wrote Smith, "flings himself headlong at right angles to the flight of the ball, for an instant his body is suspended in midair, then somehow the outstretched glove intercepts the ball inches off the ground. He falls heavily, the crash drives an elbow into his side, he collapses . . . stretched at full length in the insubstantial twilight, the unconquerable doing the impossible."

Yet, just as with the boy whose face he once described as "black as doom," Smith hadn't really attempted to put himself into Robinson's shoes in 1947. But a year later, he seemed to begin to understand when he wrote about Charley Thomas and Rickey.

Rickey later sent Smith a note that said, "You understand me better than most." Smith saved that note.

But Smith was also criticized in that area. In 1948 he wrote what he considered "a rave column" on Larry Doby, the first black player in the American League. Smith described him crouching at bat, "a thin strip of darkness at the plate." Smith recalled, "I got attacked by the Afro-American newspapers in Baltimore. And I wrote back innocently, explaining that I was only trying to describe the man as I would have described him if he had red hair. I got a fierce letter back saying red hair never kept anybody out of the Chase Hotel and so on." The Chase in St. Louis refused to allow Robinson and Doby to stay there. "I didn't answer the letter," said Smith, "because they obviously wanted a continuing argument."

Smith was still struggling to understand the subject and the powerful drama that had been taking place. But his own deep sense of decency did not allow him at first to condemn the men—many of whom, as he had said, were "good men"—who were racists. He seemed unable initially to view this issue in the cosmic terms that he had dealt with the war issue. He seemed unable, in this case, to let go of the "froth" that he had wished sports to be. It seemed that, despite tough reporting on many issues, he basically believed that sports was the place where everyone got treated fairly.

He was heartened, but not for the obvious reasons, when Yale players elected a black man, Levi Jackson, captain of their 1949 football team. On November 24, 1948, Smith wrote a column titled "What's Wonderful?":

. . . Here's the first Negro who ever made the team in all the long history of Yale football, everybody's been saying, a kid whose father worked as a steward in the Yale Faculty Club for more than thirty years, and isn't it wonderful to think that now he can have his picture taken sitting on the same prop fence where photographers posed Clint Frank and Tom Shevlin and Ted Coy and Frank Hinkey?

Everybody's been saying that except Bill Corum, whose column (in the New York *Journal-American*) yesterday expressed, better than this one will, a feeling that has been trying to force its way out in words here ever since the election on Monday. Bill said in effect, "What the hell's so wonderful about it? This is America, isn't it?" A small echo answers, "Hooray!"

Look, what the Yale kids did wasn't anything wonderful. . . . Tolerance can be a fine word, but in connection with cases like this it can be a sickening word. When you say the Yale football players have struck a solid blow for tolerance, then you are condescending to Levi Jackson. It is an injustice to the Yales and an insult to suggest that the players have smugly invited the world: "Look how broad-minded we are." . . . Do you tolerate right guys?

CHAPTER
8

Red Smith captured the mood of America in the second half of the 1940's. After the four long, murderous years of the war, Americans wanted—just as they had after the First World War—to return to a light-hearted and light-spirited routine (though they would have to confront the beginning of great change in race relations). Entertainment in the country was booming, from ball parks to bedrooms. In each case, records were being set: More people were going to baseball games and more people were buying baby cribs than ever before.

The general level of Smith's writing became more polished in New York. He had more time and thereby took more time with stories, and seemed to rise a level through sheer effort and concentration in order to satisfy a more sophisticated audience than he had had in either Philadelphia or St. Louis. He was maturing as a craftsman, a thinker, and a man.

He was a storyteller, one who knew how to keep a reader reading, no mean feat. His richness of language, of metaphor, of observation, his ear for quotes and dialogue, his eye for the small but significant detail, and his humor hooked a reader and didn't let him go until the last of one thousand or so words were happily consumed.

Smith was sailing along—readers laughing with him, feeling with him, admiring him. His columns were read in English literature classes at Columbia University as the work of an "American stylist" (although a "minor" one). He was also studied at Yale. On May 5, 1948, Smith wrote a column that drew considerable attention. He called it, "A Very Pious Story":

At the Derby, Walter Haight, a well-fed horse author from Washington, told it this way:

There's this horseplayer and he can't win a bet. He's got patches in his pants from the way even odds-on favorites run up the alley when he's backing them and the slump goes on until he's utterly desperate. He's ready to listen to any advice when a friend tells him: "No wonder you don't have any luck, you don't live right. Nobody could do any good the way you live. Why, you don't even go to church. Why don't you get yourself straightened out and try to be a decent citizen and just see then if things don't get a lot better for you?"

Now the guy has never exactly liked to bother heaven with his troubles. Isn't even sure whether they have horse racing up there and would understand his difficulties. But he's reached a state where steps simply have to be taken. So the next day being Sunday, he does go to church and sits attentively through the whole service and joins in the hymn-singing and says "Amen" at the proper times and puts his buck on the collection plate.

All that night he lies awake waiting for a sign that things are going to get better; nothing happens. Next day he gets up and goes to the track, but this time he doesn't buy a racing form or scratch sheet or Jack Green's Card or anything. Just gets his program and sits in the stands studying the field for the first race and waiting for a sign. None comes, so he passes up the race. He waits for the second race and concentrates on the names of the horses for that one, and again there's no inspiration. So again he doesn't bet. Then, when he's looking them over for the third, something seems to tell him to bet on a horse named Number 4.

"Lord, I'll do it," he says, and he goes down and puts the last fifty dollars he'll ever be able to borrow on Number 4 to win. Then he goes back to his seat and waits until the horses come onto the track.

Number 4 is a little fractious in the parade, and the guy says, "Lord, please quiet him down. Don't let him get himself hurt." The horse settles down immediately and walks calmly into the starting gate.

"Thank you, Lord," says the guy. "Now please get him off clean. He don't have to break on top, but get him away safe without getting slammed or anything, please." The gate comes open and Number 4 is off well, close up in fifth place and saving ground going to the first turn. There he begins to move up a trifle on the rail and for an instant it looks as though he might be in close quarters.

"Let him through, Lord," the guy says. "Please make them horses open up a little for him." The horse ahead moves out just enough to let Number 4 through safely.

"Thank you, Lord," says the guy, "but let's not have no more trouble like that. Have the boy take him outside." Sure enough, as they go down the backstretch the jockey steers Number 4 outside, where he's lying fourth.

They're going to the far turn when the guy gets agitated. "Don't let that boy use up the horse," he says. "Don't let the kid get panicky, Lord. Tell him to rate the horse awhile." The rider reaches down and takes a couple of raps on the horse and keeps him running kind, just cooling on the outside around the turn.

Wheeling into the stretch, Number 4 is still lying fourth. "Now, Lord," the guy says. "Now we move. Tell that kid to go to the stick." The boy outs with his bat and, as Ted Atkinson says, he really "scouges" the horse. Number 4 lays his ears back and gets to running.

He's up to third. He closes the gap ahead and now he's lapped on the second horse and now he's at his throat latch and now he's past him. He's moving on the leader and everything behind him is good and cooked. He closes ground stride by stride with the boy working on him for all he's worth and the kid up front putting his horse to a drive.

"Please, Lord," the guy says, "let him get out in front. Give me one call on the top end, anyway."

Number 4 keeps coming. At the eighth pole he's got the leader collared. He's past him. He's got the lead by two lengths.

"Thank you, Lord," the guy says, "I'll take him from here. Come on, you son of a bitch!"

Marc Connelly, the Pulitzer Prize–winning playwright, was then a professor in the Yale Drama School and read that column to each of his classes. "Those of you with hope should consider it a must to read Red Smith's column every morning," Connelly told his students. "He is one of the truly great writers of our day."

More papers were beginning to buy Smith's syndicated column (now being written six days a week), including the *Boston Globe,* the *Washington Post,* the *Chicago Sun-Times* and, how satisfying, the *St. Louis Post-Dispatch,* the paper that wouldn't hire him some fifteen years before. He was making about $5,000 in syndication money each year—it would eventually rise to about $25,000—and soon was the second most widely syndicated sports columnist in the country, behind Grantland Rice.

Time magazine said that Smith could "paint a miniature portrait with a few swift strokes." *Mademoiselle* ran an editorial called "Bouquets for Red Smith." When Robert Frost's publisher gave him a birthday party in New York, the poet specifically requested that Red Smith—whom he read regularly—be invited.

Smith received the following postcard from an American in Paris: "Read your story on the recent heavyweight fite [*sic*] and I just wanted you to know that I thought it a *great* yarn. The English paper today, commenting on the Series opener, said Black 'dismissed' six batters. The 'match' was closely played. Regards, Bing Crosby."

A letter arrived from another noted American:

My dear Red Smith:

I get a lot of pleasure and fun out of reading your column.

As it happens, in your piece today [letter dated September 1, 1949] there are references to two quotations I often use—"Ye call me chief" and "I lay me down to bleed awhile and rise again to fight." I believe the latter quotation goes like this—

"I am wounded but I am not slain," Sir Andrew Barton said. "I will lay me down and bleed awhile and then I will rise and fight again."

Sincerely yours,
Bernard M. Baruch

Smith became a regular and honored patron in the celebrity-filled Toots Shor's, which Smith called "the mother lodge." He delighted in the rough-talking owner who described himself as a "saloon-keeper," and Smith found the crowded, noisy Shor's "the easiest place in the world" to find a column. Besides being a haven for journalists and publicity people, Shor's drew ballplayers like Joe DiMaggio and Stan Musial, as well as celebrated personalities like Hemingway, Sinatra, Supreme Court justices, and President Harry Truman. And even in that galaxy, Smith was now a star.

The *Herald Tribune* began a campaign to promote its bylined writers and used famous people to contribute encomiums. Soon, on billboards all over town, Beau Jack, the former lightweight champion, was pictured saying how much he liked reading Red Smith. Smith particularly enjoyed that. "Everyone knew except the *Trib* advertising department," recalled Smith, "that Beau Jack couldn't read or write."

Best of all was the recognition Smith received from his fellow sportswriters. Perhaps the most appreciated tribute came from the man Smith may have respected above all others in the business—his boss, that tough individual, Stanley Woodward. "In my judgment," Woodward wrote at the time, Smith "has become the greatest of all sportswriters, by which I mean that he is better than all the ancients as well as the moderns."

Yet in the midst of all this, suddenly the *Herald Tribune* received Red Smith's resignation.

But Smith didn't hand it in. Woodward did.

During an economy wave in 1948 the *Herald Tribune* ordered Woodward to cut two people from his staff, two older men who were near retirement. He said, "Give me some time and I'll arrange their retirement and we won't fire anybody."

Helen Rogers Reid, who owned the *Herald Tribune*, told him, "No, you've got to do it right now."

Woodward, the 230-pound former lineman, lost his temper. "All right," he said. He received a resignation form from the payroll department and wrote alongside the names of Stanley Woodward and Red Smith: "Incompetent."

Woodward told Smith about it at the bar at Bleeck's and laughed, considering it a great joke. Smith blanched. He didn't think it was so funny, and he couldn't believe it.

Neither Smith nor Woodward knew it, but in fact Stanley's job *was* on the line. "The last straw was the silliest thing," recalled Smith. "*The New York Times,* which had a lot of space, had a banner headline on one of the inside pages on a women's golf tournament in Westchester. It wasn't of interest to anybody but the players, but some of Mrs. Reid's Westchester friends were offended because the *Tribune* didn't carry anything on the tournament. She raised Cain."

Woodward wrote a snide note to Mrs. Reid, saying he wouldn't insult one of his staff members by sending him to such an event, but would send a copy boy. "She lost her temper," recalled Smith, "and had him fired."

Smith would say that Woodward was fired for "insufficient servility." Sometime after Woodward's departure, Smith attempted to explain Woodward to Mrs. Reid. "I said to her, 'Didn't you understand that he was fighting with you to help improve your paper?' But she simply fluttered. She said something fluttery. I didn't know what the hell she was talking about."

Al Laney remembered that the staff was "terribly upset" at Woodward's firing, and many discussed leaving the paper. "Red, of course, was upset, too," recalled Laney, "and I don't remember if he had talked about quitting. But if he had, I'm sure Stanley would have said to him, 'Don't be a dope.' And a day or two later we all began to settle back down."

At home, Kay was decidedly pleased that her husband was still employed at the *Herald Tribune.* After having struggled through the Depression and the war years with a growing family and an often shrinking bank account, she was finally living as comfortably as she ever had as the spouse of Red Smith. In June 1952 the Smiths moved from the Malverne house that Smith said "keeps the rain off, and that's about it" to a house on a hill in a higher-income area, at 4 Cedar Tree Lane, Wire Mill Road, in Stamford, Connecticut. The house cost $25,000, about $5,000 more than Smith thought he could afford.

He was earning $250 a week, or $13,000 a year, nearly three times what he had been earning in Philadelphia. Plus he received another $12,000 or so from free-lance pieces and syndication. But he went ahead with the purchase.

It was a white wood-frame house with a lovely setting on one and a quarter acres. The house was comfortable, with two bedrooms upstairs for the children, a bedroom downstairs, a breakfast nook, living room, and kitchen. In the basement there was a fireplace and a small area where Smith could make an office. There was also a little screened porch and a swimming pool—"the smallest swimming pool in Connecticut," he said. The office, which he said he arrived at after making his way through the hanging wash, was a small room, formerly a toolroom. He called the office "The Sweat Shop" or "Torture Chamber."

He had a carpenter build a desk and floor-to-ceiling walnut-stained bookcases into the pine-paneled room. Smith typed at a forest-green painted desk and sat on a wooden swivel chair upholstered in green leather. He sometimes pondered a single phrase for a half-hour as the ashtray beside the typewriter grew increasingly littered with his cigarette butts. Hanging on the wall were a few awards he had won. And beside him were a host of dictionaries and sports books. Pointing to the books, he once said to a visitor, "These are my brains."

Smith also bought a new car, an MG, to go with the Mercury. "Pop," recalled his son, Terry, "had a sweet tooth for cars."

Smith was having a good time, but the column came first. Terry Smith, thirteen years old when the family moved to Stamford, remembered that warm June afternoon. While his mother directed the movers into the new house, his father set up a table under the oak tree in the backyard and typed his column.

Red Smith said that he spent most of his waking hours with the column "perpetually lurking around the corners" of his mind. He said, "I don't mind the eighteen hours a day thinking about the column." It wasn't always eighteen hours a day because he liked sleeping late and would sleep about ten hours a day when he could. Then he would rise—sometimes close to noon because his nights were late nights—and, if he wasn't covering an event, would look through the newspapers for an idea.

When Jerry Izenberg later began writing a column for the *Newark Star-Ledger,* he spoke to Smith about it. Izenberg was having "a terrible time, everything seemed labored," he said. "Red's advice was to 'take a week and try to go to an event every day. If you write off an event, it's much easier. Just make your mind like a big wet piece of clay, and then the event makes an impression on you and that's what you write. You're trying to make it much more complicated than it is.' I was a nervous wreck, and that helped. It helped a lot."

Perhaps the hardest part of column-writing for Smith was pushing himself to the typewriter. It was always a chore. He said he must "lash himself to the chair and bind his ankles with heavy cords." In reality, he moved around a bit when he had the time. When writing in the *Herald-Tribune* office, Al Laney recalled, "he'd go to the water cooler a dozen times when he was starting a column." He said he never enjoyed the actual writing, "but that's how I pay for this nice job."

He cared and labored over each sentence, each word. That was clear in his correspondence to me. After I sent him the columns I had written for my college newspaper, Smith wrote a critique. He circled my phrase, "Howie Carl worked and thought and improved. . . ." Smith wrote, "Thought how? Brooded? Pondered? Schemed? Plotted? Dreamed?" And after my line "improved on his faults," Smith wanted to know, "Remedied? Overcame? Reduced? Eliminated?" Such noodling had become second nature to Smith at the typewriter, and he struggled for the trenchant insight, the shorter version, the succinct and telling metaphor that would pierce the heart of the matter. He took great pains to "explain less," to "knock out the unnecessary adjective, the over-done adverb. . . . You sweat blood to make it sound so smooth, so natural, it reads as though you knocked it off while running for a bus."

Sometimes he had not done enough legwork or, as he admitted, "was too lazy to get good enough material for a column." He would make his calls, talk to sources or subjects, and then begin the act of composition. "It's like laying bricks," he once said. "You put one brick on top of the other until the wall is built." He rose late and usually wrote late in the afternoon, and as an old rewrite man had no inordinate fear of deadlines. He had that now-practiced knack for being able to extract his nine hundred or so column-words from the typewriter, and as the term goes in the newsroom, to make them sing. As Wilfrid Sheed, the writer and critic, once pointed out, ". . . For clowning around, his gifts were formidable: a computer-bank mind crammed with anecdotes, a deadly retrieval system, and a tongue that liked to play, viz. the following on the occasion of Ted Williams being fined $5,000 for spitting: 'It was a $4,998 mistake when Ted Williams chose puritanical and antiseptic New England for his celebrated exhibition of spitting for height and distance. In easygoing New York's sanitary subway the price is only $2. . . . The price the Boston general manager set upon a minute quantity of genuine Williams saliva, making it the most expensive spittle in Massachusetts, suggests that the stuff is rarer than rubies,' and so on. No pair of desperate TV announcers on a rainy afternoon could go further with less."

The column would take a toll on the family. Though Kay loved the money, recognition, socializing, and travel that it brought—she would go to events and make as many trips with him as possible—she still would have to vie for his attention. They argued occasionally, but always intentionally out of earshot of the children.

Terry may have felt the deepest sense of loss with his father's frequent absences. "When I was growing up," Terry recalled, "it seemed to me that my father was always writing a column. He was never around to play ball with me like some of the other fathers, and at times I resented this bitterly." Terry believed his father wasn't always aware of Terry's concern. Much of the time Smith spent with his children was taking them with him to boxing camps, race tracks, and ball games. Terry loved it. Perhaps Terry's favorite time was when he and his father made an overnight trip to a fight camp in the mountains. "What a sight," recalled Terry. "The characters, the atmosphere around the gym and the workouts were really exotic, especially for a kid in school in the suburbs. I met Rocky Marciano and Floyd Patterson, people like that. Pop and I had a great time together." Terry also remembered waiting for his father after a football game in late fall. The sun had gone down, and he was sitting in the stands, not far from the press box. He watched his father work, one of the last left in the press box—invariably because he was so painstaking—and there was only one little light bulb on. Terry remembered, "Pop is wearing a hat in the press box. It's getting chilly and the wind is picking up and blowing cups along the aisles with a clatter. The stadium cleaning men are coming along, sweeping up. As they do, they keep snapping up the seats, and I'm watching them and listening to the snap of the seats. And I'm getting cold, and I'm wishing that Pop would hurry up and finish so we can go home."

Everything was fodder for Smith's column, including taking young Terry fishing. Smith wrote in a column on August 4, 1951: "A task force of three was made up swiftly. It included a young man of twelve, going on thirteen, who had never before attempted to mislead a trout with a tuft of feather and a barb of steel. He had, however, shown an encouraging spirit several summers earlier when he was eight or nine and used to accompany his parents on forays against the smallmouth bass of Wisconsin. [Smith regularly took his family to visit his parents during his summer vacation.] The pair would angle lazily through the mornings from a rowboat until the noonday sun drove them ashore. Then they'd seek out the nearest crossroads tavern, where each would satisfy his appetite according to his needs.

"On one such day the young man stuffed his face with a ham sandwich, slaked down the mess with a Coke, and observed: 'Gee, dad, this is the life, ain't it? Fishing and eating in saloons.' "

Terry, though, never really cared for fishing, especially when sitting for hours in a flat-bottom rowboat on a still lake with the sun beating down on him and not catching any fish. But he loved sitting in the middle of the boat between his father and grandfather, and listening to them joke with their gentle humor, and hearing stories of the family and of Green Bay.

Smith didn't get angry easily, but he had occasional displays of temper. Terry remembered one "ferocious" fight. It was over whether he should go to a party after a dance that a girl had invited him to. He had "a big crush" on her and wanted to go. Terry was fifteen or sixteen. "I think my parents thought that for my age, the dance was enough," said Terry. "Pop really dug in his heels, and I dug in mine. I accused him of being arbitrary and mean. He would listen to a certain amount and then get angry and cut me off. He could be very stubborn. I don't remember how the argument ended, whether it was with a bang or if we blew ourselves out like a storm." Terry didn't go to the party.

Smith sometimes got angry while the family was driving to Wisconsin for their month's vacation. Kay would be behind the wheel; Red, wasting no vacation time, would be behind a portable typewriter that he had placed on his lap in the passenger seat. Kit and Terry tried to be quiet while their father worked and would whisper to each other. "Don't whisper," Smith barked. "If you can't be quiet, then just talk normal." He could write through reasonably routine talking, but whispering was a pesky gnat in his thought apparatus.

Several times a year when Terry was a boy, his father would take him on an outing to New York on a Saturday afternoon. Father and son would be tourists. They'd ride the ferry to the Statue of Liberty, or see the city from the top of the Empire State Building, or eat at old Fraunces Tavern in lower Manhattan, where Washington's troops were quartered during the Revolutionary War. Sometimes Red would take a busman's holiday and go with Terry to a football game.

When Terry was in high school and in his early college days, he remembers being with his father in New York and the two often winding up for lunch or dinner at Toots Shor's. Terry had hoped to go somewhere where they just might be able to talk quietly. "Basically, he always wanted to go to Shor's," said Terry. "He liked the attention he received, such as being given table No. 1—Toots had kind of a hierarchy of table placement—and he liked the fact that his son was watching all of this, all the famous people coming up to him. I had mixed feelings about this. Sometimes I also enjoyed myself and felt a little bigger by extension, but I often didn't like sharing Pop with half the people in the restaurant."

Terry thought his father was oblivious to his feelings about wishing not to be there. "It was hard to talk to him about things like that," said Terry. "I don't think he would have understood. I think he would have been startled at the very notion. It would come as a great shock to him. A great shock."

Though Smith delighted in the attention at Shor's, said Terry, he knew why men were "stroking his fur." Somewhere down the line, maybe this important columnist could do one of these people some good. "It's not my beautiful blue eyes that bring the people around," Smith said to his son. "But I think he would have agreed, if it had been pointed out to him, that he basked in it," says Terry.

Terry recalled, though, that his father was invariably complimentary to him. When Terry got a job after college as a reporter for the *Stamford Advocate,* he said his father was "attentive and supportive. He'd read my stuff and if he liked it, he'd tell me, or he might complain about a phrase or a construction, or that a piece didn't contain 'the sense of presence.' He used to talk about that so much. He'd say, 'The one thing you can do is try to get into every piece, whether it's politics or sports, the sense that you experienced whatever it is that you're describing, even by some small detail of description that will bring it off and give it color. It puts you into the scene without artificially becoming a player.' " And Terry would notice little "moves" in his father's prose, such as describing a man with "a red handkerchief blossoming from his jacket pocket," which put the reader right there. "He praised my stories," said Terry, "but would earn his credibility by being critical of, say, a verb I might use, like 'hosted.' And throughout the years people would always tell me how proud he was of me, and of the nice things he said about me. That always made me feel good."

Kit didn't have quite the same problems with her father that Terry did. She recalled, in fact, being "envious" of the relationship that Terry enjoyed with their father. "It was just something that a girl couldn't enter into," she said. Kit did find particular joy in the days when she and her father would go to the race track together and walk between the sheds on the backside, looking closely at the horses and talking with the trainers and jockeys.

Before one of Kit's first dates in high school, she asked her father what time she should be home.

"After the cake and ice cream is served," Smith said.

"What does that mean?" she asked.

He told her about a birthday party he had gone to when he was six years old. His parents instructed him to be home at a specific time, and it turned out to be before the cake and ice cream were served. Young Brick drooped home, feeling cheated.

After cake and ice cream, Kit understood, meant after a reasonable time. She was to make her own decision. Red and Kay tried to allow their kids to act on their own consciences. But Kit also understood what too late was. Once, when she returned home near dawn, her parents were at the door to greet her, without smiles. They said they had been worried and were disappointed that she had gone against their trust.

But Smith believed in Kit's maturity. When he had heard about the house in Stamford, and Kay wasn't available, Smith told a friend, "I'll drive up with Kit. She's got a good solid mind and she'll know what to do about it."

Kit was barely five feet tall in high school. "I couldn't see over crowds, couldn't wear hats, couldn't reach anything," she said. "And I was complaining. I always got paired with guys who were short, too, and that was terrible. Pop said, 'Be happy with the way you are. Don't worry about it. You make the small guys feel good and you make the tall guys feel really great.' "

In her last year of high school, Kit looked for a college to attend. But the schools that offered her scholarships were not the schools she wanted. She had been to a Catholic grade school and an all-girls Catholic high school so she had set her sights on something different, a small New England co-ed school, Middlebury, in Vermont. She was accepted but without a scholarship.

"I was troubled," she recalled, "because how could I not accept a financial scholarship? But I sat down and talked it over with Pop. He said, 'I believe scholarships should be awarded primarily on the basis of need. I'm not really flush, but we have enough money to send you to college. I wouldn't let you accept a scholarship because I feel that it should go to somebody whose family doesn't have enough money to send him or her to college. Kit, go where you want to, and don't worry about the money.' " She went to Middlebury.

At home in the "Sweat Shop," Smith typed on yellow paper. Upstairs, Kay would "walk softly" and hear "moans and groans and calls upon the Deity."

Smith would sometimes read the finished piece aloud to whoever was home. "What do you think?" he'd ask. Or, "Here's one I think made it." Sometimes he'd say, with a sigh, "I'm not sure I brought this off." Kit thought that he was never quite sure until the piece was in print. "I think it was important for him to see it in the paper," she said.

When Smith worked at home, he usually finished in the early evening, before dinner. He and Kay would have a drink—he liked Scotch and soda, she bourbon and soda—and they and the children would crack walnuts from the bowl on the coffee table in the living room. "It was a very special time," recalled Terry. "We caught up on each other's news."

After dinner, Kay and Red often sat and read. "There were incredible stacks of books around the house," said Terry. "Between my mother and father, they consumed an unending diet of literature. Mother preferred novels, Pop nonfiction. But they both loved mysteries. Pop would look up a word in a dictionary and sometimes get so absorbed he'd read in it for an hour. Mother wore out library card after library card. She churned through several books a week, mostly from the library."

The Smiths' small circle of friends included the Grahams, the Rices, the Woodwards, the Bill Heinzes—it was Heinz who lived near Stamford and had recommended the Smiths' new house—and the Joe Palmers. Palmer had come to the *Herald Tribune* as its turf writer in 1946, a few months after Smith arrived. Palmer had been a highly regarded writer for *The Blood Horse,* a racing magazine, and had also taught English at the University of Michigan while working on his doctorate. After Smith had made his quick impact at the *Herald Tribune* and then Palmer, with a lofty writing reputation, was hired, Tom Meany, sports editor of *Look* magazine, said, "The next thing Woodward is going to do at the *Herald Tribune* is hire Thomas Edison to turn out the lights."

Palmer was a dark-haired, full-faced Kentuckian whom Smith had recommended for the job. The two men became neighbors in Malverne and close friends. Smith described Palmer as "the best writer I ever knew" and delighted in his horse-racing columns, such as the one about Lyin' Fitz, whose wooden-legged stable cat could catch mice with one paw and blackjack 'em with the other, or about Man o' War, "as near to a living flame as horses get," wrote Palmer, or about his affection for old Saratoga "because it is a graceful, irresponsible, gay tradition, and its ghosts are pleasant ghosts."

Smith admired not only Palmer's writing but envied *how* he wrote. He was a touch typist, compared with Smith's two-finger hunt-and-peck style. And, Smith noted, he gave the appearance of writing with "infuriating" ease, especially when seen in the press box by one who had come to "bleed" at the typewriter.

Palmer, who wrote one column a week in addition to his regular racing coverage, often constructed his column in what Smith described as "his wonderfully organized mind." Palmer could also do square roots in his head or quote from *Beowulf* in the original Old English. Smith said that Palmer's "quicksilver mind" intimidated him and delighted him.

"One night," Smith would write, "we were having a drink after attending an amateur boxing card in the recreation hall maintained by backstretch workers in Saratoga. Joe was telling a story about cockfighting. What, he demanded, was wrong with cockfighting?

" 'It's cruel,' I said, 'inhuman.'

" 'Inhuman?' he said. 'Of course it's inhuman. And that stuff we were watching tonight—that's unchicken!' "

Smith took great pleasure in talking with such friends. The conversations ranged widely from politics to the theater to sports but frequently focused on writing and language.

One night the Smiths and their children were visiting at the home of Bill and Betty Heinz. The women were talking in one room and the men in another when Kay looked at her watch and sent Terry to tell his father it was time to go home.

Terry left and returned a few minutes later.

"Did you tell him?" asked Kay.

"No," said Terry, "they don't stop talking."

"Well," said Kay, "the next time one of them comes to a period, interrupt and say it's time to go home."

Terry left and came back a second time. He looked at his mother and shrugged. "They don't even stop when they come to the end of a paragraph."

Heinz recalled that one of Smith's pet peeves in language was "two in a row." Heinz said, "During his St. Louis days, a copy editor pointed out that it takes at least three to make a row." *Webster's Collegiate,* however, does not agree and says that a row is "a number of people or things arranged so as to form a line." "Number" may mean "two."

Smith and Heinz once had an argument over the word "climb." Smith said, "You can't say, 'climb down.' " Heinz argued that you could. "Climb," retorted Smith, "means up. You clamber down, or struggle down." Smith then made an imaginary well in the middle of the living room and said, "Here, now try to climb down. You can't." Heinz said, "It's easy. You just climb down."

On Smith's fiftieth birthday, in 1955, Kay invited the Grahams and the Heinzes over for drinks and dinner. The Heinzes had a few spruce saplings in their backyard, and Bill dug one up, put a ribbon on it, and gave it to Red as a present.

"Oh, that's nice," said Smith. "I'm going to plant that right down there." They looked out the window and there was another house a short distance from Smith's. "It'll grow up there and be a nice screen from the other house," said Smith.

One afternoon the following year, Heinz drove up to Smith's house to return books he had borrowed. No one was home, but the front door was open. Heinz let himself in and placed the books on a table in the living room. Heinz recalled:

I decided to go down to look at the tree I had given him, and I couldn't find it, though I could see where it had been. There was a ripped-up hole. Nearby there was a boulder, and I saw that the little tree was lying on its side and its stem had been scarred. I figured Terry was running the lawnmower and he ran it under the tree. So I went home, dug up another spruce tree, came back—there was still no one home—and planted the new tree where the other one had been.

A year goes by. One night Red and I were at a fight camp in the Catskills and had gotten home around eleven at night. I asked him in for a drink. As we were getting out of the car, he noticed a maple tree I had planted in the driveway. He said, "Do you remember that little tree you gave me for my birthday?" I said, "Yeah, how is it?" He said, "Oh, it's all right." I said, "What do you mean, it's all right?" "Well," he said, "you'll think I'm crazy." I said, "Try me." He said, "You know, that tree was gone for a while." I said, "Gone? What do you mean, gone?" He said, "No, no, it's back. It's the damnedest thing. That tree was gone and now it's back."

I started to laugh. I said, "You schnook. You've a hundred papers in the United States. You have x-millions of readers who think you're Mr. Smart of Broadway. How could it go away and come back again?"

He said, "I don't know."

I said, "I'll tell you how. I was at your house one day and it was missing so I went home and dug up another one."

He said, "Oh, thank God. I wake up nights wondering about that tree."

Besides the English language and social drinking, Smith's greatest hobby was fishing, preferably trout-fishing. He fished for trout in lakes and streams all over the world. "I've hung my backcast in treetops from Finnish Lapland to the Chilean Andes," he wrote. His fishing columns were always filled with humor and description. But they were not for everyone's taste. Wayne Ambler remembered, "I was joking with him once and said, 'You know, Red, I love your articles. I love when you write about horse racing and baseball. But I'm not interested in fishing. What the hell are you writing about that for?' I saw a look come into Red's eyes, and I hadn't realized that I would hurt his feelings. I was sorry as hell I said it."

One day, Jimmy Cannon, the streets-of-New York sports columnist for the *New York Post,* wrote that fishing is "cruelty disguised as a sport!" He added, "Fishing is the vice of the shirker and the rummy. . . ."

Smith wrote in defense of his passionate pastime: "Mr. Jimmy Cannon, a Florida tourist who dislikes bloodshed, came upon the cadaver of a small fish 'untimely ripp'd' from Tampa Bay the other day and the sight moved him to such a paroxysm of compassion that he devoted his entire column . . . to a cry for vengeance upon all fishermen." Smith, who always wrote as though he were the victim of fish, responded, "The true sportsman among anglers is the trout-fisherman, who wades right into the fish's territory and battles it out hand to hand, taking an honest man's chance of being swept down the rapids and bashed against the rocks.

" 'I have,' says Cannon, 'done a little research with waitresses, bellhops, and bartenders. The waitresses say fishermen abuse them most and tip with a miser's caution.'

"Well, if Mr. Cannon says he has done research with waitresses, nobody has the right to dispute him. But if he talked fishing with 'em, it was the biggest form reversal since Jim Dandy won the Travers.

"This is all we have to say in the matter, except to recall that Mr. (Izaak) Walton mentioned a Sir George Hastings, 'an excellent angler, and now with God.' This is documentary evidence of what happens to fishermen when they die. Does Mr. Cannon hope to do better?"

It seems that when away from home, Smith and his other married friends primarily socialized in bars and traded stories, worked their typewriters, and, with certain friends, went fishing. Smith had one woman in his life and that, apparently, was enough for him.

"Red," he was once asked, "what if Marilyn Monroe climbed into your bed? What would you do?"

Smith thought for a moment. "I don't know," he said with a shrug.

Smith once recalled, "We never looked at other women except our wives. This always interested Toots Shor. He used to crow about his 'special guys.' They didn't worry about dames. Drink, yes, and he applauded that, but they didn't need dames. There are some guys in the business who are satyrs and are always on the make. But it just happened that, of my immediate crowd of friends, that wasn't one of their sins. They had plenty of sins but that wasn't one of them."

One of Smith's pals, Doc Greene, the sports columnist for the *Detroit News,* was perhaps one of the best in his circle at the gentle art of courting. Smith described Greene as "a genius in a free-style, catch-as-catch-can sort of way." Greene was a Marine lieutenant in World War II and when he landed on Guadalcanal he was carried off with about thirty-five wounds, "including," wrote Smith, "one so close to the heart the doctors couldn't understand why the pump kept working.

"As Doc told the story, a whole team of specialists around his bed in Hawaii were trying to discover why he wasn't dead. Also present was a nurse who had given the patient considerable attention. Doc never admitted that he had, as the saying used to go, toyed with her affections, but he was a free agent in those days. At any rate, she listened while the doctors reviewed the case history, conjectured, theorized and marveled. At length she spoke up.

" 'I'll tell you the answer, gentlemen. He's meant to hang.' "

Of the vices or supposed vices possessed by Smith's friends, liquor consumption probably headed the list. Many times they did not come back home or to their hotel rooms until dawn.

But drinking rarely interfered with Smith's work. He somehow kept his antennae working even under what for most others would have been difficult circumstances.

Ted Atkinson, the jockey, wrote him this letter:

Dear Red,

I've just read your column on the Wood Memorial. How I've always admired your work—but this takes the cake! I was almost sure you were about two and a half sheets to the wind that evening at Tom Stix when we talked about the race. But it could not have been more than one and a half, if that, for you have not used a syllable in quoting me that I didn't. Even the ——s are there! You are uncanny. That was real reporting. (That is not an insult to a columnist?)

Very Sincerely,
Ted Atkinson

As a practical joke, Fred Russell, the columnist for the *Nashville Banner*, once called Smith's room only a few hours after they had returned from drinking all night.

"This is Abbott's Pool Room," said Russell, trying to disguise his voice. "Someone left a hat here last night and I wonder if it's yours."

In a grainy voice, Smith said, "If there's a head in it, send it right over."

Another time, someone at breakfast said, "Red, your eyes look terrible." Smith replied, "If they look bad from where you are, you should see them from where I am."

Ever since the late 1940's, Smith's hands had a tendency to shake. It was especially noticeable when he was holding a drink. There was never a medical explanation for it, according to Smith, but he believed at one time he knew the cause. Once when a young couple, a magazine writer and his wife, were having breakfast with Smith, he noticed her watching him as his hands shook when lifting his coffee cup. He smiled at her and said, "It's an old Irish affliction." Years later, Smith said that when he traveled through Ireland, he noticed to his surprise that he was the only person in the country whose hands were shaking. There may have been another explanation for the trembling of his hands. Perhaps the pressure—much of it self-imposed, as it is with artists—to write so well, and so often, nearly every day for forty-eight weeks a year, year after year—took a toll in a physical sense. Even though he said he didn't "mind" the eighteen hours a day of thinking about the column, it seems possible that there would be some nervous manifestation after his having, as he put it, bled out the column.

Smith was a late riser but Sunday morning, after a long Saturday night, might be latest of all.

Smith generally tried to make Mass, but didn't always succeed. He remained a thorough-practicing Roman Catholic, but at the same time he admitted to doubts. Smith once said, "Somewhere I read, 'Oh God, I believe. Help my disbelief.' I'm a Roman Catholic who necessarily is assailed by God." He felt most people had some doubts about their beliefs.

In church, Smith sometimes dozed off. "The good father," Smith would explain, "simply does not know how to end a sermon."

Smith thought shaking hands in church was foolish, and compared it to the Rotary. "And he was pro birth control while the Church was against it," Kit Smith recalled. "And that didn't bother him. His religion was there, his belief in God was there. And besides, he never thought that the Pope was a special conduit to God. He thought the Pope was simply the Bishop of Rome."

When people asked Smith how he wrote a column so often, he would say lightly, "God is good, God will provide." Kit said that he lived by the Jesuit saying, "Pray as if everything depended on God, but do as though everything depended on you."

In Smith's writing, his views of religion were often presented with a light approach. He once wrote about the pastor of St. Peter's in Saratoga Springs announcing the annual fuel collection for the long winter ahead. The priest told his parishioners, Smith wrote, " 'I understand that yesterday the daily-double windows were kept open longer than usual, and when they closed there were still lines waiting and 150 people were turned away. If any of those people are here this morning, we will cheerfully accept those bets in the collection basket.'

"The cheerful words came pleasantly from the pulpit. Maybe there are churches where tolerant mention of gambling would seem out of place, but not in Saratoga, where racing remains a recreation first and a business enterprise last. It has often seemed here that there is a happy affinity between horse playing and piety, and that it is an established fact of theology that men who live on the race track live long and do good deeds."

On another occasion, Smith was asked if he had any superstitions. "Only one," he said, "the Holy Roman Church."

CHAPTER
9

A collection of Red Smith's columns, *Out of the Red,* was published in 1950 by Alfred A. Knopf, perhaps the country's most distinguished publishing house. There was some concern about the title because Senator Joseph McCarthy of Wisconsin was then claiming to find Communists under every desk in Washington. Eventually, though, the name was deemed appropriate enough to stand on its own. Smith sent a copy to his parents, then living in Sturgeon Bay, Wisconsin, and inscribed it, "To the authors of the author."

Newspaper pieces, generally written swiftly and on deadline, with no inclination toward literature, were seldom published in book form. Rarer still were collections of sports pieces, often considered the most ephemeral news of daily journalism. Smith said that it was difficult if not impossible for a newspaperman to take his work as "living literature." "You know," he said, "that today's column wraps tomorrow's fish." Yet the book received reviews from serious literary journals and reviewers, and most of them applauded the contents.

In a review of *Out of the Red,* in the *Saturday Review,* Hollis Alpert wrote: "When practically every other sportswriter in the country is covering the World Series and pulling out all the clichés, Red will manage to find some corner of the event that is all his own and relate it as no one else can: no heroics and a fine eye for the zany."

One such column in the collection, written on October 3, 1947, began:

The game has been over for half an hour now, and still a knot of worshippers stand clustered, as around a shrine, out in right field adoring the spot on the wall which Cookie Lavagetto's line drive smote. It was enough to get a new contract for Happy Chandler. Things were never like this when Judge Landis was in.

Happy has just left his box. For twenty minutes crowds clamored around him, pushing, elbowing, shouting hoarsely for the autograph they snooted after the first three World Series games. Unable to get Lavagetto, they were unwilling to depart altogether empty-handed. Being second choice to Cookie, Happy now occupies the loftiest position in baseball. In Brooklyn, next to Lavagetto is next to godliness.

At the risk of shattering this gazette's reputation for probity, readers are asked to believe these things happened in Ebbets Field:

After 136 pitches, Floyd Bevens of the Yankees had the only no-hit ball game ever played in a World Series. But he threw 137 pitches and lost, 3 to 2.

With two out in the ninth inning, a preposterously untidy box score showed one run for the Dodgers, no hits, ten bases on balls, seven men left on base, and two more aboard waiting to be left. There still are two out in the ninth. . . .

The unhappiest man in Brooklyn is sitting up here now in the far end of the press box. The "v" on his typewriter is broken. He can't write either Lavagetto or Bevens.

The short-story writer Shirley Jackson reviewed *Out of the Red* in *The New York Times.* She was no sports fan, she admitted, and rarely read the sports pages. But, she wrote, "reading *Out of the Red* has been, actually, an educational experience unlike anything I have known since first looking into Chapman's Homer."

An unsigned review in *The New Yorker* took a somewhat different slant. "An entertaining collection of columns," the review said. "It might be thought that sportswriting is the world's most perishable form of literary endeavor, and, indeed, it is so, as Mr. Smith unconsciously shows in his few straightaway accounts of long-gone baseball games, horse races, boxing matches, and such. What makes Mr. Smith's book diverting is that he can be, and often is, very funny; has a sharp and affectionate ear for the kind of ravaged English spoken in locker rooms and training camps (he also has the proper attitude toward baseball announcers who call the first inning the 'hello chapter'); and is an accomplished judge and raconteur of anecdotes. If there is one flaw in his attitude toward sports in general, it is that he now and then gets his foot caught in the bog that has swallowed other sportswriters whole—tear-stained sentimentality."

The two points most critical of Smith—"straightaway accounts of long-gone" sports events and occasional over-sentimentality—are noteworthy. *Out of the Red* covered only his writing at the *Herald Tribune,* from late 1945 to 1950. Few people read Smith to find out the score. People read Smith to see the game through his unusual perception and wit. Smith also believed people read accounts of games to relive the enjoyment of their experience at the game. And with a colorful and respectful use of language, the enjoyment of the game could last a little longer.

There was certainly sentimentality in the collection, though "tear-stained" was totally in the eyes of the beholder. Smith, for example, wrote of his "shock" when hearing of the "tragic death" of the former Yankee second baseman, Tony Lazzeri, at age forty-two, who was found "all alone in a dark and silent house—a house which must, in that last moment, have seemed frighteningly silent to a man whose ears remembered the roar of the crowd as Tony's did." Smith's accounts, even when centered on pathos, had enough facts and even humor to lighten the load they were carrying. And with Lazzeri, a quiet man, Smith recalled a reporter grumbling, "Interviewing that guy is like mining coal with a nail file."

Though *Out of the Red* received warm and generous critical acclaim, it sold only about 7,500 copies—not a bestseller by any means, but satisfying from the publisher's standpoint. Satisfying enough, that is, for Knopf to publish a second collection in 1954, *Views of Sport.* The experience was nearly identical—fine reviews and sales of about 7,500.

Though Smith was surely enjoying his status, he was saddened on another front. On July 13, 1954, Grantland Rice, while typing out a column in his office, suffered a stroke. His head fell forward and he died with his head on his column. He was seventy-three years old.

The loss was a great one for Smith. "Granny wrote of men he

137

loved and deeds he admired and never knew how much bigger he was than his finest hero," wrote Smith. The death of Rice also established Smith as the most widely syndicated sports columnist in the nation, with about seventy papers and some 20 million readers. He was earning $30,000 a year, and riding another wave of superlatives.

In March 1955, *Harper's* magazine published an article about Smith, "The Case for the Red Smith Irregulars," and the writer, Charles Einstein, began: "It is considerably easier to say that Red Smith is the best sportswriter in the business than to prove that Walter Wellesley Smith is a sportswriter at all." In January 1956 *Life* magazine ran a feature entitled, "The Gifted Mr. 'Red' Smith" and called him "the most literate and widely read sportswriter in the U.S."

If Smith had any competition then as the most highly regarded sportswriter in the land, it was either from the ghosts of Ring Lardner and Damon Runyon or from Jimmy Cannon, then with the *New York Post*.

Cannon was syndicated through the Hearst papers. A short man with dark hair and thick dark eyebrows, he favored checked sport jackets with striped ties and wide-brimmed hats. Unlike Smith, Cannon didn't rely on memory. His notebook was out and ready during an interview. He said he saved the tough questions for last. "I don't want to go back to the office with an empty notebook."

Cannon was born in Greenwich Village and was a product of the tough streets of his Irish neighborhood. Often he wrote that way and sportswriter Robert Lipsyte later described Cannon as appearing "as a romantic tough guy—Humphrey Bogart at the typewriter."

Cannon once had written scathing pieces about Jake LaMotta, the former middleweight champion, for throwing a fight; years later LaMotta saw him in a restaurant and walked over. LaMotta stuck out his hand and said, "Jimmy, let's let bygones be bygones." Cannon never looked up from his meal. "I don't shake hands with creeps," he said.

Cannon, who didn't go to college, became a copy boy with the *New York Daily News* when he was fourteen years old, in 1924. By age twenty, he was a reporter with a growing reputation. When he covered the Lindbergh kidnapping, in the mid-1930's, he attracted the attention of Damon Runyon, who thought Cannon had "a natural style." After a short while, Cannon switched to sports and became a columnist. He was quick-witted, passionate, crusading, and sometimes insightful. He could also be very self-centered, maudlin, and prolix. But almost always he was entertaining, on paper or in person, intentionally or otherwise.

Dave Anderson, a *New York Times* sports columnist, recalled:

Cannon always ran everything. He was the self-appointed traveling secretary when some of us were on the road. He would tell you the plane's at 12:15. "Be in the lobby at 10:30. See you at checkout, all set to go." I remember one time, it was the late morning after a fight and Jimmy and I and two other sportswriters get into a cab to go to the airport.

I say, "We've got to get something to eat. They won't feed us on the plane for an hour." We get to the restaurant in the airport and the dining room isn't open, but nobody has told us that. So we wander into the restaurant and sit down, and there are waiters off in a corner setting up tables.

Finally, Cannon stands right up and says, "They don't want us here." Everybody is staring at him, and the place isn't even open. So he's screaming they don't want us here and there's not even a hostess or a maitre d'—nothing. He says, "We gotta find the coffee shop." Now we are losing time. We get to the coffee shop and we have about forty minutes until the flight. And there're a few people on line.

Cannon goes right past the people, goes up to this nice old lady who's got the menus in her arm, the hostess. He says, "My darlin', we only have twenty minutes and we have to catch a plane"—so did everyone else in line have to catch a plane—and he says, "Can you get us a table right away?" He says that there are only four of us, we know exactly what we want, we don't need menus, but we do need a table. And she's kind of baffled by all this. But she sits us down.

Jimmy looks up and says to her, "I want a club sandwich, but only two pieces of bread, not three. I'm on a diet." She stares at him, but she takes the order and she's not even the waitress. She disappears and she's back in what seems like forty seconds with everything we've ordered. Puts it down. Cannon looks at it. You could see him counting with his finger. He goes, one, two, three pieces of bread. He looks up and says, "God gets even with me in small ways."

Cannon never married, and his life was his typewriter. Smith would recall passages of Cannon's that he liked, like the one that began a column about a boxing match: "Once, dreaming with morphine after an operation, I believed the night climbed through the window and into my room like a second-story worker. . . . The night had the dirty color of sickness and had no face at all as it strolled in my brain. . . ."

Smith would write that Cannon "might devote half a dozen paragraphs to a description of cellar-door dancers he had seen as a boy in Greenwich Village, and only then get into the splendid meat of the column. 'What Jimmy doesn't understand,' Hemingway said, 'is that the stuff up top is just the warm-up. You write it all, then throw away the first three paragraphs.'

"Jimmy's spoken lines were as swift and pointed as the ones he wrote. . . . [One] time Bill Heinz remarked on Ben Hecht's predilection for referring to Germans as 'those people with short necks, thick ankles, and watery blue eyes.' 'Means Marlene Dietrich,' Jimmy said."

Cannon used to ask other writers, "What do you think of my stuff?" He once asked that of Frank Graham. "Jimmy," said Graham, "you remind me of a young left-handed pitcher with all the speed in the world and no control."

Cannon said, "Overwriting. Yes, that's my greatest fault."

Smith concurred, though he would say, "the mother tongue behaved for Jimmy as it behaved for hardly anyone else. At his best, he could make any writer wonder what the use was."

On occasion Cannon wrote a column he called "Nobody Asked Me, But . . ." It featured one-liners such as: "The plainest of women look exciting in a polka-dot dress," and "I've never seen a circus clown I thought was funny," and "The sautéed smelts at Sweet's in Fulton Fish Market are a treat."

Once, Cannon asked Smith how he felt about the "Nobody Asked Me, But . . ." column.

"I don't give a damn whether you like celery or not," said Smith.

"Funny," said Cannon, furrowing his brow, "I get most of my mail on that."

Cannon, though, never again asked Smith what he thought of his "stuff." Cannon confided to friends that he thought Smith's views were sometimes too narrow, though he respected Smith very much as a craftsman. "But sometimes Red doesn't see beyond the foul-lines," said Cannon. That is, that Smith took sports and life too lightly. Smith believed Cannon felt competitive with him, but Smith said he didn't feel competitive with Cannon. Smith liked to say that he was in competition with nobody. "I have my own little peanut stand," he said, "and if you like 'em, you'll buy; if not, you won't."

Smith recalled, "Jimmy was very insecure. I couldn't make Freud's weight, anyway, so hell, I don't know where that insecurity came from but it was monumental."

The two men were friendly with each other and chatted, and often sat with the same group at Toots Shor's. They would write near each other in press boxes across the world, at the Olympics in Europe or the World Series in Brooklyn.

"In some ways," recalled Bill Heinz, "Cannon bothered Smith. Cannon could be a brilliant writer, and Red may have resented that some. I feel sure Kay did, more than Red. I always felt that Kay thought Cannon was a threat to Red's prominence. And Red used to say about Cannon's 'Nobody Asked Me, But . . .' column, 'Oh, that's not so hard,' and he'd reel off about three nobody-asked-me-buts of his own that were very good. I'm sure he didn't just sit there and make them up; it just came to him."

On Monday afternoon, May 7, 1956, Smith and Kay were standing in line to check out of a hotel in Cincinnati, on their way to the Kentucky Derby in Louisville. Kay walked over to a newsstand to buy the morning paper. When she came back, she was ashen.

"You'll never guess who won a Pulitzer Prize," she said.

Smith jokingly mentioned someone in sports who was relatively new to the newspaper business.

"No," said Kay. "You get one more guess."

"Arthur?" he said, joking again.

"Yes," she said.

Arthur Daley, sports columnist for *The New York Times,* became only the second sportswriter to win the Pulitzer Prize, and the first to win it for general sportswriting. In 1935, Bill Taylor of the *Herald Tribune* had received a Pulitzer for news coverage of the America's Cup yacht races. In 1952, Max Kase of the *New York Journal-American* had earned a special citation from the committee for his coverage of the college basketball scandal.

Smith was not envious of Daley, who he thought was a pedestrian writer, but he was wounded that he should be passed over by the committee. "My father," recalled Terry Smith, "was a fierce competitor who drove himself, who wanted and sought the kind of recognition that the prize represented. And he felt plainly and simply that if anyone was going to get the award, he should be the one."

Smith sent Daley a telegram: "Congratulations. From now on only one a day." Smith meant that despite the award, Daley, like any columnist, couldn't rest on his laurels and had to keep churning out the column.

It was less than Daley might have hoped for from Smith, for whom he had the highest regard. "I suspect," said Robert Daley, Arthur's son, "that Red never praised my father, and I know he would have liked it.

"If the positions had been reversed, he would have been clapping Red on the back. I think he wanted genuine congratulations from Red and never got it.

"My father always thought that Red was the best and was wonderful, and at the same time, he felt that Red didn't work as hard as he did. I mean, Red wasn't there interviewing ball players night and day. Red might do a piece off the top of his head. But my father never said a catty word about Red Smith."

Arthur Daley had won a number of prizes, and most surprised him. When he won the Pulitzer, he was astonished, "He had always imagined that Red would get it, if any sportswriter did," said Robert Daley. Arthur never gloated over the award. "He always wrote to each of us when we were away, and that week's letter to me read only: 'This will be short, but very, very sweet. I have just won the Pulitzer Prize. Love, Dad.'"

Arthur Daley was nearly the opposite of Jimmy Cannon. Daley was tall, quiet, self-effacing. He sometimes seemed so shy he had a difficult time speaking. On assignment, he carried a clipboard and often stood on the periphery of a group of writers talking with a ball player or a manager. Joe DiMaggio once said of Daley, "He'd be there at a mass interview, hanging at the edges. Then he'd get his man in a corner, alone. He'd never come on strong . . . he'd look you straight in the eye. I knew I could trust him from the first day I met him."

Writing gentle, fairly prosaic columns that were filled mostly with anecdotes and reminiscences, Daley generally took a solid establishment position. He rarely wrote critically of individuals; he said he didn't like writing about a "louse when there were plenty of nice, amusing guys around."

Daley had joined *The Times* three months after graduation from Fordham in 1926, at age twenty-two, and had been a general assignment sports reporter for sixteen years. Then on Christmas Eve, 1942, the erudite John Kieran gave up the "Sports of the Times" column to devote more time to nature-writing, and Daley was asked to take it over. He wasn't sure he could handle it. Robert Daley remembered overhearing his father and mother, Betty, talking about it. "Of course you can do it, Arthur," she told him.

Daley's somewhat stilted style had the saving grace of earnestness. And his hard work added to a column that brought pleasure to even sophisticated readers. In his quiet way, he once told someone how he had run into Robert Kennedy and the politician had complimented him, saying he had read his column and enjoyed it for years. "And," Daley said softly, "he said it in front of my son, which made it very nice."

When Daley was given the column, it was with the provision, "until further notice." That "notice" never came. But Daley, while writing a thousand words a day, seven columns a week, forty-eight weeks of the year, seemed worried about being stripped of the column. When Smith was making his reputation at the *Herald Tribune,* Daley was feeling pressure. He once said to Shirley Povich, sports columnist for the *Washington Post,* "How would you like to have my job, writing against Red every day?"

Smith knew Daley's feelings and took it as part of the writer's insecurity. "But can you imagine having a job in which you're frightened all the time?" said Smith.

Smith accepted Daley as a "nice guy," said Povich, "but when he was awarded the Pulitzer, Red said privately, 'Hah! Why? Because he's with *The New York Times*? Or he's been around a long time?' It made Red angry, and he pointed out that they gave Arthur Daley the Pulitzer Prize for General Excellence of his columns. Red said, 'Name one.' "

On mornings afterward, Smith would sometimes pick up *The Times* and go to Daley's column. "And when one was especially trite in his view," recalled Terry Smith, "Pop would say, 'Aha, another Pulitzer Prize winner.' "

Still, Smith felt no writing competitiveness with Daley. "The reason he didn't," recalled Kit Smith, "is that Pop thought Daley had a fantastic gift for being slightly off on the words all the time. I was treated to daily readings of Arthur's columns. If I was around the house in the morning, I was told how many words he had managed to just barely miss."

Sometime after he won the Pulitzer, Daley wrote that the Air Force tied the Army "in the beginning of a historic service rivalry in mist-shrouded Yankee Stadium yesterday." Two days later Smith sent this missile from his column: "One essay identified the game as 'the newest of service classics.' Another declared that Army and the Air Force had 'begun a historic service rivalry.' Well, if Kentucky can age bourbon to mellow ripeness in a matter of weeks, chances are a football game can become a classic of historic description within twenty-four hours."

At home, Smith would describe to Kay or Kit or Terry the way Daley would make ballplayers talk. "In backward sentences," recalled Kit. "Arthur would do the whole string of conversation, and he'd have a ballplayer, for example, saying, 'A hitting slump is something I'm having a problem with these days.' Pop explained that a ballplayer just doesn't say it that way."

Smith would never discuss any of this with Daley in person. He never felt the need.

One spring afternoon, Smith and Frank Graham and Daley were driving across Florida from Vero Beach to St. Petersburg. "We had filed columns from Vero Beach and so no deadlines threatened us," Smith would write. "It was a glorious day and the convertible was open to a spotless sky. In the conversation the name of a doctor came up, a lovely guy whom we all knew was an alcoholic.

" 'I know why a lot of doctors drink,' said Arthur, who didn't drink. 'Same reason newspaper guys drink. It's the pressure we're under.'

" 'Like now, Arthur?' Frank Graham said."

Smith didn't add whether Daley laughed, though Daley probably did. Smith's anecdote was a light jab, and the intention seemed not to make Daley the butt of a barb but to show how pleasant the life of a sportswriter can be, though sometimes sportswriters lose sight of that. For the moment, perhaps, Daley, at least to Smith, had done just that. It also indicated the pressure Daley generally felt. It was Smith's contention that, though one has to keep beating out the stories, "Sportswriting is the most pleasant way of making a living which man has yet devised."

When Arthur Daley died in 1974, Robert Daley found a newspaper clipping that his father had been saving in his wallet. It was an anecdote about a man who was troubled by a ringing in his ears and by his eyes bugging out. The man went to a series of specialists to get cured, and each did something terrible. One told him it was his teeth, so he went and had "his fangs yanked and replaced by crockery." The man's eyes still bugged out, and he still had a ringing in his ears. Finally he went to a specialist who told him his disease was fatal. With that the man decided to get himself outfitted in the best that money could buy. He went to buy custom-made shirts and told the clerk he had a size fifteen neck. The clerk measured and said, No, it's eighteen. The guy said fifteen. The clerk said, You keep buying these fifteen-inch shirts and your eyes will bug out and you'll hear ringing in your ears.

The clipping was from a column by Red Smith.

. . .

Of those writing sports in the 1950's two whom Smith regarded highly were John Lardner, the sports columnist for *Newsweek,* and Joe Liebling, who wrote boxing for *The New Yorker.* Each was a humorist, but in Smith's view they were also fine reporters and meticulous researchers informed on a wide range of subjects.

About Liebling, Smith wrote, "The fact that he wrote for a magazine deadline and not a daily paper made infuriating reading of 'The Wayward Press,' another department Joe handled for *The New Yorker.* A working stiff would write a story for deadline, doing an imperfect job, as most of us do most of the time. Weeks later, an omniscient Liebling would pick the story apart, honing his wit with cheap shots. Perhaps he was compensating for his failure as a reporter on dailies.

"Still, the guy did write the pure crystal stream and his boxing, in particular, was a joy to read."

John Lardner, Smith said, "wrote the greatest lead I ever read anywhere: 'Stanley Ketchel was twenty-four years old when he was fatally shot in the back by the common-law husband of the lady who was cooking his breakfast.'

"As Joe Liebling would say, that is what Colonel John R. Stingo would call a 'labyrinthine digression.' "

In August 1956, Smith received an assignment out of sports. It resulted in Smith's first writing on a purely political subject since he interviewed Trotsky nineteen years before. A *Herald Tribune* editor thought it would make a sparkling addition to the paper to have Red Smith cover the Republican National Convention in San Francisco and the Democratic National Convention at the International Amphitheater in Chicago. And to cover them not as a political pundit, but as he would a sports event. Though Smith read the front pages and certainly was aware of the political world, he was not an expert on politics. The editors didn't care. Seeing the convention through Red's unorthodox spectacles should prove entertaining. Smith happily accepted the assignment.

After Frank G. Clement, governor of Tennessee, delivered the Democratic keynote address in the International Amphitheater, Smith wrote: "For volume, endurance and unflagging pace, no sports figure could have matched the bull-throated boy wonder of the corn-pone belt. . . . A news account of the speech (one reporter suggested) should begin: 'The Democratic Party smote the Republicans with the jawbone of an ass.' "

The convention would nominate Adlai Stevenson to run a second time against the incumbent President Dwight Eisenhower. When Harry Truman, who left the presidency in 1953, made a surprise appearance in the Amphitheater, Smith wrote, "The old champ came striding down the aisle with outriders in front of him and cops behind, and memory recaptured the classic lines which once described Jack Dempsey's entrance in a ring: 'Hail! The conquering hero comes, surrounded by a bunch of bums.' This was Harry (Give 'em Hell) Truman, last Democrat to hold the heavyweight title, coming out of retirement now to slug it out with the clever contender, Ad Stevenson."

Following the convention, *Newsweek*'s press section reviewed the coverage. Under the headline, "One Was the Brightest," *Newsweek* said, ". . . Though newsmen insisted—as they always do—that the convention was the most thoroughly covered in history (there were 4,200 reporters on the scene), they admitted that the reporting was, with rare exceptions, unimaginative. One exception was Red Smith, the *New York Herald Tribune*'s brilliant sports columnist, who proved the journalistic adage that a crack reporter can turn out good copy on almost any subject."

On Smith's first day back in the office, a *Herald Tribune* editor suggested that Smith switch from sports to the other national pastime—or "go global," in the phrase of Westbrook Pegler, a sportswriter who had switched to political writing years before. There were other precedents: Heywood Broun, Herbert Bayard Swope, Arthur (Bugs) Baer, and James Reston. "No," said Smith, "I'm having much too good a time in sports to quit."

Smith didn't agonize over his decision. He was simply not interested in going off into something new. He even turned down the chance to be sports editor of the *Herald Tribune.* He was comfortable being at the top of his profession in sports, enjoying broad latitude in writing and travel. Besides, as he said, "You spend a lifetime learning to find your way to the dugout at Yankee Stadium. It would be a shame to waste it."

Nor was politics ever a consuming interest of Smith's. He voted liberal Democrat and his leanings were influenced, it seems, by Robert LaFollette, the progressive and reform politician from Smith's home state, Wisconsin. LaFollette served in the United States Senate from 1906 to 1925, from Smith's infancy to his junior year in college. Smith was an admirer of Franklin D. Roosevelt and his New Deal programs, which he thought were courageous and imaginative in helping the country climb out of the Depression. Smith voted for

Roosevelt in each of FDR's four campaigns. In 1948, he voted not for Truman but for Henry Wallace, the Progressive candidate. Smith had disparaged Truman as simply a former haberdasher, but later came to respect him.

"My parents really idolized Roosevelt," said Terry Smith, "but I think my mother had a keener political sense than my father. I think he believed the things he said he believed, but I don't think he spent a tremendous amount of time arriving at it."

There were few political debates in the Smith home. "But I remember when the Army-McCarthy hearings were on, which were so riveting, and it was my mother who sat watching them hour after hour in front of the television in the downstairs parlor," said Terry. "It was very dramatic and my mother was absorbed in it. Half of America was watching. My father was interested, but so absorbed in his own work and perhaps his own schedule of traveling, writing seven columns a week then, that he didn't have time. He was a newspaper junkie and a sports junkie to a degree, and he liked literature and fishing, but politics didn't come up very high on his list of passions."

Smith would recount when, covering the Olympics in Helsinki in 1952, the name of Richard M. Nixon first made an impact with him. Nixon had been nominated to run as Eisenhower's vice-president on the Republican national ticket. Nixon was then a U.S. senator from California and had made headlines in the 1940's in the Alger Hiss case.

Smith asked his roommate in Helsinki, Lew Burton of the *Journal-American,* "Who the hell is Richard M. Nixon?"

"He's the California McCarthy," said Burton.

That prompted Smith to "read up" on Nixon when he returned to the United States. He concluded that "the truth wasn't in the man at all. He was absolutely untrustworthy, a sleazy liar." And nothing ever shook Smith from that view. He saw Vice President Nixon a number of times at Toots Shor's, or around press headquarters of some games. "He's holding forth on football techniques, and I just made haste to get out of the way," said Smith. Years later, when Nixon was in the White House, he selected his all-time baseball team —three all-time teams, in fact—for *The New York Times.* Smith wrote Nixon, "in 2,800 cliché-ridden words," discredited himself as an authority on at least one crucial selection: "Nobody who saw Hack Wilson play the outfield could pick the fat man over Joe Medwick, not even the year Hack batted in 190 runs. Perhaps Mr.

Nixon never heard of Jimmy Wilson, whose wondrous skills as a catcher he ignores in favor of lumbering, lovable old Ernie Lombardi. And as for relegating Frank Frisch to a utility role—well, words fail."

Smith concluded, "The man wrote that picking these teams was one of the hardest jobs he ever attempted. Doing a fair critique of his performance is no easier. When you regard him as a sportswriter, you can't help feeling that he really ought to go back to being President of the United States. That's a dreadful, difficult line to write."

While Nixon dropped into Shor's on rare occasions, Ernest Hemingway, when in New York, appeared there regularly. Smith met him there in the late '40's. Hemingway was a fan of Smith's, and the admiration was returned. In Hemingway's novel, *Across the River and Into the Trees,* a dispirited colonel "noted how the wind was blowing, looked at the portrait, poured another glass of Valpolicella, and then started to read the Paris edition of the New York *Herald Tribune.* I ought to take the pills, he thought. But the hell with the pills. . . . He was reading Red Smith, and he liked him very much."

Smith was tremendously pleased. Smith, thought Kit Smith, was somewhat awed by the famous novelist. When Smith next saw Hemingway at Shor's, he said, "Thank you for putting me in the book." In late February 1958, Smith traveled to Cuba to cover some sports events and took the opportunity to visit Hemingway. "He was warm and companionable, quick with wit and laughter, with a strange but genuine shyness," Smith wrote. " 'Here we can talk,' he said in his home outside of Havana. 'When we meet in New York it's always somewhere like Toots's or 21. Those crowds make me nervous.'

"The talk," Smith added, "could be wonderful. . . ." To Smith, Hemingway was not anything like the "drunken braggart" as he was sometimes portrayed. "After he won the Nobel Prize, he was quoted as saying that he used the first $25,000 to get even. I had the bad taste to ask him why he was broke. 'What bothers me,' I said, 'is that with the exception of Edgar Guest, you are the best-selling author in America, and the top guy should be able to afford anything.'

"He said that with his first successful book—*The Sun Also Rises* —he gave the royalties to the mother of his son. With the next—*A Farewell to Arms*—he gave the royalties to his own mother.

"Then, he said, 'Red, a fellow's only got so many books like that in him.' "

Later, the hotel manager, Tony Vagun, invited them to the Hotel

Nacional in Havana. On the terrace, they were "ostensibly" watching the Gran Premio de Cuba auto race on the Malecon, Havana's beautiful seaside avenue, where crowds stood several deep, but "we were actually . . . talking about bullfighting," Smith wrote later.

"No aficionado like Hemingway, I had nevertheless been captivated some years earlier by Armallita, who was good enough to be honored with Manolete himself to open the new bullring in Mexico City. Hemingway remembered him well: 'Skinny guy, high-waisted like Alvin Dark with the crotch clear up here.'

"Just then a car plunged through the crowd. The race ended in gory disorder. In Hemingway's face, anger struggled with concern as he viewed the scene.

"'A cruddy sport,' he said. 'In bullfighting, the matador can take as much risk as he chooses, but these creeps always take somebody else with them.'"

Back in New York, in the spring of 1958, Smith wrote: "News of a gold strike at Sutter's Mill reached Horace Stoneham, so he hitched up his Conestoga wagon and hauled the New York Giants out to California. . . ." The major story was big-league baseball's debut on the West Coast. Smith abhorred the Dodgers and Giants moving out of New York, and later said that something went out of baseball for him after that. But he would cover the major story by flying to California. At the airport newsstand, he found himself looking at a familiar face on the cover of the April 21 issue of *Newsweek*. The cover read, "Red Smith: Star of the Press Box." Inside, the article described Smith as "the world's most widely read sportswriter," syndicated in more than ninety newspapers with a combined circulation of 20 million. Smith described himself as "a seedy amateur with watery eyes behind glittering glasses, a retiring chin, a hole in his frowzy haircut, and a good deal of dandruff on the shoulders. . . ."

About being on the cover of *Newsweek*, he later said: "Exhilarated is too big a word. Oh, I was gratified. I was pleased, but to my astonishment the magazine was like poison to me. I skirted the stands widely and shied away from them. It made me self-conscious every time I passed a newsstand to see my kisser looking up from there."

In the following year, the world's most widely read sportswriter became aware that the new ownership at the *Herald Tribune* planned some changes in the paper. One apparently would involve the sports editor, Bob Cooke. Smith then thought he could repay a favor for the man who, some thirteen years before, had hired him, Stanley Woodward.

"The Coach," after having been fired as sports editor of the *Herald Tribune,* had gone on to a succession of jobs, including sports editor of the *Miami News* and now the *Newark Star-Ledger.* Smith had missed Woodward very much, and expressed his feelings in a letter, dated January 23, 1959, to John Hay Whitney, who had bought the *Herald Tribune* and assumed the posts of editor-in-chief and president of the paper:

Dear Jock:

Quite a few months ago, Red Blaik phoned from West Point, said he had heard changes were impending on the *Tribune* and if so, how about Stanley Woodward? "It's a shame," he said, "that there shouldn't be two strong sports pages" [meaning another besides *The Times*]. I told him I knew nothing, had heard no rumors, but that seeing Stanley back on the *Tribune* had been my dream for years.

Last night Bob Cooke told me of his meeting with Howard Brundage. The news will be out soon, making an early decision on a successor imperative. I've put my own convictions in writing for George Cornish. [Cornish was the executive editor of the paper.] I repeat them for you.

Ten years ago we had the best sports section I ever saw. Now it needs desperately a major rebuilding job. (I'm not blaming Bob Cooke for this. We've lost many fine men, like Joe Palmer and Woodward himself, who haven't been replaced.) I believe deeply that Stanley is the best man to do the job.

Jock, in thirty years of knocking around the country I've never known another sports editor, or the head of another newspaper department, who deserved to be compared with Stanley. I believed, and said, that it was a ruinous mistake when he was fired ten years ago—for fighting too loudly for a better newspaper.

I'm a prejudiced witness. Stanley is my friend (so is Bob Cooke . . .) and I'm eternally grateful to him for giving me the opportunity I probably wouldn't have got except for him. Still, I don't think you have to discount anything I say on this ground; among qualified newspaper men everywhere, he has a huge reputation to support me. What seems most important to me now, though, is not his acknowledged excellence as a newspaper man but rather his rare qualities as an executive.

The job to be done on the *Trib*'s sports department is more administrative than editorial. Stanley is a quick and accurate judge of men. Where a newcomer might need months to orient himself, Stanley has kept in close touch with the situation. He is the kindest guy I know, but he can be as tough as the situation demands. He is so dead honest, so fair and so full of fierce integrity that he gets unquestioning loyalty from any staff. . . .

As to Stanley's age, I don't know how well you know him but he is in excellent health and he is a bull of extraordinary vitality. I think the big job on the *Tribune* sports department has to be done in the next few years. I believe deeply that there's nobody else who could do it half so well. Long before his age could become a factor, he would have the best sports department in America and he would have a man ready to succeed him. . . .

Because of his great reputation, Stanley's return would be a shot in the arm for the newspaper. Because of his ability, it would be the breath of life in the sports department. . . .

A decision has to be made fast. They think highly of Stanley in Newark and wouldn't willingly let him go. There are others who could be had, but none like him.

> Yours,
> Red

Smith's answer came about a week later. It was announced that Woodward, at sixty-three, was returning as the *Herald Tribune*'s sports editor after an eleven-year absence. It was sweet vindication for Woodward, who began his first column: "As I was saying, before I was so rudely interrupted. . . ."

Smith had realized his "dream" of having Woodward back as sports editor. And Woodward did brighten the section. He brought in Tom O'Reilly, an excellent racing writer, added Art Smith, Red's brother, to write the rod-and-gun column, reshuffled the copy desk and added some talented young reporters, such as Jerry Izenberg. And again Woodward seemed to get more out of the staff when he took over. His story ideas were stimulating to the department.

But he was not quite the Woodward of eleven years before. He was suffering from arthritis, asthma, and a cataract. Understandably, he lacked some of his earlier fire. "It's been a long eleven years," he said, "and I'm wrung out like a sock." No longer was he playing his favorite game at Bleeck's—sitting across the table from some friend and trading shin kicks and guzzling highballs to numb the pain—and he even apologized in his way for his actions in 1948. "I was," he said, "an awful popoff."

With failing health, Woodward lasted only three years on the job. "The press boxes are cold," said Woodward, "and there are too many steps to climb." He retired in early March 1962.

Red was offered the sports editorship and said, "No, I'm not going to do that stuff in there. I want to do what I'm doing. Besides, you've got a man there who can do the work—that's Harold Claassen."

Claassen, an assistant to Woodward, was named sports editor in April 1962. Smith stayed with his column.

CHAPTER
10

Inside Red Smith's home in Stamford, men were moving furniture around and setting up cameras and lights. Outside, on his front lawn, two television control trucks and an equipment truck were parked. Newly installed towers, looking like giant erector sets, stood in his backyard. Power cables stretched from Wire Mill Road to the nearby Merritt Parkway. These power lines would be strung until they connected to the CBS studio in Manhattan, some thirty-five miles away. From there the images to be seen in the small white house on the hill at 4 Cedar Tree Lane would be transmitted to nearly ten million homes in the United States.

"My God, they're tearing up my house," Smith said on the phone to Bill Heinz.

All the activity was for *Person to Person,* the popular thirty-minute television show with Edward R. Murrow as host. Smith and Kay would be the subjects for the second half of the Friday, January 30, 1959, segment, to be seen at 10:30 Eastern Standard Time. Dagmar and her husband, actor Danny Dayton, were on for the first fifteen minutes.

Though the show was supposed to be an "intimate chat," Smith and Kay sat rather stiffly on their living-room couch, as Murrow, smoking his ever-present cigarette, sat on the edge of his chair in the New York studio and spoke to them over television screens. Then Smith and Kay took Murrow and the television audience on a tour of their home, from living room to downstairs parlor with fireplace to Smith's writing room. Smith talked about how he worked—"with difficulty"—and told a couple of anecdotes. One concerned a Yankee coach, Charlie Dressen, telling a young Yogi Berra, who often swung at bad pitches, to think while batting, and Yogi striking out and mumbling, "How do they expect a guy to think and hit at the same time?"

Though television in this instance would expand Smith's celebrity, it would, conversely, in later years begin to remove some of the luster of his national image. Not just his, but that of the printed word and its practitioners in general. In the ensuing years, television would dramatically alter the newspaper business and cause some newspapers to fold. It would compete with newspapers and magazines as the prime source of sports coverage and eventually would reshape the entire world of sports.

From the late 1940's, when television began to expand, the networks treated sports as a kind of second-class citizen. In those days, wrote the television critic Ron Powers, "Television sports had been a passive illumination of what people already cared about. Television did not invent the Rose Bowl or introduce Americans to the heavyweight championship or generate the money necessary to form the National League. Television responded to an existing demand."

In the 1960's, the American Broadcasting Company introduced the *Wide World of Sports* and put up the television money to allow the American Football League to survive and to challenge the National Football League. The challenge was so powerful, of course, that the NFL would eventually be forced to absorb the AFL in a merger. Then, said Powers, television networks "could make people interested in events *because they were on television.*"

If any one moment could be credited with changing the future of television sports by exciting Madison Avenue and its advertisers to its huge commercial possibilities, it was the televised climax of the NFL championship game between the New York Giants and the Baltimore Colts. *Sports Illustrated* immediately labeled it "the best football game ever played."

The date of the game was December 28, 1958, just a month before Smith appeared on *Person to Person.* Smith covered the game in Yankee Stadium. "For the first half, it was the dullest game ever," Smith wrote in the press box immediately afterward.

"For half the game, the Eastern champions of the National Football League floundered and fumbled, peewee upstarts foolishly challenging superior forces from the Western frontier town of Baltimore. Then suddenly they were giants." The Colts led at half time, 14–3. But the Giants came back, and took the lead 17–14 at the beginning of the fourth quarter. Then the Colts charged back with quarterback Johnny Unitas time after time hitting his favorite receiver, Raymond Berry. Berry, said Smith, "catches passes—to borrow a line from Bill Heinz—the way most of us catch the common cold." The Colts finally kicked a field goal to tie the game with seven seconds remaining.

For the first time in pro football history, a game went into overtime. "Now the game changed character altogether," wrote Smith. "Where time had been the vital factor, the very essence, it suddenly lost all meaning in an unprecedented fifth period. A 'sudden death' period it is called, but it was as lingering as leprosy."

After eight minutes and fifteen seconds of overtime the Colts' Alan Ameche, Smith wrote, "plunged for six points and the title." At the time, however, neither Smith nor anyone else could foresee the impact this game would have on the world of sports and television.

Besides guest appearances, Smith had a few other experiences on television at sports events. Of course they provided material for his column. "For reasons never clear . . . ," Smith wrote, he was asked to do "color" for CBS on the Preakness and Belmont Stakes in 1953. The Preakness went along fairly well, except for Smith introducing George Humphrey, Secretary of the Treasury, as Senator Humphries. The Belmont day was different. It "came down pouring rain. Pounding, insistent rain . . . ," wrote Smith. "Maybe the patter of rain on a bare skull adds a quality of immediacy to the telecast of a horse race. Maybe not. Having bifocals awash doesn't do a thing for the wearer's vision. . . ." Native Dancer, owned by the Vanderbilt family, won the race. "I squinted through the downpour trying to pick the gray horse's owner out of the horde of Beautiful People who always show up for the Belmont. . . . Suddenly I was face to face with a handsome couple.

" 'Hello, Red,' the man said, offering his hand.

" 'Uh, hello,' I said, eyes still searching the area.

" 'This is my wife,' he said after a moment.

" 'How do you do?' I had an uneasy feeling that this dialogue might not be slaying the great unseen audience in New Mexico, but I was desperately rubbering around for a Vanderbilt. Those kind people who wanted to help stood there in awkward silence. At last they turned away. An instant later, truth dawned.

"Oh, Lord! That was Mr. Roberts!" Also known as Henry Fonda. "They were gone," wrote Smith, "and in the years since there never has been an opportunity to apologize."

Smith liked a few sports announcers such as Don Dunphy, Phil Rizzuto, and Red Barber, but he was highly critical of most. Of one Smith wrote: "Suppose—maybe it's an outlandish hypothesis, but we're just supposing—he should lapse into English."

The end of the fifties heralded changes that would affect Smith greatly, and though he could not have been fully aware of the impact, he certainly felt something.

"It was a decade of disillusion," he wrote on December 17, 1959, in a wrap-up column on the fifties. But he referred primarily to the college basketball "sellouts" in which players shaved points, and the West Point "cribbing scandal" in which football players cheated on tests to remain eligible.

It was also a decade in which two of his favorite athletes would bow out, one gracefully and one not. Joe DiMaggio, whom Smith called "a matchless craftsman," retired from the Yankees in 1951. "He hit the ball so often and so far and patrolled center field with such surpassing grace that his ability as a baserunner was largely overlooked," wrote Smith. "Yet Frank Crosetti [a Yankee coach], who saw every game Joe played in the majors, testifies that he was never put out going from first to third."

And Joe Louis, in a comeback attempt, fought his last fight in 1951 and was knocked out in the eighth round by Rocky Marciano, who was "young and strong and undefeated. . . . It is difficult to see how he can be stopped this side of the heavyweight championship." As for Louis, Smith wrote, "An old man's dream ended. A young man's vision of the future opened wide. Young men have visions, old men have dreams. But the place for old men to dream is beside the fire."

Soon Smith himself would be considered out of step with a younger generation—at least in the eyes of Seymour Krim, a young writer who said he was speaking for the "hip modern reader." In the essay "Sportswriting: Square and Avant-garde," included in his 1961 book, *Views of a Nearsighted Cannoneer*, Krim wrote that sportswriters of the day had "a shockingly meager idea of what a first-rate adult writer can do with thought and language.

"Suffice it to say," Krim wrote, "that Walter Wellesley 'Red' Smith, currently regarded as the number one newspaper sportswriter in the country and a man who regards himself as a suave litterateur, is not troubled by the fact that he has never read a word (at last report) by Dylan Thomas or e.e. cummings. This is Mr. Smith's privilege. But in a time when American popular culture is seriously wooing mature creative minds in order to add a cubit to its stature, sports journalism in our country remains a primitive backwoods mostly inhabited by second-rate wordslingers who have been trapped on the sports beat and feed the public a daily ration of mind-softening squash." Krim was hard on all the current sportswriters, except for John Lardner and A. J. Liebling, who wrote for magazines.

Krim said that Smith offered "a cute sweet poisonless narcotic" and that "old standbys like Frank Graham and our friend 'Red' Smith keep the formularistic conservative approach shined up for the tory sports fan."

The points Krim made, though overstated in some instances, had validity. There was a lot of "squash"—melodramatic and over-wrought prose—produced, and many if not most sportswriters were content to spew the party line of promoters and team owners. As for Smith, he considered the point of his "conservative" approach. He had not been a consistent moralist or a crusader, and his style often emphasized the fun, or light side, of the games. He had thought that his primary job was to entertain, to do "a soft-shoe dance and stay within the bounds of truth and propriety."

Times did change in the 1950's, and Smith occasionally expressed strong feelings about important issues, such as the basketball scandals. "It is unfortunate, of course, that these young men have to be put away," wrote Smith. "It is even more unfortunate that when they go behind the wall, they will not be accompanied by their accomplices—the college presidents, the coaches, the registrars, the alumni, who compounded the felony." In 1957 he criticized the baseball reserve system, calling it "the slave trade." When owners said that collective bargaining "would destroy baseball," Smith countered: "That's what the publishers told us in the early days of the Newspaper Guild: 'It may be all right for steel puddlers,' they said, 'but you are artists, professional men, possessors of unique and precious talents. Union regimentation would destroy your objectivity.'

"They did not explain why artists had to work sixty to eighty hours a week for twenty-five dollars."

But Smith, fifty-five years old in 1960, was spending less time in the dugouts. He was no longer the age of the players, as he was when covering the Cardinals and the A's, but more the age of the front office executives and owners. And he enjoyed their company. At a race track one day, he was standing with Alfred Vanderbilt, who, wrote Smith, "pointed to horseplayers standing four deep and peering into the shadow paddock.

" 'I look at them," Alfred said, 'and I ask myself, How can they do it? Where do they get the money to come out here every day and bet? I think maybe I've found the answer. It's the money they save on neckties and razor blades.' "

The fact that Vanderbilt's arch comment, and perhaps the aura of that world, found its way into a Smith column may have been evidence to some that he was a "tory."

Smith was well aware of Krim's piece. "He hated it," recalled Terry Smith.

One of the sources quoted in Krim's piece was Roger Kahn, who described the narrow world of baseball people and baseball writers who read no poetry and little beyond the boxscores. Kahn had not mentioned any specific sportswriters.

When Krim was working on the piece, he had asked Kahn about Smith. Kahn had worked for the *Herald Tribune* in the early 1950's and liked Smith very much. When Kahn, as a young reporter, covered his first spring-training camp in Arizona, Smith sent him a telegram: CONGRATS. MAYS ARRIVAL STORY A HONEY. Later, when Kahn had an offer to go to *Newsweek*, he had asked Smith for advice. "Either decision is a right decision," Smith said. "But stop agonizing and make a decision." Kahn went to *Newsweek*, where he eventually wrote the cover story on Smith.

"Does Smith know poetry?" Krim asked Kahn.

"As far as I know," said Kahn, "he doesn't read e.e. cummings or Dylan Thomas, no." But Kahn did say that he had heard Smith quote Browning by heart.

"Anyway, I thought I was talking off the record," Kahn recalled. "And Krim used it."

The next time Smith saw Kahn, whom he often addressed as

"Sire," Kahn recalled, "There was no 'Hello, Sire.' He said, 'I like e.e. cummings. I'm not crazy about "The night above the dingle starry." That's a line from a poem by Dylan Thomas.' I called up Krim and chewed him out for using stuff that I thought was off the record, though he obviously had a different view."

Smith didn't hold the slighting reference by Krim against Kahn, and they continued as friends.

Krim's writing, along with that of Norman Mailer, who wrote the foreword to Krim's book, represented a new school of writing that Smith disliked. "It was the 'I-I-I first person school of writing,'" recalled Terry Smith. Red had enjoyed Mailer's first novel, about fighting men in the Second World War, though he thought some of the language was unnecessarily rough. When the novel first appeared, Smith described New York Yankee outfielder Hank Bauer in a column as being "a tough ex-Marine as starkly realistic as *The Naked and the Dead.*" But Smith also thought that Mailer hadn't written anything worthwhile since then. Terry, who had now begun work at the *Herald Tribune,* argued that Mailer's language in particular could be powerful, "one writer's way of getting across his perceptions. But Pop couldn't get past what he called the self-indulgence. Mailer was the polar opposite of what Pop considered good, tasteful writing."

In September 1962, about a year after the Krim book appeared, Smith went to Chicago for the first Sonny Liston–Floyd Patterson heavyweight championship fight. There, he ran across Mailer who, by Mailer's own account, was "unavoidable Mailer." Mailer, like Krim, took an equally dim, though funnier, view of the American sporting press. "An old fight reporter is a sad sight," Mailer would write in *Esquire* magazine. "He looks like an old prizefight manager, which is to say, he looks like an old cigar butt." It is a dull, unthinking, "conformistically simple" kind of occupation, he added, and fraught with freeloading: "Every last cigar-smoking fraud of a middle-aged reporter, pale with prison pallor, deep lines in his cheeks, writing daily pietisms for the sheet back home, writing about free enterprise is himself the first captive of the welfare state." The press was provided with everything by the fight promoters from the cash-free bar at press headquarters to chartered limousines to the fight camps. Meanwhile, Mailer was having a good time—at least, an excessive time—and a verbose one.

In the days leading up to the fight, Mailer, boisterous and seemingly inebriated at times, according to Shirley Povich and Barney

Nagler, got into encounters characterized by erratic behavior. One such incident occurred the day after the fight. Liston had knocked out Patterson in the first round in Comiskey Park the previous night, and now reporters went to the Liston news conference.

"At noon," Smith wrote, "the flower of American letters assembled to gather for posterity pearls from the new champion's unbruised lips. Instead of Liston, they found Norman Mailer, an author on parole"—Mailer months before had pleaded guilty and received a suspended sentence for stabbing his wife in the abdomen—"in possession of the microphone, floodlights in his face and television cameras grinding. He was assuring posterity that he planned to prove in public debate that Patterson actually won the fight by a sixth-round knockout." Smith continued:

The champion arrived to take the seat of honor and the author was supported to the door. There was nothing sullen about Liston now. He sat with huge arms folded on the table, a big smile gleaming. He had waited a long time for this day. . . .

Mailer, on his feet throughout [the press conference], had been demanding to ask a question and others had been shouting him down. The champion lifted a vast, imperious hand, palm out. "Leave the bum talk," he commanded, grinning wide.

"I picked Patterson to win in the sixth round," the author said, "by a one-punch knockout—"

"He's still drunk," Liston told the crowd. At the end Mailer made his way to the front. "You called me a bum," he said. Liston gazed down at him.

"I call you a bum," he said tranquilly, "and you are a bum. Everybody call me a bum. I'm a bigger bum than you because I'm bigger."

He thrust out five great fingers.

"Okay, bum," he said.

In Mailer's piece, in *Esquire,* he wrote that in the aftermath of the fight, newspaper writers and magazine writers "kept taking little bites at me." And the first, he said, "was a little jaybird named Mr. Smith."

Barney Nagler recalled: "Red said that Mailer was talented, but that he behaved as he wrote—flamboyantly, rhetorically, and much too loud."

Two months after the Liston-Patterson-Mailer encounter that made him laugh, Smith observed an incident that chilled him. It occurred between halves of the Army-Navy football game on December 1, 1962. Smith watched as cadets and midshipmen formed a double row across the field and then the young President of the United States, John Kennedy, walked across the field from the flag-draped box in the east stands to another in the west. Traditionally, presidents sat on one service's side of the field for the first half, then changed sides.

"This President," Smith would write, "was a Navy veteran but he was also Commander in Chief of the Army.

"Hatless and without an overcoat in the [December] cold, he went jauntily, one football fan among 100,000. Halfway across, a drunk broke through the line and was almost within arm's reach of the President when Secret Service men grabbed him. Laughter started in the crowd but choked off.

"Suppose the drunk hadn't been drunk? Suppose he had a gun? It could have happened there in Philadelphia, before 100,000 witnesses. . . ."

On Friday, November 22, 1963, it happened before thousands of people lining the area around Dealey Plaza in Dallas. As the smiling young President sat, hatless, beside his wife, in an open limousine driving in a motorcade, someone with a rifle in the window of a nearby building took aim, shot, and killed him.

Two days later, the National Football League played its full Sunday schedule of games. Smith angrily opposed it. "Maybe it's important to determine whether the St. Louis Cardinals can upset the Giants in Yankee Stadium today, whether the Bears can push on against the Steelers in Pittsburgh," he wrote for that Sunday's papers. "There's a race to be finished and there's money invested. Money." Money not just from gate receipts, but also from the lucrative television contracts.

The decision by Pete Rozelle, commissioner of the National Football League, to play the games was controversial. Some writers took up the stand along with Smith and hoped to have the games postponed while the nation was in mourning and preparing for the President's burial on Monday. But other writers thought, like Rozelle, that the President, being a sports enthusiast, would have wanted to see the games played, and the country not come to a standstill.

Smith, though he personally liked Rozelle, would never forgive him for that decision. "It was the public display of indifference that bothered me," said Smith.

The assassination ended a year that had begun sadly for Smith and many other New Yorkers. A printers' strike had closed all nine New

York daily newspapers from December 8, 1962, until April 1, 1963 —a strike lasting 114 days. After it ended, one paper, the *Mirror*, didn't reopen its doors, and others, like the *Herald Tribune*, would begin to totter. At the *Herald Tribune*, advertising and circulation dwindled (from 411,000 in 1962 to 303,000 by 1965). Morale sank as publishers tried to compensate by cutting editorial expenses. "I remember," said Harold Rosenthal, who covered baseball for the *Herald Tribune*, "that travel began to be cut down, and even pencils were becoming a premium item around the copy desk."

Outside of New York City, Smith's circulation was actually growing. One hundred and ten newspapers were running his syndicated column, and a third collection of Smith's columns appeared in book form. Crown published it as *Red Smith's Sports Annual, 1961*, implying that a new one would come out every year. But 1961 would see the first and only *Red Smith's Sports Annual*. Fewer than 5,000 copies were purchased.

Why didn't it sell? Why does any book sell or not sell? Stanley Walker, in reviewing—and praising—the *Annual* in the *Herald Tribune*, might have touched upon one reason: "There is, of course, nothing new in this little volume of 223 pages, and the question of whether Smith columns 'stand up' under hard covers is debatable. It seems that all collections of newspaper stuff, even the very best, lose something in their flavor, their immediacy, or whatever it is, when put in book form. This is nobody's fault; it is simply a fact."

However, it didn't discourage two other publishers from putting together two more collections in 1963. One, published by Doubleday, was on a single subject, and titled, *Red Smith on Fishing*. The other collection, *The Best of Red Smith*, was published by Franklin Watts, which, unlike the massive Doubleday, was a relatively small publishing house. It was also published simultaneously in softcover by J. Lowell Pratt Inc. *The Best of Red Smith* comprised columns from the dozen years since the release of his previous encompassing collection, *Views of Sport*. Neither the fishing collection nor *The Best* made quite the critical or even the financial impact that the first two collections did.

Unspectacular book sales didn't trouble Smith. He felt fortunate to get an advance against royalties for what, in his view, was simply a recycling of material. Years later, a fellow newspaperman thanked Smith for writing a foreword to a published collection of his own columns. "If the book sells anything," the other writer told Smith, "it will only be because of your introduction."

Smith put his arm around the man to reassure him. "Guys like us," said Smith, "don't make any money writing books."

During the summer of 1964, Smith's father fell gravely ill. On October 8, after Smith had written a column following the second game of the World Series in St. Louis, he received a phone call that his father, Walter Philip Smith, was dead at the age of eighty-two. Over the years, Red had continued to take his family to visit his parents in Wisconsin until his mother died in 1957. Then his father moved to Avon Park, Florida, to live with a cousin. Smith stopped there for visits during his tour of spring-training camps. Responding now to a condolence note from Johnny Shevalla, a friend from his Philadelphia days, Smith wrote, "My father was the finest man I ever knew. I only hope to live and die as my dad did."

Smith's respect and admiration was genuine. Walter Smith may have had a shaky sense of self-worth, but Red had a different view. "For Pop," said Terry Smith, "Grandpa Walt was a symbol of strength and integrity. He was an honest person who dealt with people honestly. Grandpa Walt seemed to think of himself as a failure in business, but Pop felt he was caught in a squeeze—the Depression—that was not of his making." Smith seemed to respect his father's sense of obligation in sticking with a family business in which he really didn't have his heart.

Smith also admired the love that his parents shared for each other, which made for a stable home. "My grandparents were almost cornily in love," said Kit Smith. "They held hands, they went everywhere together." Kit remembered her grandfather talking about his wife preparing to go for a cancer operation. "He said she had a stubborn courage, and that on the day she went to the hospital she dressed up and wore a pretty hat on her head. Grandpa said it was as though she were making a slightly unpleasant duty call."

Red liked his father's sense of dedication, his perspective, and his humor. Kit remembered them spending hours together fishing by themselves. "It obviously wore well," she said. In the last ten years or so of Walt Smith's life, Red sent him a check every month. "Pop," said Terry Smith, "was happy to do it."

Smith left the World Series and went to Green Bay for his father's funeral. Then he skipped the rest of the Series and traveled directly to Tokyo to cover the Olympics.

As was often the case, Smith, at the Olympics, looked for the offbeat. He found it at a geisha bath and wrote a column about it.

Twelve years before, at the Olympics in Helsinki, he had written about taking a Finnish sauna, in which he was "boiled like a missionary in the cannibal islands."

After reading the geisha column, Frank Graham asked, "Red, why is it that every time you take a bath you feel you have to write about it?"

Graham hadn't gone to the Tokyo Olympics, and Smith was primarily with Shirley Povich, sports columnist for the *Washington Post*, Arthur Daley of *The New York Times*, and Jesse Abramson, the track expert from the *Herald Tribune*.

About Abramson, Smith wrote that he was "an incredible character who has known all track records since the cradle and can quote every record clocked since *Pithecanthropus* stood *erectus.*"

"Red and Arthur and I," recalled Povich, "were lost and Abramson was our leader. We set out every day for the Olympic Village and Jesse would outline where we'd go, how we'd get there. He knew how to get around, and we followed like sheep. Jesse would say, 'We're going to have dinner later tonight at such and such a place at such and such an hour.' Now, the final day comes, and of course we write the story. When the Olympic flame was turned out, Red wrote, 'The gas man cometh.' It was one of his pet sayings. Afterward, we went back to the hotel and this is our final night after two weeks in Tokyo, having Jesse take us all over. Now Jesse says to us, 'And tonight we are all going to eat at so-and-so restaurant.' Red looks at him and says, 'Who needs you?' "

The next spring, Smith was in Florida again for his annual tour of the training camps, and this time he was not traveling with Frank Graham. Graham had been very ill with what was believed to be cancer and was in a Bronx hospital. One evening, while having drinks before dinner in his hotel room in Miami with Shirley Povich, Kay, and Povich's wife, Ethel, Smith received a phone call from his office.

"Frank Graham died," he was told.

Smith slowly put down the receiver and turned to Povich. "Let's have a drink to Frankie," said Smith. Povich recalled that Smith, who had written a column for the next day's paper, sat down and substituted one about Graham, the man he considered one of his best friends. He recalled Graham's contribution to the art of column-writing and referred to their having been nicknamed, in the horse-racing terms, "1 and 1-A"—that is, they were both from the same stable and ran as an entry, and that a bet on one was a bet on the other as well. "I am prouder to have been part of that entry than anything else in the world," wrote Smith. ". . . The news [of the death] was hard to take, but it wasn't unexpected. Frank had been failing badly for several years, and making jokes about it, of course. When he got down to ninety-eight pounds he gave Mr. Fitz first call on his services in the event that great trainer needed a real light-weight to ride for him in a handicap.

"He didn't stop losing weight at ninety-eight, but he didn't stop fighting or laughing, either. He was proud of his ability as a street fighter when he was a kid attending P.S. 89 in Harlem. 'You went to the same school?' Frank said one day to Sugar Ray Robinson. 'Well, when I was there, buffalo ran wild on Lenox Avenue.' 'You're kidding!' Ray said.

"Lordy, but the old street fighter gave it a battle this last couple of years."

Nine months later, Smith suffered another blow when Stanley Woodward—"the best and kindest man I ever knew . . . my idol" —died.

During this time, the *Herald Tribune* was having serious financial troubles. There was a twenty-five-day newspaper strike in 1965, and circulation had by now dropped by more than 100,000 and was close to 300,000 in the less than two years since the last strike. Jock Whitney said that 400,000 was a break-even point. On April 24, 1966, yet another strike hit—this one called by the Newspaper Guild —and on August 17, after four months, the *Herald Tribune* corporation announced it saw no future and that it would not bring back the paper. A newspaper that could trace its ancestry back 131 years was dead.

Smith was stunned. Like so many others, he had found it hard to believe that the paper, which had become a foundation for him, had collapsed. He was angry at both management and the unions for being so stubborn. He had been an early organizer of the Guild and sympathized, but told Kit, "Why do they make it so hard for me to support them now?" And management, he felt, had allowed the paper to deteriorate by indecisive leadership.

On August 17, the last day of the newspaper, Smith wrote:

When you have lived with a woman for twenty-one years, parting comes hard no matter what the cause. When you know she has been kicked to death, there is blind anger along with the grief.

But writing in blind anger is seldom recommended. Presiding at the funeral of the *New York Herald Tribune,* Jock Whitney said it was a time for mourning, not recriminations. Fair enough, let others point accusing fingers, as others will.

Chances are all will speak some truth. None will tell the whole truth, for so many factors over so many years led to the death of the *Tribune* that to say, "This is where the deed was done, and how" would be foolish oversimplification.

Usually this space is reserved for fun and games, but there is no heart today for writing about base hits or left hooks or the safety blitz. Whenever any newspaper dies, everybody loses. When a great paper passes—and in its day the *Trib* was one of the very best in the world—the loss is immeasurable.

That fact won't keep the deep thinkers from trying to estimate what the silencing of another voice means to New York, to the nation, "and indeed," as Brownie Reid used to say when he was the boss, "to the whole free world." What it means here is that my best girl is dead.

The love affair began September 24, 1945. We came to know each other's faults and deplore them. There were irritations and spats and once—in 1948 when Stanley Woodward, the greatest of all sports editors, was fired—an outright break was close. Yet always there was affection, at least on one side. We were happy together.

No matter what one may read in textbooks or hear in journalism school, generally called the school of communications arts today—"I can't get anybody to sign up for my courses," complained Tom Stritch of Notre Dame when the new term was adopted; "they think 'communications' means stringing wires on poles"—no matter what you read or hear, only one ingredient can make a great newspaper: great newspapermen.

The truth should be self-evident, and yet it escapes many publishers, that a newspaper cannot possibly be better than the newspapermen who put it out.

Well, by 1945 there was no James Gordon Bennett around to snap an order to Henry Morton Stanley—"Find Livingston"—nor were the presidential ambitions or editorial opinions of Horace Greeley much remembered. But the *Trib* still had a staff anybody would be honored to join.

Joe Barnes had a small but nifty crew who set standards for lively but distinguished foreign correspondence. As a war correspondent Homer Bigart hit more beachheads than the United States Marine Corps. Bert Andrews in Washington, Tex O'Reilly—wherever he happened to be—these and dozens of others made morning coffee with the *Tribune* a daily adventure.

As to the sports department, there never has been a staff to match the one Stanley Woodward put together after World War II. A guy had to count himself the most fortunate of mortals to be working alongside pros like Joe Palmer, Rud Rennie, Al Laney, Tom O'Reilly, Tommy Holmes, the incomparable Jesse Abramson, and Stanley himself.

It was not by accident that such talent was concentrated in a single department of a single newspaper. All employers want good men, but Stanley didn't sit around wishing.

He went searching for the best.... Once he got the man he wanted, he turned him loose, allowing him complete freedom and backing him at every step.

Nobody ever had more fun than this crew, in press boxes, in the office, or playing the match game at Bleeck's. Stanley ran the happiest ship afloat in this business. Perhaps it is just as well he didn't live to see the old bucket go down.

That afternoon Smith went to Bleeck's, the last time he would do so as a member of the *Herald Tribune*. Richard Wald, the thirty-five-year-old managing editor of the paper, was dejected. Smith took him along. Wald recalled that Smith was not wearing his heart on his sleeve, as he had in his column. "He told me that 'changing papers is no big deal. You tend to think rather better of people you didn't have to work with anymore, so it has its blessings.' He was, of course, right. But he was also taking care of me, and I appreciated it."

Shortly after, Smith received a typed note sent to his home. It began, "Dear Red, I don't want to be sentimental but I do want to thank you personally, and with all my heart, for the work you did in behalf of the *Tribune,* and I am sorry it had to end...." In pen, across the bottom, was written, "I guess this is the emptiest day of my life." The note was signed "Jock"—John Hay Whitney.

Smith continued to write for the newspaper syndicate, now Publishers-Hall, which had bought his contract from the defunct *Herald Tribune* syndicate, and then about a month after the *Herald Tribune*'s demise, a New York daily began publishing in mid-September. It was named the *World Journal Tribune—WJT*. It picked up many of the columnists from the three merged papers, including, on opposite sides of the first sports page, Red Smith and Jimmy Cannon.

After nearly five months, Smith was again appearing in a New York daily. Yet there would be little rejoicing. For one thing, the *Herald Tribune* was dead; for another, the *WJT* was a rather uncertain successor. It seemed unfocused in appearance, with a wide scattering of features and columns. Smith called the *World Journal*

Tribune "that bewildered relic of three New York newspapers." Labor problems always threatened; and no one knew if readers would warm to the hybrid.

Besides all these uncertainties, Smith had something else to worry about: Kay's health.

As had been the case since the children had grown up—Kit was now married (she was Kit Halloran) and the mother of four, living in Wisconsin, and Terry was married to Ann Charnley, who was expecting their first-born—Kay had joined Smith whenever possible. In 1966 they had traveled together to Florida in March for spring training, to Louisville in May for the Kentucky Derby, and to Ireland in July for their vacation.

Shirley Povich recalled his wife and Kay waiting outside the press box at the 1966 Derby. "Kay was saying how she loved the life, liked being, as she said, 'one of the boys.' It was a long, long love affair, and she and Red had a grand time together."

That summer Kay complained of physical pains and felt weak. One afternoon she told Terry: "I love your father so much. I wonder if I'm good enough to be Red Smith's wife."

Terry said, "Don't say that—it's ridiculous. I know Pop doesn't think that in any way. The two of you have worked for all this." Terry said later, "I think she had begun to suspect her illness."

In late August, she visited a doctor, who told her she had a touch of pleurisy. At the end of September she went into the hospital for a gallbladder operation. It was then doctors suspected something worse, that Kay might have cancer of the liver.

When the doctor received the results in early October, while Kay was recuperating from her operation, he called Smith. Kay has cancer, the doctor said. He didn't know exactly how long she would live, but it would not be more than six months. Smith called Terry at *The New York Times*—Terry had moved there as a reporter—and asked him to go with him that evening to the hospital in Stamford.

"Pop was at loose ends," recalled Terry. "He couldn't even find the keys to the car to drive to the hospital." Smith told his son, "This is the toughest thing I've ever had to do in my life." He meant seeing Kay in such pain, feeling the pain of losing her. "Their relationship," said Terry, "was the linchpin of his life. They had been married more than thirty-three years."

Kay would not be told the facts of her illness; she was informed that she had a gallbladder condition. That was Red's decision. He felt that Kay might just give up if she knew her sickness was terminal. Let her live with hope, he decided.

Red called Kit in Wisconsin and told her the news. Red told her not to visit immediately because her mother would think something was radically wrong. In a month, in November, Kit would have a birthday and that would seem an appropriate time to make the trip East.

"I think Pop misjudged Mother," recalled Kit. "He remembered her getting nervous when there was a big dinner party, and he and I would have to put the finishing touches on things, getting the roast out of the oven, putting the meal on the table. But she didn't fall apart when she was left alone so much with two small kids. I think she handled all the big things well. I remember one time saying to Mother, 'Most people may not see this, but I've always thought you were a really strong person.' And she said, 'You're kidding.' She meant, You mean they doubt my strength? That was her vision of herself."

Terry and Red visited Kay right after hearing the test results, "We kept a stiff upper lip," recalled Terry. "And then Pop and I went to dinner. Just the two of us, in a place called the Stamford House. We sat there and talked all night." They decided to refuse to accept the test results as the final word. They agreed to get other doctors' opinions and, as Smith said, "to pursue this thing."

"It was a great shock, a tremendous shock," Terry recalled. "I went home with Pop and spent the night in the house in Connecticut with him."

The next morning, Smith sat down and wrote a column.

"I don't remember the subject," said Terry, "but when I saw it the next day, I was amazed. It was a good column, and a funny column, almost light-hearted. I said something about that to him later. He said, 'It's the only way I can deal with this. I just bury my head in it, and for those three or four hours I don't think about anything else. I don't think about this news or what's going to happen or anything. I concentrate on the column.' "

To be close to Kay in the hospital, he stayed home and watched on television the first two games of the World Series, which were played in Los Angeles. Smith told Kay he wasn't quite feeling up to the cross-country trip but would pick up the Series when it resumed in Baltimore. The Orioles unexpectedly whipped the Dodgers in the first two games. Smith wrote, ". . . All the deep thinkers insist that the terrazzo infield, the salubrious smog and the ennobling atmosphere of Los Angeles give the home team a distinct advantage, but if the Dodgers found aid and comfort in their gaudy kraal, they must have got it out of a bottle in the clubhouse. . . ." Smith then traveled to Baltimore and reported on the Orioles' victories in games Three and Four, for a sweep of the Series. He returned home to Kay, and during the fall and winter spent much of his time with her in the hospital or at home when she was an outpatient.

In February, Smith called Kit in Wisconsin and said that her mother was dying. He wasn't sure if Kit should come East. "He was really trying to spare me," said Kit. But she left for Connecticut immediately. "When I saw her, I was shocked," said Kit. "She was so thin I didn't recognize my mother when I walked in."

On February 15, 1967, Catherine Cody Smith died. "It was a hard struggle, and Pop suffered, watching her suffer and feeling helpless," said Kit. "By the time she died, there was a lot of relief."

For much of this time, Smith continued to write, though he wasn't pleased with much of his stuff. A few weeks before Kay's death, around the time of the first Super Bowl, Smith told Bill Heinz, "I know I'm looking terrible"—he was referring to his column—"but once this thing is over, then watch me go."

CHAPTER
11

The Smith house was very quiet without Kay. For the first time in thirty-four years Kay wasn't there to share Red's home. Smith had a housekeeper come in once a week, and he wondered if he shouldn't hire her full-time, just to give a sense of life to the rooms. He tried to fill his empty feelings, for a while, with travel, with going into New York City more, staying until closing at Shor's, and sometimes just checking into a hotel late at night.

In the months following Kay's death, Smith never missed a writing assignment and was intent on not missing any important sporting events. He was sixty-one years old and white-haired, but determined to stay youthful in his column. The way to do that, he was convinced, was "to be there." It was what he always told young sportswriters who had asked him for advice.

Amid strong, disturbing rumors that the *World Journal Tribune* was in deep trouble, Smith flew to Louisville for the Derby. On Thursday, May 4, he did what he enjoyed so much, visiting a horse farm in Lexington and writing about the beginnings of a Derby contender. His column in the May 5, 1967, *World Journal Tribune* began:

The delivery room where Damascus was born is the second stall on the right as you enter a great brick barn on John A. Bell's Jonabell Farm here. Cattle used the barn before Bell's time, and now the stall is occupied by a mare named Mabe Lee and her five-day-old colt.

It was the summer in the Blue Grass country today with the sun bright and hot on the lovely acres where the Kentucky Derby favorite romped through his first six months. Clamorous Louisville seemed a million light-years away.

In Louisville's streets, clogged traffic hooted and snarled. Hour by hour hotel lobbies grew more crowded. Authorities fretted over threats by agitators for open housing legislation to make Churchill Downs the scene of disruptive demonstrations tomorrow, the biggest day in the racing year and one of the biggest on the whole American sports scene.

It was impossible for a visitor, and probably impossible for a horse, not to feel the nervous excitement in the stable area where Damascus awaits the call to post.

There was still in his writing the youthful excitement so necessary to lively prose. He felt this exhilaration about many sports events. He still got "dry in the mouth" before a heavyweight title fight, and he had been thrilled at horse races since he began covering them in Philadelphia. In Philadelphia, he had written that he was "a guy so screwy about horse racing that he could not watch a heat through binoculars without some steadying support for the elbows." In 1967 he may not have been quite as "screwy" about horse racing as he had been thirty years before, though he still loved it.

But his life and the world around him were changing rapidly. His use of the word "agitators" revealed his feelings that there should be another way to get open housing without "disruptive demonstrations" that would "threaten" his favorite sports event, an event he had been covering with joy for more than two decades. "There is excitement in the air," Smith once wrote, "mingled with the scent of orchids and mint and bourbon."

Early Friday afternoon, May 5, Smith was in the aisle of the outdoor pressbox at Churchill Downs when Jimmy Cannon excitedly went over to him. "I just heard," said Cannon, "that the paper folded."

Smith reacted calmly—stunned but not surprised. He spoke to Cannon for a moment more, then walked slowly back to his seat and his green portable Olympic. There was sadness, though it did not compare to his despair at the termination of the *Trib.* But who could measure the cumulative impact of all that he had suffered recently? The last two and a half years had been the worst period in Red's life. One blow had followed another: The death of his father, the death of Frank Graham, the death of Stanley Woodward, the death of the *Herald Tribune,* the death of Kay, and now the death of the eight-month-old *World Journal Tribune.*

Smith still had the syndicate to write for, but for the first time since he had come to New York nearly twenty-two years before, he had no New York City outlet and was without immediate expectations of one.

The other New York dailies seemed set with columnists—the *Post* with Milton Gross and Larry Merchant, the *News* with Dick Young, and *The Times* with Arthur Daley. Smith was four months short of his sixty-second birthday. Would anyone hire him at this age, even if they could squeeze in another sports columnist? What now? Where would he go? What would he do? These were staggering questions to answer for a man who had never wanted to be anything but a newspaperman, and who had been nothing but a very fine newspaperman for forty years.

"I saw Red one night, and he looked ill-attended, with spots on his tie," recalled Shirley Povich.

Smith was drinking heavily after Kay's death, and his friends were worried. "He might tell the same story two or three times the same night," recalled Skipper Lofting, a press agent and friend of Smith's. "And he could draw some doozy blanks. He could wake up in a motel and look at the matches to see where he was. He could lose typewriters. He'd always say, 'I could sleep on a picket fence, and often have.' "

One day, Smith asked Lofting if he thought Smith was an alcoholic. Lofting drank hard and would become a member of Alcoholics Anonymous. He told Smith no. "Because," Lofting theorized, "your personality doesn't basically change when you drink."

Terry Smith was troubled, though. He knew his father had fallen a few times on the sidewalk in front of Shor's after a long night of drinking. "I was worried that he would really drift loose from his anchors and drink too much without someone telling him, 'Let's get outta here. Let's go home,' " said Terry. "My nightmare was of Pop driving home alone to an empty house after a late night in the city. He's on the Merritt Parkway, and he isn't focusing well, and there is a glare of lights, and he slams head-on into a tree."

Smith might have been hired by another big-city newspaper outside of New York. But New York had been his home since 1945 and he felt too settled to start over in a totally new area. To leave would be a psychological and emotional blow. He had struggled to make it to New York and had established his reputation as the best in his field in, as he called it, the "capital of the world." There could be no stepping down from there.

Besides, possibilities remained in New York. *Time* magazine was testing the market and laying out "dummy" pages for a new afternoon paper, and so was *The New York Times*. Smith was mentioned as a columnist if anything should materialize. Nothing did.

Smith's column survived in seventy newspapers across the country. Smith continued to be carried in many of the major newspapers in America. He still appeared regularly in, among other places, the *Washington Post,* the *Chicago Sun-Times,* the *Boston Globe,* the *Los Angeles Times,* and the *San Francisco Chronicle.* In the New York area, he appeared in the *Newark Star-Ledger,* the *Long Island Press,* the *Jersey Journal,* and the *Staten Island Advance.* "I've got the town surrounded," Smith said.

He could still joke, but Smith's syndicated column was not always given prominent display and might be found—if it appeared at all—as a kind of afterthought anywhere in the sports section on a given day. Jeffrey Landau, who became an editor of the *Baltimore Sun,* recalled reading Smith with delight when growing up on Staten Island. But the *Advance* "would sometimes run him in the back of the sports section and cut it heartlessly," he recalled.

It angered Smith that his column would be cut for space reasons or simply because of a desk editor's whim. It angered him and it depressed him. (On occasion, though, Smith could be pleased. He once told Jerry Holtzman, then with the *Chicago Sun-Times,* that the trims that paper made on his column for space showed him he could write shorter and still be as effective.) Smith also believed that the syndicate could do a better job of selling and distributing the column. It was sent out on a news and feature wire but wouldn't get top priority—sports rarely did—and newspapers received it late and would often run Smith's column a day later than they would have if he'd been writing for the *Herald Tribune* news service. Or papers would not run the late column at all. On occasion Smith would receive a phone call from an editor asking how his newspaper could get the column, or get it quicker. Smith would complain bitterly to the syndicate officials. Some of these problems had also occurred when he was with the *Herald Tribune,* but they hurt more now that he was more vulnerable.

Not long after the *World Journal Tribune* folded, the *New York Post* made Smith an offer. "It was for very low pay," recalled Terry Smith. The offer was significantly less than the $50,000 he had received from salary and syndication at the *Herald Tribune.* "It was handled poorly, kind of on a take-it-or-leave-it basis. And Pop resented it. He told one of the editors, 'Look, I just lost a paper and a wife in the last year, and I'm not interested.' "

Kit visited Red and went out to dinner with him one night. Sportscaster Howard Cosell was in the same restaurant and happened to be eating alone. They spoke to Cosell when they entered. Later, when he came over to their table to talk, Kit, jealous of this time with her father, said under her breath, "Oh, no." When Cosell left, Red said, "Don't be too hard on Howard. It's no fun to eat dinner alone."

Smith didn't like eating alone, nor was he happy staying by himself in the house in Connecticut. He talked to Terry about selling it and moving into the city, and began a casual search for an apartment in Manhattan.

In the spring of 1967, Terry was offered an assignment to become a correspondent for *The New York Times* in Israel. One of his major concerns was leaving his father.

Terry and Red met for dinner at Mamma Leone's on West Forty-eighth Street in Manhattan, "a place we knew and liked and where we could talk quietly as opposed to Shor's," said Terry.

His son discussed *The Times*'s offer and asked "very candidly about what effect it would have on him," recalled Terry. "I wondered how he would manage with no one around."

Red Smith looked hard at his son. "You want to do it, go and do it," he said, becoming emphatic. "Don't look back. Don't worry about me. I'll be fine." Terry recalls Red saying this over and over, and "with such strength and force that he convinced me he'd be all right." Terry took the assignment.

As the months went on, Smith continued to phone in his five columns a week to the Publishers-Hall Newspaper Syndicate. He seldom saw them in a newspaper. He told Terry, "It's like writing the column and flushing it down the toilet."

Shortly before leaving for Jerusalem, Terry acted on an idea. The *Wall Street Journal* had no sports columnist. It wasn't the New York general circulation daily that his father would have preferred, but it was a distinguished newspaper with a circulation of over one million. Terry recalled that "it was kind of cheeky of me" but he didn't ask his father—he told his father—that he was going to check the *Journal* on his behalf. "He didn't stop me," recalled Terry.

Terry called Vermont Royster, the editor of the *Journal,* whom he did not know. Terry introduced himself on the phone and asked, "Do you know what your paper needs?"

"Well, no," said Royster.

"A sports column. And I've got the columnist for you. My father." Royster asked, "Who's your father?"

"Red Smith."

"I know his work well," said Royster, "and I admire him very much."

"He hasn't put me up to this," said Terry, "and I haven't asked him. But I know my father, and I know he would love to be appearing in New York again, and I think he'd be great for it."

"I'm interested," said Royster. "I'll take it up with some people here."

A week passed. Royster called Terry Smith. "There was a lot of divided opinion here," said Royster, "but the answer is no. It came down to mortgaging the space, and it was decided not to give any of it up to sports. But everyone agreed that if we wanted a sports columnist, it would be Red Smith."

When Terry informed his father of the *Journal*'s decision, Red took the news evenly. He had not expected to get it—"it was from left field," recalled Terry—though he would have liked the position. Sometime afterward, Shirley Povich recalls seeing Smith and getting the impression that Smith felt himself much older. "He talked about 'these old bleached bones,' " said Povich.

Smith had other friends who were also concerned and who hoped to stimulate his interest in things beyond his column. "All the people in Stamford are introducing me to all the eligible widows from miles around," Smith told Povich. "They're in a hurry to get me married off to the widow of their choice." He added, "Women, especially married women, can't bear the sight of a house-broken male who isn't supporting someone. As soon as they get wind of it, they start inviting him to dinner and having a spare gal around."

One concerned friend was Tom Stix, whom Smith described as "my literary agent if I had a literary agent." He also referred to Stix as "an old friend, a pipesmoker, raconteur, Baker Street Irregular, and amateur of the running horse." Stix had fielded numerous offers for Smith to write books, from memoirs to sociological studies. Smith turned them all down. For the first, he said, "I don't have any memoirs"—not even liking the stuffy sound of the word. For the second, they were "too weighty." A collection of columns was one thing, but a full-blown "actual book" was another. "I wouldn't know where to begin," he said.

In the spring of 1967, Smith was invited to Stix's home in Manhattan for dinner. "A spare gal" joined Stix and his wife, Regine. Her name was Phyllis Warner Weiss. She was a widow and was working to complete a fine arts degree at Sarah Lawrence. She had dropped out of Radcliffe after two years to work in New York. She later met and married John Weiss. Phyllis was not familiar with Red's writing and was no sports fan. The evening was very pleasant, nonetheless, and Red was animated, telling stories of the *Herald Tribune,* enjoying Phyllis's company. When they left, Smith offered to drive her home. She lived on his way home, in Harrison, New York.

When they arrived at Phyllis's, she invited him in for a nightcap. And when he said good night to her, at dawn, on the porch, he kissed her. He told her that since his wife had died, he had had no real interest in women, but now he could feel something inside stirring again.

"Red," she said gently, smiling, "shut up. The kids are sleeping upstairs."

Phyllis, at age forty-six, was fifteen years younger than Smith. She was a slight woman with short brown hair and glasses, reserved, almost shy, with a responsive intelligence and a generous laugh. Her late husband, John Weiss, was a newspaperman and publicist in New York who had even done some sportswriting for *P.M.,* a rather short-lived daily in New York. But he and Smith had never crossed paths. John Weiss had died in a plane crash ten years before, and Phyllis was left to bring up their five children, three girls and two boys. When Red and Phyllis met, Kim was twenty-three, Karen twenty-two, Robin eighteen, Peter seventeen, and Jenifer fifteen.

The night they met, Red and Phyllis had spoken about their families. Smith told how Terry's then fiancée, Ann, had called the *Herald Tribune* to get the dates of the Kentucky Derby, Preakness, and Belmont Stakes so that she could set the date for her June wedding in 1964. "That," said Smith, with a twinkle, "is my idea of a proper daughter-in-law."

The day after the Stixes' dinner, Smith called information and got Phyllis's phone number, but didn't call. "I was interested enough to think we would have another date," he would recall. Meanwhile, the Stixes had invited Smith again for dinner, at which he had met "another gal and I had a few dates with her right away."

He continued, however, to think of Phyllis Weiss. And perhaps hesitated to call because even taking a first step toward an involvement would be unwise since she was considerably younger and the mother of five kids. Where could that lead?

Phyllis had liked Smith. "He talked almost like writing," she said. "And I liked his mouth. I thought it was sensual." She hoped he would call.

One evening a few weeks after the Stixes' dinner, the Weiss family was seated at dinner when the phone rang. Peter Weiss, Phyllis's seventeen-year-old son, answered. "I'm sorry," he said, "she can't come to the phone. We're having dinner."

When he came back, Phyllis asked who the caller was. "Someone named Red Smith," he said. Peter had never before told anyone that his mother couldn't come to the phone. Oh, Peter! she thought.

After dinner, Phyllis called Red back. "I'd been worrying what had taken him so long," she said years later. "I knew he was going to call—it was clear. There was electricity."

Though neither Phyllis nor her kids were familiar with Red's work, Ray Weiss was. Ray Weiss was Phyllis's mother-in-law. "She thought he was wonderful," recalled Phyllis. "She was a big fan."

Smith lived a half-hour drive from Phyllis's house by way of the Merritt and Hutchinson River parkways, and his Mercedes-Benz had a way of finding itself heading toward 111 Harrison Avenue, the Weiss residence. "Once we went out," recalled Phyllis, "we never stopped going out."

They went to dinner, to the movies, to the theater in Manhattan. Sometimes he just took her food shopping. Smith would rise earlier than was his custom, write his column, and then pick up Phyllis. They would motor around in the daytime, in the dappled New England fall, through the Connecticut and New York countrysides, looking at old houses, and then would spread a picnic blanket beside a pond. Red was "filling her in" on his life, as baseball writers did in the pressbox when one came a few innings late. He talked about his youth. He spoke of his love for his father and how they fished together and had once caught a herring and went to see an eclipse and how tears would come to his father's eyes when he heard music that he loved. He spoke of his mother with affection but recalled scolding her for being a gossip, and he said that his parents "were crazy about each other." "I had never known anyone who had so idyllic a childhood," Phyllis recalled. And he told her about his brother, who now suffered from alcoholism, how with heavy heart he took Art periodically to an upstate home to dry out, and that this was a burden Smith felt he had to bear.

"And he talked about newspapers he had known," she said, "but not much about his columns."

Smith called her "my school girl" because she was taking classes at Sarah Lawrence. Phyllis was uncomfortable calling him "Red"—"it sounded like a trade name," she said. "Walter" somehow didn't do, so she decided to call him "Wellesley." It was what his mother had called him, and it was fine with him.

Shortly after he met Phyllis, Smith traveled to Jerusalem to visit Terry and Ann, a trip he had planned months before. Smith was moved by Israel, a country then just twenty years old. He was impressed with its vitality, its creativity, and even its abruptness. "The people there don't practice amenities," he said, "because they're too busy building a country."

While traveling through Israel, he and Terry and Ann stayed one night at the King David Hotel in Tel Aviv. From there, Smith wrote this letter:

Phyllis my dear,
When young I was taught that personal letters should never be typed but then they neglected to teach me to write long-hand. And I've been wanting to talk with you.

There's been considerable confusion here, not only involving the sinking of Israel's Navy. A few days after arrival I learned that Ann was radiant with hope that she was pregnant. (Having a family is the most important thing in life to these kids and Annie's only pregnancy three years before ended with a miscarriage. . . . Annie has even suggested to Terry that they adopt a couple of Arab kids but Terry said no, Arab kids just sat around drinking coffee.) . . .

Terry has a little time off and we're taking off today for six days in

Cyprus. . . . (I'm due back in the papers of November 6, but I am not required to deliver the body at any special time.) . . .

He went on to tell her of his travels around Israel, including the hike up to Masada. "Somehow my saloon legs managed the climb. . . ." He described a race track on the desert near the Dead Sea which was

1,291 feet below sea level, the lowest gambling hell on earth. . . .

And now the phone has rung and I'm off to Cyprus to lounge in the sun and impersonate Somerset Maugham in frayed white linen, puffing a melancholy pipe and deploring the dissolution of the Empah.

Ever thine, Red? Walter? Wellesley?

Cyprus turned out to be less restful than Smith anticipated. He and Terry decided to swim on a popular beach five miles east of Kyrenia on the open coast. It was about five o'clock in the afternoon and the lifeguard and nearly all the sun-bathers had gone. Red and Terry, both good, confident swimmers, dived into the water. Terry recalled:

We got carried out by this exceptionally strong undertow. We didn't pay any attention to it and found ourselves about 150 yards from shore. We started to swim back. After a few minutes it became obvious we were not getting in. We sort of buckled down and swam harder. We made some progress, but the surf kicked up more and more and getting over the curlers was an incredible struggle. It occurred to me we might not make it. He was flagging badly.

He said something like, "I'm getting winded, I'm getting pooped." We kept swimming, and at one stage I reached out and sort of put a hand on him, and he'd do the same to me, and we'd ride a wave. We didn't say much more, except that we gotta really get through this. It was damn serious and we knew it. And with a final push, both of us together broke through the surf and then were splashed up on the beach. We dragged ourselves up to the sand, breathing very hard, exhausted.

He looked over at me and said, "That was close." After our incident, "Five Mile Beach" became for Pop kind of an expression of trouble.

Flying home from Cyprus, the tourist carried with him several stories he would write, the first being on the race track he called the "Dead Sea Downs." And, after the swimming drama in Cyprus, the idea of death may have been on his mind: He wrote, for example, that "in the Maccabean War about 170 B.C., Lydias led a force of 100,000 foot-soldiers, 20,000 horses, and thirty-two elephants to subdue the

Jews. The campaign was bad for Eleazer, brother of Lydias. He got hit on the head with a falling elephant and snuffed it."

Smith returned to his home in Connecticut and to Phyllis. He had missed her. "I had fallen in love," he would say later. "There was a second time around. I didn't know that. It came as something of a surprise to me."

He hadn't said anything to Terry about Phyllis, but he told Kit when talking to her on the phone. "He was almost apologizing for doing this so soon after mother died," said Kit. She had no complaints. She knew he had been lonely.

Over Christmas, Smith drove out to Wisconsin to spend the holidays with Kit and her family. Smith was giving the Hallorans his Buick, the second car, which he no longer needed. He had left Phyllis a present to open at Christmas, a string of gold beads. On Christmas Day, Smith called Phyllis and said that he had thought about her all the way to Wisconsin. He joked about the old Victorian saying that until you're married, you're allowed to give flowers, books, or candy, but not personal jewelry. He flew home shortly after his visit.

On Valentine's Day 1968, Phyllis answered her doorbell and found a florist delivering a dozen roses to her. She opened the attached envelope and read, "From the Fairfield County Archery Association." The sender, she knew, was an elderly, cherubic arrowbearer, and she was delighted.

On a rainy Saturday night in early April, Smith took Phyllis and her red-headed sixteen-year-old daughter, Jenifer, to Roosevelt Raceway. A harness-racing horse, W. W. Smith, had been named in his honor, and Joe Goldstein, the track publicist then, recalled that Smith was "so anxious to show this woman the horse. He seemed very eager to get along with her and her daughter and to impress them. We went down to the paddock, and it was muddy and terrible, and I thought, this might be the end of the love affair."

Smith wrote about the night in a column the following day:

W. W. Smith is a dark bay gelding with one white hind foot, a long plain face, and a name of rare distinction.

"Kind of a rangy dude," said his trainer, Steve Demas. "Not much to look at, as horses go."

"Oh, well," somebody said [it was Smith], "neither is his namesake, even as horses go."

This was a rainy evening at Roosevelt Raceway, a night for planting mud-spattered shoes under a table in the clubhouse dining room, for prodding sluggish corpuscles into action with a touch of the craythur, for a whirl of light-hearted gambling over the chicken chow mein. Perhaps there are pleasanter ways to spend a rainy evening in New York, but they are not recommended by the clergy. . . .

Down on the floodlit track, horses had water in their ears and the climate dripped clammily down drivers' necks, but all was cozy where the glassed-in sinful dwell. . . .

Smith and Phyllis put ten dollars on W. W. Smith, a horse that the form chart disclosed had a history of inconsistency. Smith wrote:

. . . W. W. Smith, with Carmine Abbatiello in the sulky, was sixth in the stretch, leading only the odds-on favorite, Romulus. At the finish, Romulus was sixth and W. W. Smith last.

Witnesses who had invested their savings on W. W. Smith for what might be termed sentimental reasons, watched with quivering lip as Abbatiello's red and gold silks receded. Then, out of the corner of the eye, they spotted the number of the winner. He was Hodgen Special, stablemate of W. W., scoring for the entry at $11.80 for $2—and how sweet that is.

But why, Steve Demas was asked in the moist paddock while W. W. cooled out under a red blanket, why had the old boy finished last? Steve smiled fondly.

"He's never been sound," he said. "He's temperamental. He's kind of homely, and when one drop of rain falls he can't handle the wet track. The rest of the time he's beautiful."

For several years, Phyllis had wanted to take a vacation in Europe, and the coming summer seemed the right time. "Hell," Smith said, "I can take a vacation any time. Do you need a companion?" They decided to go together by ship—Phyllis rarely flew after her husband's fatal plane crash—but there were complications, namely Jenifer. At sixteen, Jenifer was a modern-thinking high school junior, but not modern-thinking when it came to her mother traveling to Europe with a man. "She thought it was scandalous," recalled Phyllis.

Jenifer and Smith at first got along relatively well, as Smith did with Phyllis's other children, until there was talk of marriage. Then, Smith would recall, "Jenifer didn't need me in her close-knit family. In fact, she now hated my guts."

In early July 1968, Phyllis carried through with the plans, but purchased a separate stateroom for Smith on the Dutch liner *New Amsterdam*. This didn't appease Jenifer. She shed tears as the day approached, and at the pier. As the ocean liner pulled away, and Phyllis and Red waved to all her children, they saw only Jenifer's bright red hair covering her face as she sobbed goodbye.

The couple sailed to London, then drove through Holland and along the Rhine in Germany and Switzerland, and then down to Rome, where they met Terry and Ann.

Smith and Phyllis stayed at the Hotel Eden, near the Via Veneto. Before departing America, Smith had written Terry a letter describing the trip and telling him when they would be in Rome. Smith told Terry, "We'll book separate rooms lest we be accused of living in sin —if that sort of thing is possible these days. And if anybody really cares."

It had been Smith's suggestion to meet Terry and Ann in Rome, a two and a half-hour flight from Jerusalem for them. "I was filled with all kinds of apprehensions, knowing that I'd be meeting someone for the first time who might become my stepmother," recalled Terry. The group spent a three-day weekend together sightseeing in and around Rome. Smith was funny and solicitous—and the time went smoothly.

Terry had mixed feelings. There was a "natural resistance" to "someone who might replace my mother in my father's life," he recalled, but Terry was also delighted and relieved that "someone would keep an eye on him—who obviously cared for him a great deal —and would provide the support system that had been stripped away from him."

After Terry and Ann returned to Israel, Smith and Phyllis continued sightseeing. He wore a tie and powder-blue blazer at the Coliseum, he carried a green Michelin guidebook up the stairs to St. Peter's, and they drove along the Amalfi Coast and stayed overnight at Positano. In Naples, he sent a boy for a bottle of wine and the boy never came back. Smith was mad at himself for being taken.

After a week in Italy, the couple left for home on the ocean liner *Michelangelo*. One evening, on the Atlantic, Smith asked Phyllis to marry him. He told her that since he was so much older, she might expect to be widowed a second time. Also it might not be easy for the children on either side. "Didn't get any yes right away," Smith would recall. Not right away, but he did get the yes.

Upon their return he learned that his column would appear again in a New York City outlet, but it wasn't quite what he had hoped. Publishers-Hall had added as a subscriber to his column the Fairchild Publications, which published *Women's Wear Daily,* the women's fashion-industry newspaper, and the *Daily News Record,* its men's fashion paper. They were lively papers, well-edited and well-written, with a combined nationwide circulation of about 160,000. The papers' publisher, James Brady, who had read and admired Smith in the *Herald Tribune,* had only recently learned that Smith's column was available—at $100 a week. "A steal," he told John Fairchild, chairman of the corporation, and bought the column. *Women's Wear* would call the column "Sportif," a French word that Smith said "was a bit lacey." Even though he would be appearing between the hosiery and lingerie, the fabrics and the knits, the furs and the cosmetics, it was better than no New York outlet at all.

Smith suggested to the syndicate editor that he cover the Republican National Convention in Miami Beach and the Democratic National Convention in Chicago. It would be a reprise of his 1956 political convention coverage for the *Herald Tribune.* He had got "a big kick out of covering a political convention as a sportswriter viewing a very popular spectator sport. And I'd try to have fun with it." The editor said great, go ahead.

The first Smith columns that appeared in *Women's Wear* were in August from Miami Beach, and ran on the front page. On the night the Republicans nominated their Presidential candidate, Richard Nixon, who had been defeated the last two times he had run for office, Smith wrote:

"Congressman Gerald Ford, the Clyde Beatty of this carnival, made his entrance at 5 P.M. armed with a gavel in lieu of the traditional whip and kitchen chair. . . ."

During the nominating speech for Nixon, Smith continued, "there was a moment of apprehension when Spiro Agnew said of Nixon that: 'You don't create such a man, you don't discover such a man —you recognize such a man.'

" 'I was afraid he was going to say you exhume such a man,' a listener on the press stand whispered hoarsely."

The "listener" was Smith, who still was no fan of Nixon. But he could nonetheless view Nixon's nomination for president in the wry, detached approach of old. Smith interviewed a favorite of his, Beau Jack, the former lightweight champion, was a bootblack in the Fontainebleau Hotel barber shop. He told Beau Jack about Nixon, the former vice-president.

"He's an experienced boy but he hasn't won an election on his own since 1950," said Smith. "Not one win in eighteen years."

"Eighteen years?" Beau Jack said. "Seems like a commission wouldn't hardly okay him to fight."

For the most part, though, it was a soporific convention—"ordeal-by-oratory," wrote Smith.

The Democratic National Convention in Chicago later that month would be dramatically different.

President Lyndon Johnson's policy of continuing the war in Vietnam had stirred the passions of many Americans, particularly young ones. The growing opposition to Johnson had convinced him not to run for a second term. The field of Democratic presidential hopefuls was then dominated by Vice President Hubert Humphrey; George McGovern, senator from South Dakota; and Eugene McCarthy, senator from Minnesota. In the previous five years, the country that had seemed so tranquil during the 1950's under President Eisenhower had experienced upheavals coming from the civil rights movement and the assassinations of three national figures: President Kennedy, his brother Robert, a Presidential candidate, just a few months before the convention, and the black leader Dr. Martin Luther King, shot and killed two months before Robert Kennedy.

Thousands of young people now converged on Chicago to protest the Vietnam policies and try to give voice to what they considered an enlightened and humane approach to politics.

Smith followed these events and didn't always approve of the young. He had criticized Muhammad Ali—still called "Cassius Clay" by some, a symbol for many of the young—and his refusal to be inducted into the Army because, Ali said, "I ain't got nothin' against them Vietcongs." Two years before, Smith had written:

Governor Otto Kerner of Illinois finds Cassius Clay's shrill complaints about his new draft status "unpatriotic and disgusting." So do millions of other Americans. Equally objectionable to many are the posturing of patrioteers in political office who miss no chance to take bows wrapped in righteousness and the American flag.

As published, Clay's remarks on being reclassified 1-A have been stupidly odious. . . .

[He is] heavyweight champion of the world, twenty-four years old, unmarried, rich and superbly healthy, and begging to be let out of his duties while other kids are dying. . . .

None of which justified Kerner's request to his Illinois boxing commissioners that they reconsider their approval of Clay's match with Ernie

Terrell in Chicago. . . . Clay's loud and tasteless quarrel with the Louisville draft board has nothing whatever to do with his defense of the heavyweight championship.

Squealing over the possibility that the military may call him up, Cassius makes as sorry a spectacle as those unwashed punks who picket and demonstrate against the war. Yet in this country they are free to speak their alleged minds, and so is he. If he burned his draft, library, Diners Club and American Express cards together, this would not excuse a politician for singling him out by denying him the right to work at his trade as long as the Army leaves him free to work. . . .

Smith had strong reservations about Ali the man and the boxer; he thought Ali was a braggart as well as a relatively untested fighter who may have benefited from Sonny Liston's losing both title fights to Ali "for business reasons." (Smith always questioned Liston's integrity in those bouts.) Beyond that, Smith's political column on "Clay" was, oddly, at once a most liberal and a reactionary position, right-leaning even to the point of not accepting Ali's name change, a practice that was in the mainstream of American sportswriters. (Ali abhorred Cassius Clay because it was, he said, "a slave name".)

Among the young protesters going to Chicago—the "unwashed punks," as Smith depicted them—was a sixteen-year-old redhead named Jenifer Weiss, whose mother he soon would be marrying and with whom he would be sharing a house.

"I was in the midst of the rebellion," recalled Jenifer, "and I thought Red was, well, not conservative, just mainstream. I was very stubborn and wouldn't see his perspective, but he listened to what I had to say, and I don't know whether he embraced it or threw it away, but he would always think about it."

What impressed Jenifer about Smith at the convention was that he "wanted to see what else was going on besides just what was in the convention hall. He spoke to people who weren't in the limelight. He'd get another side. Like when I saw him covering racing, he would talk to the owner of the horse, but he'd also talk to the groom."

Smith covered the Yippies and the Hippies and went with Jenifer to hear Phil Ochs, the folk singer, in concert and sat in the Chicago Coliseum with, as he wrote, many "unbarbered kids." But that was more descriptive than critical, and he added that those "shaggy heads have been targets of nightsticks this week," a reference to confrontations between young people and the Chicago police of

Mayor Richard Daley. Smith told Jenifer he thought Ochs had "a terrible voice" and, beyond that, wondered if the people leading the movement were "the best people for it." But he was appalled by cops knocking "kids through plate-glass windows."

Smith came away from Chicago with a broader view:

In the past, it seemed to make some sense for a sportswriter on sabbatical from the playpen to attend the quadrennial hawg-killings where Presidential candidates are chosen, to observe and report upon the politician at play. After all, national conventions are games of a sort, and sports offer few spectacles richer in low comedy—with the possible exception of a Sonny Liston swooning at the sight of Cassius Clay—than the exhibitions of yahoo statesmanship which used to move Henry L. Mencken to sulphurous laughter.

It is sadly different this week in the police state which Richard "The Lion-Hearted" Daley has made of the city he rules. There is no room for laughter in this city of fear. . . .

Up to the time of this writing there has been no violence or sabotage of the sort Mayor Daley feared when he brought in thousands of troops to reinforce his army of 11,000 policemen. Only minor headbreaking resulted last night from the effort of several hundred Yippies to test the cops' love . . . in Lincoln Park. . . .

The International Amphitheater where delegates convene is an armed fortress behind a barbed-wire stockade. To reach the hall, delegates and visitors must stop and show credentials at checkpoint Richard.

This is easier than getting through the Berlin Wall and the examination isn't as thorough as the frisking which the Fruit of Islam gives visitors entering a mosque for a sermon by the Muslim divine, Muhammad Ali.

Yet it is a bitter thing to feel that measures like these are deemed necessary to the democratic process in America. We used to make fun of the banana republics to the south where bullets accompanied ballots.

For Smith, "the presence of guns, the sadistic gestapo tactics of Mayor Daley's guardians of law and order" produced in him "a depressing feeling."

Jerry Izenberg, sports columnist for the *Newark Star-Ledger,* was also covering the convention and saw Smith becoming concerned with social issues in a way he never did before. "I got the impression that what he saw there, and the fact that he had an adolescent in his life for the first time in many years, made Red rethink some of his positions," said Izenberg. He also referred to the fighter as Muhammad Ali and not Cassius Clay.

It was clear that Smith had developed an understanding—and even a sympathy—for the views of Jenifer and other young people in Chicago. He never again described them as "unwashed punks," even if they were still "unbarbered." He would say after the convention that he was "really disenchanted." He was unhappy not only with the political goings-on, but also with his work at both conventions. His reporting "didn't come off as well" as it had in 1956, he said. "It was a good gimmick back then, but not anymore." The world had changed, and politics wasn't as much fun as in the gentle days of the mid-fifties and didn't lend itself to the light, wry approach Smith had sought. Smith decided he would stick to sports from that point on, though continuing to include political or nonsports views when they coincided with the sports events of the day.

The 1968 Olympic Games would include just such a mixture.

After the World Series games in Detroit and St. Louis, Smith traveled to Mexico City for the 1968 Olympic Games and covered a wide range of events. He watched George Foreman, who would win a gold medal and later become the heavyweight championship of the world. In one of Foreman's Olympics bouts, Smith was intrigued by the referee. "During the intervals when they were permitted to fight," wrote Smith, "George outpunched his man by a substantial margin. The referee was Gualtiero Checki, imported from Italy to interfere with the boxers. . . ."

Smith kept his coverage typically tongue-in-cheek for the first few days of the Games, until the dramatic 200-meter race and its aftermath, which caused an international furor.

. . . The sun was gone. On the rim of the stadium the Olympic flame guttered and blazed against the blue-black sky. The lighted figures on the scoreboard were a golden dazzle. Only on the floodlighted field was night held off. . . . On the [victory] stand were Tommie Smith, complete with goatee, a painful muscle pull, a new world record in the 200 meters, and a deep sense of involvement in the cause of American blacks. At his right was a little Salvation Army worker from Australia, Peter Norman, who had nipped the whiskered John Carlos for second place.

Smith and Carlos wore knee-high black stockings, symbols of Negro protest. Each had one black glove, a button of protest on his chest, and one white track shoe in the ungloved hand. As the band played "The Star-Spangled Banner," they dropped their heads, not looking toward the American flag as it climbed, and each lifted a clenched fist in a gesture meaning "we shall overcome."

Chances are there were mixed feelings among the 70,000 looking on, but nobody booed. Dignity and justice and angry courage stood there in the dusk. . . .

Shortly after, U.S. officials threw Tommie Smith and John Carlos off the American track team and ordered them to leave the Olympic Village.

Red Smith objected. He wrote that the pair had made a protest "of the sort every black man in the United States had a right to make." As for punishing the runners, Smith said, "the playground directors put their pointed heads together" to come up with a decision. "They are, as Marc Antony observed on another occasion, 'all honorable men,' who consider children's games more sacred than human decency."

He concluded: "If sports suffer some discomfort as a result of it [the blacks' statement in Mexico City], that is too bad, but if a just cause is promoted through this method, I think the end justifies the means, although I was taught in school it never did."

Smith's views of politics when it mingled with sports was stronger than ever, and he wrote with much more conviction and empathy about Smith and Carlos than he had about Jackie Robinson breaking into baseball.

Before leaving Mexico City, he also remembered to buy presents for Phyllis, whom he was marrying in a couple of weeks, and for the rest of his new family-to-be. He had spoken to Phyllis by phone, and she had referred to another impending marriage, that of Jacqueline Kennedy and Aristotle Onassis.

"Will you buy me an island, too?" asked Phyllis.

"Would a nice Mexican dress do as well?" Smith asked.

He never did buy her an island. "But he got the next best thing," she recalled. "He bought me a house on an island." The island was Martha's Vineyard, and the house was built in the summer following their wedding.

Six days after the Olympics ended, on Saturday, November 2, Smith and Phyllis were married in St. Gregory the Great, a Catholic Church in Harrison. The ceremony was held in the rectory and not in the main church because Phyllis, raised in the New England Congregationalist faith, was not Catholic. (She was now an agnostic.) Red was "very nervous," recalls Phyllis, and when he arrived in his dark suit to pick her up, he realized he had left the wedding ring at home in Stamford. She went upstairs to her bedroom, got the wedding ring from her first marriage, and gave it to him. Then, in her cream-colored Italian damask dress, she took Smith's arm, and on that mild day they walked the three blocks to church.

Art Smith was the best man. Neither Terry nor Kit attended. Terry was in southeast Asia, and Red had told Kit that the wedding would be small and brief and that it wasn't necessary for her to fly all the way in for it.

Phyllis's five children were there. Though there was still a rather uneasy truce between Red and Jenifer—and to some extent, Peter, Phyllis's seventeen-year-old son, and Robin, the eighteen-year-old daughter—the wedding went off without incident.

Red gave Phyllis pearls for a wedding present, and she bought him a tweed sports jacket "because I liked it and because he needed one," she recalled. They spent one night at the Westbury Hotel in Manhattan. In regard to a full-scale honeymoon, Smith told the society reporter for *The New York Times,* "We're both too busy."

Smith and Phyllis understood the various problems they would endure between themselves and their families, such as the generation gaps, the age gaps—"his mother and my grandmother dressed in the same fashions," said Phyllis—and the conventional problems of two people trying to get along together.

They shared interests in literature and socializing with friends. Phyllis had little enthusiasm for football and abhorred boxing. She would recall going to Kingston, Jamaica, for the George Foreman–Joe Frazier heavyweight championship fight and not wanting to attend the fight itself, sitting in her room and "feeling the tension of the fight in the warm air." She did have a mild interest in baseball and enjoyed the color and excitement and the characters around the race track. Mostly, she liked being with Red. Sometimes she would read the lead of his column, and if she didn't care for the subject, she wouldn't continue with it. Other times, he would read her a column that pleased him. "I loved to hear him read it, so clear and expressive," she recalled.

They went to art museums on occasion, though it wasn't Smith's first choice of things to do. He liked representational art and tried to comprehend modern art. "But," said Phyllis, "I don't think he ever understood Picasso." When the ballet and a football game were on television at the same time, Smith usually won out and watched the football game on their color TV set.

Phyllis was a social drinker and saw Smith as perhaps more than that. She was concerned with how much he drank, and what he drank. For years, he had preferred Scotch, but Phyllis eventually persuaded him to change. "She read that vodka contained somewhat less poison than whiskey," Smith recalled, "and that of our popular drinks the ingredients most likely to give you a hangover are bourbon, then—going down the scale—rye, Scotch, gin, and least of all, vodka. I think she read that in *The New York Times* and, Virginia, if you read it in *The New York Times,* it must be true." Smith, under Phyllis's watchful eye, also began to cut back somewhat on the amount of liquor he consumed.

Smith took his wife to Toots Shor's. Once, while sitting at a banquette with Phyllis and Shor, Smith was called away. Phyllis and Toots, the large, long-time "saloon-keeper," sat there alone, uncertain of what to say to each other. "Then he put his hand on my knee and patted it when he talked," recalled Phyllis. "He didn't mean anything by it. It was just a habit that he did with men. He was uncomfortable with a woman. This was a man's world."

Toots was having other problems as well. Financial problems. He suffered, he said, because television and night baseball had cut into the night life and saloon life of New York City. In 1971, Shor, unable to pay $269,576 in federal, state, and city income taxes, was forced to close his establishment. The shutting down of Shor's affected Smith personally and professionally. And without a sports-gathering center, Smith's trips into the city would become less frequent.

By then, Smith had sold his house in Stamford and moved into Phyllis's seven-bedroom house in Harrison. They converted a bedroom into a workshop for him. He went from living alone to living with anywhere from two to six others, some of whom resented a replacement for their real father. Eventually Phyllis's oldest boy, Kim, got married. Karen, Robin, and Peter were away at college—but returned during vacations—or they would be working and either living at home or staying nearby. Jenifer, still in high school, was living at home permanently.

"I inherited five Vietnik stepchildren," Smith would say.

The kids took to calling Smith "Redcliffe," a twist on his nickname and their mother's former college. (Appropriate, too, because Wellesley and Smith were also the names of women's colleges.)

The living arrangement was strange for all of them. "We were," said Peter Weiss, "kind of standoffish. I didn't know this man, didn't want to know him, and didn't feel I needed to know him. He wasn't our father and we weren't his kids, and he didn't treat us as his kids. There wasn't an open and free exchange at first. One thing that impressed me was that we knew he was an important man in his field, and yet he was so unpushy about himself. He never gave us lectures or speeches. I remember him saying about politics, 'I've spent most of my adult life voting against Richard Nixon.' I thought that was funny, and said, 'All the good it did you.' And Red laughed at that."

Smith would get upset when the kids came home and dropped their backpacks in the middle of the living-room floor. "It was a little hard for Red," said Phyllis. "Of course, he would leave his shoes lying around, too." Jenifer still tested Red and his differing views. Robin would drop out of college for a while. "She was a really warm person," said Phyllis, "but she was going through an abrasive period." And with Peter and Red, she recalled, "there was a little sparring going on."

None of the Weiss children were ever heavily involved with drugs, Phyllis recalled, but they experimented. Especially with marijuana. "Peter's attitude was, 'Why not? What's wrong with pot?' We worried for a time about him. And Red would grow impatient with him."

Peter recalled being home from Antioch College one Christmas and "whipping out a joint and offering it to Redcliffe." Red said, "No, thanks, I've tried them before." And he had, in a Milwaukee speak-easy some forty years before. "They aren't good for anyone," said Smith.

"They're good for some people," said Peter. "Makes them feel good. Besides, it's my life."

Smith bristled. Peter said, "You're old-fashioned."

"Yeah," said Smith, "I am."

In various ways, Smith tried to establish his credentials with Phyllis's children. When, for example, Carlos Baker's thick and celebrated biography of Hemingway was published in 1969, Smith was pleased to point out his name in the long list of people Baker had interviewed in his research. Another time, Smith received an old copy of a college textbook, *A Quarto of Modern Literature,* which contained a piece that he had written on Joe Louis. It was the only newspaper article in the book, and it was between an essay by Winston Churchill and a poem by Dylan Thomas. Red left the book on the kitchen table, with the page open to his place. He also showed them *The Harper Dictionary of Contemporary Usage* in which he was referred to as one of the "language experts."

Of all Phyllis's children, Red was having the smoothest time with Karen. Once, singing with a choir group in New York City, she invited Smith and Phyllis to a performance. Afterward, she asked Smith what he thought of it. "I always enjoy a prize fight," he told her. She threw back her head and laughed.

As time went on, all sides made adjustments. "The more he was around," said Peter, "the more I grew to like him." Smith was generous with his time. And sometimes he would discreetly help with money when needed. He and the children frequently discussed the war, and he began to see more of their side. "We came to find him," said Robin, "trusting and loving."

In 1971, Jenifer, a sophomore at Earlham College in Richmond, Indiana, dropped out of school. She was interested in horses, and Smith made a contact through a friend for her to work on a horse farm in Ocala, Florida. Part of the job involved menial tasks, like shoveling manure. She was unhappy. One afternoon Smith, traveling alone, visited her on his way to a spring training camp.

"He told me that he could help me get a job, but he couldn't help me keep a job," Jenifer recalled. "And if I wanted to leave that job, it was fine with him. It wasn't like I was doing a disservice to him. That wasn't a problem. I sort of felt like he was telling me to follow my instincts, that my instincts were good and that what I wanted to do was okay, that I'd turn out okay and not to worry." It was very much the way he had handled Kit when she was Jenifer's age.

That evening Smith picked up Jenifer to go to dinner. As they walked to his rented car, he handed her the keys and said, "Here, you drive." Jenifer recalled that when she, a teenager, was with adults, they always drove. "I don't know why he let me drive; maybe it was to make me feel important, an equal and not like a little girl," she recalled. "I remember he complimented me on the way I drove. Just sort of offhanded. It stuck with me. He paid attention to me, gave me confidence. From then on, Redcliffe and I became very good friends."

She returned to Earlham after one semester's absence and graduated in 1973.

CHAPTER
12

One rainy afternoon on the New Jersey Turnpike, Joe Goldstein, the sports publicist, was driving with Barney Nagler, a columnist for the *Racing Form;* Robert Lipsyte, a young, new sports columnist for *The New York Times;* and Red Smith. They were driving to Philadelphia to interview the heavyweight champion Joe Frazier.

Lipsyte had recently seen a Smith piece in *Women's Wear Daily* and told him how much he liked it. "I'm sorry you don't have an outlet on a New York daily," said Lipsyte. "It must make you unhappy."

"It does," said Smith. "I wish I wasn't just in the garment center."

Sometimes, when sentiments similar to Lipsyte's were expressed to Smith, he'd joke and talk about being "big in the rag industry" and that he was "the lead sports columnist for *Women's Wear Daily.*" "I'd better get this on the wire," he once said to Jerry Izenberg, "*Women's Wear Daily* is waiting." By his tone, Izenberg recalled, Smith "wasn't putting down *Women's Wear Daily.* He was putting down Red Smith."

On the other hand, Brady, editor of *WWD,* admired how Red

handled being in his paper. "He was never apologetic," said Brady, "at least not in my hearing. I never heard him say anything but good things. I think he felt, 'I'm a professional.' "

Smith and Brady rarely had reason to see each other, but one evening they found themselves at the same party after a fight. "Ali was there and all these huge athletes stuffed into dinner jackets, and Red was small and courtly but he seemed totally at ease," recalled Brady. "We talked and he asked me how the paper was doing. He said, 'When I didn't have an outlet in New York, you gave me one, and I want you to know I will always appreciate that.' "

While appearing in *WWD,* Smith wrote many typically thoughtful and delightful pieces, and he would still play the gadfly. After the election of Satchel Paige to what Smith called the "anteroom" of the Hall of Fame, a room reserved for those who played in the Negro Leagues, he took issue with a quote in *Sports Illustrated.* It said, "The only change is that baseball has turned Paige from a second-class citizen into a second-class immortal."

Smith wrote, "Relegating [Paige] to an anteroom was a compromise, but neither the baseball hierarchy nor the baseball writers nor the selection committee that picked him compromised on purpose. The fault is in the eligibility rules, which have kept out more deserving whites than blacks. The rules should be changed. . . ." He suggested some whites, such as Addie Joss and Bill Lange, who didn't play the required ten years for Hall eligibility but who should be in "the sacristy." He continued, "Could you write a history of baseball without mentioning [Joss]? Nobody ever has. That ought to be the measure of a man's fitness for the Hall of Fame, the only measure." Then he added a kicker that to the baseball establishment was blasphemy. "To be sure, that would qualify Eddie Gaedel, the midget who went to bat for Bill Veeck's Browns in 1951. Would that be so bad?"

A few weeks later, in sharp response to the killing of four youths at Kent State in the spring of 1970, Smith wrote: "Student protests against the slaughter of undergraduates who dissent from President Nixon's war policies have brought some dislocation of college sports schedules. This is surely the least important result of the Cambodian invasion and the Kent State killings, but it did call for decisions within the campus athletic community."

Gone not only were the references to "unwashed punks" but also the gentler references to "unbarbered" youth. Instead he wrote of "concerned young people" and of "agitation" rather than "dissent."

The Democratic Convention and life with Phyllis and her children seemed to have helped make him appreciate the antiestablishment. But he had other, more pressing, concerns. He had problems with his health—he wheezed—and a doctor had suggested, as Smith would recall, that he "stop drinking, stop smoking, and stop breathing." The doctor recommended that Smith blow up balloons to strengthen his wind. Smith followed the advice. Once, while waiting in a car for Phyllis to finish shopping, he blew up a balloon and put it down. He looked and saw a woman smiling through the window. "I saw you!" she said. He laughed, feeling only a little sheepish.

There were days, though, when he seemed tired in his column, tired perhaps from his breathing difficulties, tired perhaps from his long years as a newspaperman and public performer—especially with a diminished audience. In an obituary tribute to the fight manager and former sportswriter Lew Burston, Smith misspelled the name all the way through, including the headline, "Lew Bursten." He repeated a few anecdotes, one of them about Stanley Woodward at press headquarters before a fight when everyone was "yakking away." Smith wrote:

There came one of those accidental moments of quiet, when almost everyone fell silent. From a far corner came the voice of Stanley Woodward, the late, great sports editor of the *New York Herald Tribune.* Stanley, who may have been the most ferocious patriot of his time, was concluding a discussion with another journalist. . . .

"Yes!" Mr. Woodward was saying. "Yes! I agree it is perfectly all right to raise statues in memory of Robert E. Lee—provided you also raise them to Axis Sally, Tokyo Rose, and Benedict Arnold!"

Smith would be pleased to recall in print his dear friend, and perhaps felt a nostalgia for those vibrant days of yesteryear when Smith and his *Herald Tribune* colleagues were the center of the sportswriting universe, and Smith's columns were not "being flushed down the toilet."

There were other writing disappointments. One day during this period Skipper Lofting, rodeo press agent and friend, suggested an idea to Smith. Lofting had talked to Pat Ryan of *Sports Illustrated* about Smith writing a piece on the rodeo cowboy Freckles Brown. Smith had written a baseball column for *Sports Illustrated* when the magazine first came out, in 1954. At the time, he wrote six columns a week for the *Herald Tribune,* and this 1,500-word piece once a week for *Sports Illustrated* was draining. Also, the editors inserted words into his copy like "moreover," he said, "that I've spent a lifetime trying to avoid." And after only a few months he stopped writing for *Sports Illustrated.* Now, Pat Ryan, *Sports Illustrated's* articles editor, assigned the cowboy piece to Smith. A colleague of Ryan told her that "Smith always had trouble writing for the magazine, and are you sure you want to assign him?"

"By 'trouble,'" Pat Ryan recalled, "it meant that he had a chattier style than the magazine, that wonderful sort of quicksilver, smooth, personal style of his. I think the magazine was more third-person, detached. Also, the distance was different. The length for this magazine piece is about three thousand words, while his column is nine hundred or so. It could flatten out."

When the piece came in, Ryan, unhappily, found it flat. She thought about trying to make it work by cutting it, then said, no, she'd call him, as reluctant as she was to do so.

"I knew the baggage I was taking into this," she said. "He knew I was a helluva lot younger than he was. And of course he knew I was a woman. He didn't get angry at me, though I'm sure he wasn't happy. He was very gracious."

Ryan asked Smith to rewrite the story, and he did. It was rejected again. He would salvage the piece for a column.

Sometime afterward, on a very hot day in early June 1971, at the U.S. Open at the Merion Golf Club in Ardmore, Pennsylvania, outside Philadelphia, I heard Smith calling my name. (I was then a thirty-one-year-old sports columnist for the Newspaper Enterprise Association.) His voice had that familiar raspy sound, and in this case it came from under a shade tree, where he was sitting, wearing a floppy white hat. He waved me over and invited me to sit beside him under the tree. He had been walking the course, too, but had grown tired after a diet of hills and heat. We spoke about writing, and a particular New York sportswriter was mentioned. Smith liked him, but said that when telling a story, "he holds the bow string too long." It was an amiable chat and Smith seemed in good spirits. But seeing him sitting under the tree alone instead of with at least several others around him, as so often in the past, gave me the feeling that Red Smith, now nearly sixty-six years old, was literally and figuratively drifting on the periphery.

He still enjoyed some of his old pursuits, such as traveling to the Kentucky Derby. He and Phyllis drove down from Connecticut, with Smith taking the familiar route and stopping for picnics at a lake or woods, eating cheese and drinking wine.

But he could still be roused to anger. Once a truck brushed the fender of Smith's car. The truck driver, much younger and well-built, got out and accused Smith of cutting him off. The white-haired old man got out of his car and, with fists clenched, angrily berated the truck driver. Smith's face grew red and Phyllis grew concerned. The truck driver, thought Phyllis, was amazed at the old man's ire. "I think he thought Red might have a stroke."

Smith had another car accident with Phyllis beside him, a more serious one. She suffered a fractured vertebra and sprained neck, and he a bruised leg. When he tried to collect on his insurance, he received a run-around. He wrote a letter to the insurance company, beginning, "While in hospital, chiefly for my own entertainment, I filed an accident report. . . ." He eventually won satisfaction for his claim.

Back in New York in the late summer of 1971, Smith had lunch with Robert Cowles, president of Publishers-Hall Newspaper Syndicate. Smith asked for a larger share of the syndicate profits from his column than the fifty percent he had been receiving. Cowles said he couldn't afford it. "There was nothing he had to afford," Smith would say. "He wasn't paying a nickel for my stuff." After all, Smith reasoned, Cowles was paying no salary, only a percentage of the money received from subscribing newspapers. Smith also wanted assurances of better selling, distribution, and delivery of the column. "I wanted to hear how he could do better," recalled Smith. "I felt we just stiff-armed each other that way."

The contract was expiring and Smith felt that the syndicate would wait until he got nervous before he signed. "I'm not going to do anything about it," Smith told Phyllis. He had some leverage, he believed, because many papers still used his column regularly, and the syndicate was profiting from this.

Nineteen seventy-one was turning out to be an unfortunate year financially for Smith, as it would be for many who had investments in the stock market. Terry recalled that his father "took a terrible bath" when the market tumbled that year. Red Smith had a financial adviser he called "the Wolf of Wall Street." "He was a successful stockbroker and a horse player," recalled Terry. "And Pop invested pretty much what he had with him and lost a lot. Maybe as much as one hundred thousand dollars."

At the World Series in Baltimore that October, Smith received a phone call that made him forget some of his troubles. The caller was Abe Rosenthal, then the managing editor of *The New York Times*. Rosenthal said that Robert Lipsyte, who had been sharing the "Sports of the Times" column with Arthur Daley, was leaving and asked Smith if he could recommend any sportswriters to fill the position. Smith mentioned a few names. "How about you, Red?" asked Rosenthal. "Would you be interested?"

"Yes," he said without hesitation.

Rosenthal asked about his status with the syndicate. Smith told him the contract was expiring. "Why don't you come in and talk with us?" said Rosenthal.

Shortly after that conversation, Fred Russell, Smith's friend from the *Nashville Banner*, arrived in Baltimore and saw Smith in the hotel lobby. They shook hands. Russell recalls Smith's hand being moist. "What's the matter?" asked Russell.

"I have a meeting tomorrow morning back in New York with *The Times*," said Smith. "They approached me. I just can't think too much about it because I want it so bad. I'll be back in the late afternoon."

At *The Times* Rosenthal remembers having called Jim Roach, *The Times*'s sports editor, into his office. "Who's the best man around to fill the sports columnist's vacancy?" asked Rosenthal. Roach said, "Red Smith." Rosenthal said, "Let's try to get him. I think we can. I've already spoken to him."

Smith met with Roach, and then with Rosenthal, and an agreement was quickly reached. Roach was a long-time friend and admirer of Smith's, and Rosenthal, though not an avid sports fan, had read Smith in the *Herald Tribune* and remembered him as a witty, eloquent writer. "It was a childhood or youthful dream of mine, a wish of mine, to get Red," recalled Rosenthal. "Instead of seeing 'Read Red Smith in the *Herald Tribune*' on the side of trucks, it would now read, 'Read Red Smith in *The New York Times*.'"

Rosenthal remembers signing Smith to the contract. "It was sadly amusing," he said, "because Red was sixty-six years old and Jim Roach was approaching sixty-five and under the stipulations, executives had to retire at sixty-five. But Red was signed on as a contract employee and could stay on the rest of his life."

Did Rosenthal have any reservations about hiring a man sixty-six years old? "None whatsoever," he said. "He wrote as if he were much younger. I didn't care how old he was. I liked his acceptance of sports as entertainment and amusement. He didn't get huffy-puffy with self-importance. Besides, I enjoyed hiring the best person I could find."

Rosenthal asked Smith not to say anything about the new job until it was announced officially. A few days later Tom Wicker, a news columnist and associate editor of *The Times,* saw Terry Smith in the Washington bureau and said, "Heard your father's been hired to write the sports column." Wicker told Terry he got the information in New York from "Punch"—the nickname for Arthur Ochs Sulzberger, publisher of *The Times.*

"I haven't heard anything," said Terry.

Then Terry called his father.

"Is it true?" he asked.

"Yes," said Red.

"How come you didn't tell me?"

"Abe swore me to secrecy."

"But that secrecy," said Terry, "didn't include me." When Terry had gone to *The Times* from the *Herald Tribune* in 1965, his father had phoned him "from a pressbox somewhere," recalled Terry, "to offer congratulations and a warning: 'I hope you're going to enjoy working in a cathedral.' "

The Times, to Smith then, may have seemed a cloistered establishment compared to the looser, less "sanctified" halls of the *Tribune.* But now Smith would be appearing in *The Times*'s pages, and occasionally in its halls. He would continue to write at home and phone in his stories. He kept his traditional byline, of course, but in a newspaper that generally ran full first names—such as Arthur Daley, James Reston, and Walter Kerr, or initials, from C. L. Sulzberger to A. M. Rosenthal, and only occasionally a diminutive like "Tom" Wicker or "Dave" Anderson—his byline would be distinctive. Now a nickname, a remnant of the long-defunct and breezy *Philadelphia Record*—it folded in 1946—would appear on the pages of the "cathedral" newspaper: "Red" Smith.

Smith and Dave Anderson, who had been a *Times* general assignment sports reporter with specialties in football and boxing, would share the column with Arthur Daley. Daley and Smith would each write three columns a week and Anderson two. (Two columns would appear on Sunday.) Smith, signing "W. W. Smith," received a two-year contract as an "independent contract writer" for a salary of $38,000 a year. He received no benefits. No matter. He was back in New York.

He drove home to Harrison, where he and Phyllis broke open a bottle of champagne and even gave some to Putois, their border collie. Smith called Kit; Phyllis called her kids. "There was," Smith would recall, "a lot of electricity around the house."

After the official announcement, Smith received numerous congratulatory letters. One was from Herb Caen, the humor columnist for the *San Francisco Chronicle*. "Dear Redhead," he wrote. "Thank God! Now I can drop our subscription to *Women's Wear Daily,* but kindly run a boxscore on who ate what at La Grenouille each day to keep my wife happy. . . ."

Robert Cowles of Publishers-Hall Newspaper Syndicate, who thought he was in a negotiation of sorts with Smith, wrote that "I returned from vacation and learned that you chose to depart the fold. . . . The news brought mingled emotions." He was happy, he said, for Red to be going to the "highly regarded" *Times,* but "hated" to see Red leave.

Another letter was from Smith's predecessor. "I've been telling anyone who asks that had I known my resignation would bring you to *The Times,* I would have quit years ago," graciously wrote Robert Lipsyte. "It's not entirely an exit line. I was thrilled by the news, on several counts. As a *Times* man, at least in spirit, I saw your coming to the paper as a long-deferred marriage of the best newspaper and the best sportswriter (more than sportswriter, of course: during a brief but painful pitstop in the English master's degree program at Columbia, we discussed RED SMITH, AMERICAN STYLIST). As a reader, Smith-hungry for years now, I can hardly wait for the mornings that will begin with you. It would be presumptuous for me to wish you anything but sober typesetters, but all the best. . . ."

Arthur Daley, then sixty-seven years old—a year older than Smith —congratulated Red, but he was, characteristically, nervous about Smith joining the staff. Daley wondered what it meant for him, despite Rosenthal's words in the announcement that "Arthur Daley is a man who has earned a special respect and affection in the sports world and at *The Times*. . . ."

Lipsyte would be missed by a devoted following that appreciated his innovative, literate, and socially conscious approach to sports over the three and a half years he wrote the column. The demanding nature of the column had worn away at him, however. He said that when one column was finished, he began thinking of the next. He needed time, he said, to relax, to go scuba-diving, perhaps.

Unlike Lipsyte, there were some writers who thought Smith over the hill, that he was an old man and no longer, as one reporter said, "in the trenches." He was sixty-six and, as he had written twenty years before, when Marciano, age twenty-eight, knocked out Joe Louis, age thirty-seven, "the place for old men to dream is beside the fire."

Patrick Smith, Art's son, recalled that his uncle Red now had "more fullness in his voice, a different tone. He was spontaneous. In the few years before, he sounded a little sad, a little lonely, a little uninterested in things."

In the years that Red Smith had no New York City general-circulation daily, he had been, said Phyllis, "more unhappy than he either knew or admitted."

Now, Smith would recall, "I felt like I was back playing the Palace."

But he would open out of town, in Houston. He and Anderson went there to see Muhammad Ali, the former champ, fight Buster Mathis, who, Smith wrote, "had trained down to a svelte 260 pounds" after ballooning to 320. On Monday, November 15, two days before the fight, Smith's first piece for *The Times* appeared. "Buster Mathis is big as Texas is big, and it has been said that in this state a man can drive farther and look longer and see less than anywhere else in the nation," Smith began. "There may be more peaceable prizefighters than Buster, but none his size; pound for pound, he probably is the mildest gladiator in circulation.

"He is a decent, sensitive monster with one attribute that makes him seductively beautiful by fight-mob standards. The late Don Skene described this trait in a novel called *The Red Tiger*. 'He was kind of a marshmallow,' Don wrote, 'but at least he was a big marshmallow. . . .' "

Two and a half years earlier, Mathis, a ranking heavyweight, had lost dismally to Jerry Quarry and retired. Now he was making a comeback. So, in a way, was a slight, white-haired man in front of a portable typewriter at ringside in the Astrodome. The qualities that elevated Smith to the highest position in his profession had not diminished. His control of the language and his craftsmanship were as precise as ever, and his wit still shone, but in the months ahead *The Times* readers would see something different in Smith: that is, a greater concentration on issues, a more serious, aggressive and socially conscious journalist. These stunning changes would reflect the stunning changes in his life and perceptions—from the death of family and friends and newspaper, to a period of seeming exile, to his experiences at the Democratic National Convention in Chicago and the Olympics in Mexico City, to a new and challenging family.

Smith was aware of criticisms by some younger writers that his stuff had been "lightweight." Lipsyte, who had praised Smith's growth in recent years, had also criticized Smith for not taking a tougher stand on issues earlier in his career. "He juggled for us. He was saying, 'Yeah, baby, everything's okay.' Well, everything's not okay, and entertaining just isn't good enough."

Smith responded to such criticism in two ways: First, he agreed in part. "Today, maybe," he would say, "I feel that entertaining requires too much from me. My feet are tired. I'm a little weary of the old soft shoe." Second, he was doing something about it.

Beyond covering the sports staples of major fights, horse races, and ball games, Smith also honed in on the "cozy" tax shelters of the ball clubs that cried poverty and on the failure of Off-Track Betting and "Hot-Horse Howie" (Howard Samuels, the president of OTB) and "Honest John" Lindsay, mayor of New York, to fulfill the promise of shutting off the underworld's profits from illegal gambling.

But the major issue in sports was the labor-management problem, particularly in baseball, and especially when the Curt Flood suit headed for the Supreme Court. Professional athletes were growing more aware that the old ways of total owner domination were not only unnecessary but illegal. Flood, an outfielder, had attacked baseball's ancient reserve clause, the contract stipulation Smith had opposed as far back as 1938 in Philadelphia (in the Wally Moses holdout) and several times over the years (as in 1957, when he wrote a column headlined "The Slave Trade," and in 1966, when he wrote that "Like Hoffa, club owners are above the law"). But these were jabs, not continuing attacks. In fact, when Congressman Emanuel Celler was holding hearings on the reserve clause in 1951, Smith said he was "dragged [there] by the heels." He wrote back then, "Pardon the aside, but it would seem that the Congress has more important things to do than waste time over baseball's reserve clause." (In 1974, Smith wrote that he was "wrong" about that. Shortly after, Shirley Povich sent him a note saying, "I don't know whether I want to trust a man who changes his mind every twenty-three years.")

With *The Times,* when Smith took hold of an issue, he didn't let it off easily. "I've always had convictions," he said. "But as I've gotten older, I've gained some inward assurance that I'm on the side of the angels. I speak out more readily and approach these topics with much more conviction than I ever did before."

He also bridled when, as he once said, someone approached him
and asked, "Do you know Richard Nixon? You'd like him; he's a
real jock." Without dealing personally with Nixon, Smith would
write: "There are two reasons why this left the cockles as cool as a
proper martini. One is the implication that because a guy writes
about sports for a living he is a case of arrested development with
no interests away from the playground and a mind too simple to
entertain even small-talk of war or peace or books or plays or world
affairs or domestic problems or how to scramble eggs. The other is
the assumption that a sportswriter, because he is a sportswriter,
regards enthusiasm for football or a grasp of the infield fly rule as
a qualification for public office."

The new Smith devoted numerous columns to baseball's reserve
clause. He wrote that even though a player like Flood was earning
$90,000 a year, owners still had all the best of the situation: the
player, bound in perpetuity to a team unless the team decided to
trade, sell, or release him, was unable to test his market value. Smith
wrote that Flood was "a man of character and self-respect. Being
black, he is more sensitive than most white players about the institution of slavery as it exists in professional baseball. . . ." Smith castigated the baseball commissioner, Bowie Kuhn, for "restating baseball's labor policy: 'Run along, sonny, you bother me.' " Though
some sportswriters agreed with Smith's stand, the majority appeared
to be traditionalists, believing that baseball was fine the way it was.
And though some fans agreed with Smith, it seemed many more
believed that ballplayers were making enough money—they were
living a dream life, weren't they?—and should be satisfied.

When the Supreme Court voted 5–3 in the Flood case to keep the
status quo, Smith was angry:

Arguing Curt Flood's suit before the Supreme Court, former Justice
Arthur Goldberg reviewed the long and seamy history of buckpassing
between the Court and Congress, both of whom have stalled for half a
century over baseball's privileged position with regard to anti-trust
law. . . .

Once again the Court declined to consider either the legal and moral
complexion of the reserve system or the merits of Flood's case against the
system. Even though the majority opinion delivered by Justice Harry A.
Blackmun conceded that baseball's exemption from anti-trust regulation
was an "aberration" and an "anomaly," the Court once again backed off
and invited Congress to correct the situation. . . .

Justice William O. Douglas, dissenting, said it was high time to correct an error. . . . He said baseball should be subject to antitrust law. . . .

It is a disappointment because the highest Court in the land is still averting its gaze from a system in American business that gives the employer outright ownership of his employees. . . .

It is a disappointment because this Court appears to set greater store by property rights than by human rights.

Despite the Supreme Court ruling, the Major League Players Association was growing in strength and launched a successful battle to open free agency for players. Smith wrote increasingly about it and about the association's executive director, Marvin Miller. Smith said the owners had depicted Miller as "a master pitchman who hypnotizes the players." Smith, however, found that, unlike the owners, Miller didn't "lie" when he was asked a question. Miller recalls Smith phoning him on numerous occasions. "From the earliest days of the players association in 1966," said Miller, "I was convinced that when he asked a question, it was because he wanted to know the answer, not because he was just going through the motions. And that the reason he was calling was that there was a gap in his information and he was trying to fill it in. I didn't always have that impression from all reporters calling. I thought some reporters had their minds made up before they called. I never felt that way with Red."

To be sure, not all of Smith's column subjects felt that way, Commissioner Kuhn, who had opposed Miller, believed Smith had his opinions firmly in place before calling him. To Smith, Kuhn was a bumbling stuffed-shirt who posed as an even-handed czar. But, Smith wrote, in regard to the Flood case, "any misconceptions about the role of the commissioner that may have lingered in the minds of fans have been eliminated." In virtually every instance, said Smith, Kuhn issued press releases presenting the owners' side. ". . . Everyone must accept Kuhn for what he has been ever since he was hired —his employers' mouthpiece, a front man, a figure head." Smith gave a rundown of Kuhn's four predecessors, from Judge Landis ("a tyrant and the player's best friend") to Happy Chandler (who "left office for reasons of health; that is, the owners got sick of him") to Ford Frick ("capable and honest" but not firm) to Spike Eckert (whom "the owners played two dirty tricks on . . . hiring him" and "firing him"). Smith followed that with: "There has never been a commissioner who stood more erect, wore better clothes, or kept his shoes more meticulously polished than Bowie Kuhn." He also said that "other than a tack on his seat, nothing could make Kuhn jump up faster than when he saw a television camera."

Smith was also opposed to Kuhn's stand for World Series night games, which Smith said was a capitulation to television interests that neglected the nostalgic and traditional qualities that were associated with World Series day games. (In some ways, though, this smacked of the stiffened position of Smith's friend Frank Graham when night baseball was introduced. "Now," wrote Graham, "baseball would compete with professional wrestling and belly dancers for the entertainment dollar at night.") And Smith protested the designated hitter, which Kuhn permitted and which Smith called "that loathsome ploy."

Smith also ridiculed Kuhn's pose of sitting through a playoff game in a cold rain while wearing no coat or hat, as though it were a balmy night, and allowing the game to continue for the sake of the television revenues. Under the business suit, however, the commissioner, it was learned, was not as hardy as he appeared; he was wearing thermal underwear, a fact Smith would frequently note in his column at Kuhn's expense. One winter afternoon Smith phoned Kuhn at home for information. Kuhn was called to the phone. He had been outside chopping wood, he explained. "And Red," said Kuhn, "you won't believe this, but you'll never guess what I'm wearing." Though the commissioner could joke about the thermal underwear, Smith's critical columns pained Kuhn. He admitted to Terry Smith when he met him in a restaurant that Red's criticisms hurt, "mainly," said Kuhn, "because I always admired his writing so much."

In March 1972, four months after Smith began writing for *The Times,* he and Phyllis moved into a house in New Canaan, Connecticut, about thirty miles from the house in Harrison, and about sixty miles from Manhattan. All of Phyllis's children were living away from home then, and the Smiths wanted to move farther into the country but with a house big enough to accomodate visits from their families. They bought a ten-room, two-story, mid-eighteenth-century house made of flagstone and white clapboard with a red front door. Smith would show it off, down to the timbered-ceiling basement area, with jokes of his being a country squire. The house sat on a woodsy four-and-a-half-acre plot on West Road. Behind the house, at the end of a gravel driveway, stood a sturdy, freshly painted gray barn. One side of it became a garage, the other a small office for Smith with heat and plumbing.

He sat on a straight-back chair on wheels and wrote on a large green desk typewriter, facing a tall window and, beyond that, two pine trees. Above him at the window hung a big yellow light in a half-shell globe, which from the driveway looked like a half-moon. Behind Smith, long bookshelves lined two walls and stretched to the ceiling. The shelves were packed with books in orderly fashion according to sport, including boxing yearbooks, horse racing yearbooks, and baseball guides going back to the 1930's. The shelves also held such nonsports books as the William Strunk, Jr., and E. B. White *Elements of Style* (which, Smith said, he tried to reread once a year), the *Oxford English Dictionary,* the *Oxford Shakespeare,* and *Alice in Wonderland.*

In the little space unoccupied by books hung two English fox-hunting prints that he had received as gifts from Terry and Ann and a few photographs, including an action shot of the first Joe Frazier–Muhammad Ali title fight, one of Yogi Berra sitting on a dugout step, and, at the rear of the office, an ink drawing by Robert Riger of Ted Williams leaning against a bat beside a batting cage. Taped to the inner side of the door was a *Saturday Review* cartoon of a woman saying to her husband as he sits watching a quiz show on television, *"If you know all the answers,* Mr. Red Smith, *why don't you try to get on?"*

Alongside that cartoon was taped a piece of notebook paper with a Japanese inscription penciled on it. Below the Japanese was the English pronunciation and translation, "Bai Shun—selling springtime." While in Tokyo covering the 1964 Olympic Games, Smith had learned that that was the motto of the Japanese ladies of pleasure. He thought it had some application to his work as well. "My job," he once said, "is to provide momentary pleasure, like a good whore." He had said that his "goal was to entertain . . . and capture the grace and drama and beauty and humor" in sports. And though he didn't always believe that to be the case now, he still never wanted to lose sight of it. And even when climbing onto a soapbox, he always tried to do it with humor. He continued to see the lighter side of sports, even indulging in an occasional pun.

Upon learning that John Delamere, a New Zealand high jumper, had developed a new technique called "the Kiwi Flip," Red wrote, ". . . When you hear that the first attempt was made in major competition without a single proper practice jump, it becomes clear it was a case of love at first flight." Smith recalled that Elmer Layden, one of the Four Horsemen, "was unflappable as a seal on ice." And when something odd happened in one horse race, Smith noted that "the stewards couldn't believe their binoculars."

From the kitchen window, Phyllis could see Red writing. "He was now," she said, "an entirely different person sitting at the typewriter." When he wrote for the syndicate and *Women's Wear Daily,* she recalled, "he'd sit at the typewriter and do nothing for a long time. Once he got to *The Times* he sat differently. He'd pour himself into the typewriter."

"Yes," he said a few years afterward, "I realize that now. I didn't realize it then."

Morris McLemore, a sportswriter and broadcaster from Miami and a long-time friend, said he thought Smith was writing consistently better than he had in previous years. Smith agreed. And in 1974, when Smith selected columns for a new collection, *Strawberries in the Wintertime,* he included very few from the four and a half years he wrote exclusively for the syndicate.

He chose the title *Strawberries in the Wintertime* because it "happens to be the title of a piece about Willie Mays, and it captures, I think, some of the flavor of the sportswriter's existence, which is what the late Bill Corum was talking about when he said, 'I don't want to be a millionaire, I just want to live like one.' "

In this regard, Smith was back feeling, at least on occasion, like a millionaire. But he still had to labor to produce the column, methodically shaping a sentence until he was satisfied. He rarely went back and rewrote. "There's nothing to writing," he once said. "All you do is sit down at the typewriter and open a vein."

In the same year that *Strawberries* appeared, Smith, it happened, developed a bleeding ulcer. Several years before, his friend, Bill Heinz, had gone to a doctor because of stomach pains. Smith wrote that the doctor advised Heinz, " 'If you don't stop knocking yourself out to be the best writer in the world, you're going to get a bleeding ulcer.'

" 'I'm only trying to be the best writer I can be,' said Heinz, 'and I'll have to risk the ulcer because that's what my life is all about.' "

It was what Smith's life was all about, as well. Smith was not hospitalized, but he did miss a few columns after the World Series. When he returned to work, he did try to watch his diet, but he didn't change his writing habits. He continued "to sweat" at the typewriter. Writing a column, he said, repeating an old joke, was like being married to a nymphomaniac. "As soon as you're finished," he said, "you've got to start over again."

He was happy at *The Times,* but would sometimes fume at the editing. He had asked the copy editors to call whenever they felt a correction, substitution, or deletion was necessary. "We had an understanding," he would say about the desk, "but it was only a partial understanding." Unlike at the *Herald Tribune,* where his copy went virtually untouched, *The Times*'s copy editors made occasional changes. Sometimes they were necessary, sometimes they weren't. When the copy editors caught errors of fact, he phoned his gratitude. But sometimes he discovered changes that exasperated him. Once, he wrote that a fighter was "surrounded" in his corner by his seconds. The desk changed the verb to "circled." "You can't circle a corner," complained Smith.

Another change that infuriated him involved his line comparing the look on a man's face to that of someone who had just "bitten into an apple and found half a worm." The desk changed it to "bitten into an apple and found a worm." It flattened the entire image.

At breakfast, Phyllis recalled, "when he'd see a word had been changed, he cursed and yelled. There were a lot of goddamnits and son of a bitches. And he'd lecture me as though I had done it. I promised him I'd never do it again. He laughed, and then just fumed quietly."

If the change was "outrageous," he had said, "I'll scream to the editors. But I'd rather not be a prima donna and be screaming all the time."

One editor in particular he got along with was Arthur Pincus, then on the copy desk and later the editor of the Sunday sports and SportsMonday pages. "It was a challenge to edit him and edit him well," said Pincus. "Sometimes he'd make mistakes with dates or sequences of events, things of that nature. I think he depended a little too much on his memory on a lot of things.

"Maybe it was part of his rebelliousness, but some things he never outgrew. For example, he was always trying to get the phrase 'son of a bitch' into the paper." Pincus recalled an anecdote Smith wrote about Harry Grayson, one-time sports editor of the Newspaper Enterprise Association, whose office had been moved from New York —where Grayson had been very happy—to Cleveland. In a blinding snowstorm one night Grayson fought his way up Euclid Avenue in Cleveland. A car pulled up beside him and a man said, "Excuse me, pal, how do you get out of town?" And Grayson, Smith would write, replied, "You silly son of a bitch, if I knew, do you think I'd be here?"

Pincus said, "I called Red and suggested 'silly jerk' or 'stupid jerk' or some kind of tortured phrase. I said, 'But we can't use "son of a bitch" in *The Times.*' Smith said, 'Jesus Christ, when the hell is the Gray Lady going to wake up and learn the way language is today!' He was mad, but I think he knew all along we wouldn't use it." Though the strength of the story demanded "son of a bitch," the story ran with the watered-down phrase "silly ass."

It wasn't the desire to use vulgarity that urged Smith to continue to try to get such phrases into his column. He scorned "the gratuitous and unartistic" use of four-letter words in some books and magazines. "Someone will throw in 'you're full of shit' for no good reason," he said. "The writer thinks he must do it, that it's 'today.' " Smith had a discussion with Roger Kahn about the use of four-letter words and liked a point Kahn made. In an interview in his book *The Boys of Summer,* Kahn asked Carl Furillo, the former Dodger outfielder, how he was able to play the caroms so beautifully off the right-field wall in Ebbets Field.

"I worked at it, that's fucking how," replied Furillo.

Smith said, "Roger was dead right in quoting Furillo like that. There's no way you can get the quality of Furillo's answer if you say, 'I worked, that's how.' Or any other way except that maladroit way of using 'fucking.' "

Increasingly, Smith left his desk in the barn and went into Manhattan to get stories. For a while, between newspapers, he had been using the telephone more than in the past—"that's legwork, too, I guess." But now he was doing more legwork with his legs than with his phone. And his interview technique remained conversational, not inquisitorial. At one press conference with several athletes in the ballroom of a Manhattan hotel, reporters sat around a table with one athlete, then moved to another table with another athlete. Smith pulled up a chair near Mike Marshall, the relief pitcher.

Marshall, considered a difficult interview by some reporters, was impressed with Smith. "He listened to my answers," Marshall recalled. "He didn't just follow a prepared list."

Smith mentioned an aspect of free-agency in the news and asked Marshall, "Do you have a subjective view on it?"

Marshall, who has a doctorate in kinesiology, did. Smith, having gently appealed to Marshall's vanity with the lofty phrase in sports conversation, "subjective view," then said, "My stepson asked me, 'Are all ballplayers underpaid?'" Smith didn't say "overpaid," which might have made Marshall defensive, but put an original twist on a question that might otherwise have been a cliché. And he didn't say, "I said," but put it into the mouth of what sounded like a youngster genuinely wanting to know.

"Well," Marshall began, "ballplayers are in a unique situation," and went on to talk at length about matters such as supply and demand and "the profits of the industry."

Smith had deftly opened up a reputedly tough interviewee. Sometime later, Smith was asked about Marshall and his reputation. "I like Mike," said Smith. "You have to take people the way you find them. You can't take somebody else's word for it."

In that interview, the pitcher had a tape recorder with him. It was for the benefit of his wife at home, he said; she was interested in questions posed by the press. "It made me a little extra careful," Smith recalled. "I hadn't taken notes, and when I was unable to remember his words verbatim, I did not quote directly. I said what he said without using quotes. But every direct quote, everything with hooks around it, was verbatim. I guarantee that."

Smith went to lunch with another pitcher, and an acknowledged tough customer, Early Wynn. Roger Kahn joined them. "They were very polite," Kahn recalled, "and then Red said, 'Early, did you ever deliberately throw at a batter's head?' And Wynn said, 'There was a batter named Jose Valdivielso, a .230 hitter, and he hit a line drive into the bottom of my chin and it took stitches to close it. The pitcher's mound is my office and I don't like my office messed up with a lot of blood.' Red just fell in love with that and used it a number of times."

Smith delighted in such honesty. It was, in his view, at the opposite end of the spectrum from the hypocrisy and pomposity often exhibited, for example, by the International Olympic Committee and its president, Avery Brundage. In early 1972, the IOC banned Karl Schranz, the Austrian skiing champion, from participating in the Winter Games for "professionalism." Schranz had sold his name and picture to advertisers.

Smith wrote: "It goes without saying that Karl Schranz is a professional. So are all the state-supported athletes of many countries; so are the American kids who are hired to play games for colleges; so are all those Olympic runners who took bribes from manufacturers of track shoes during the 1968 Olympics. . . .

"The simple truth is that the whole concept of amateurism is archaic. . . ."

The man Smith singled out as "the godliest, the most intransigent and the loudest" of the IOC was Brundage. Smith called him "a rich and righteous anachronism . . . a vestigial remnant of an economy that supported the leisure class that could compete in athletics for fun alone. His wrath is more terrible because it is so sincere and unenlightened."

For years Smith had written of Brundage and his group as "the waxworks," and had spoken of Brundage specifically as "Slavery Avery." (Brundage once wrote Smith about one of the few columns in which he praised the Olympic president. Brundage concluded the letter with, "It was good work, but I don't care too much for that Slavery Avery business.")

In the summer of 1972, Smith and Phyllis traveled to Munich for the Summer Olympics. They went to press headquarters, housed in a large building and filled with computers and machines printing out information for reporters. The headquarters was crowded and raucous, yet seemed to be run with great efficiency. I ran into him there.

"I've got credentials but can Phyllis get into the Olympic Village?" Smith asked me.

"It's not too hard," I said. "I've been here for a few days and I've seen people sneaking into the Village all the time. Security is not terrific."

Security didn't seem a pressing concern as the Olympics got under way. There wasn't a problem getting into the Olympics; the problem was the many who were dropping out, or threatening to.

As with the Mexico City Games four years before, racial politics were a concern. Black African nations threatened to boycott the 1972 Games if Rhodesia, with a white supremacist government, was allowed to participate. The IOC, despite Brundage's vote against the action, asked Rhodesia to go home.

Smith wrote that story, approving the IOC's decision. Meanwhile, the offbeat still attracted him. He wrote about some of the arcane pleasures of various Olympic events, like the new Olympic sport, canoe and kayak slalom, where "Skull fractures and deaths by drowning are held to a minimum by headgear, life jackets and rescue crews."

But the fun of the Olympics ended at 4:30 A.M. on September 5, when a group of white-hooded Palestinian terrorists easily sneaked into the Olympic Village and took eleven Israeli athletes hostage in their dormitory.

Smith, like most of the hundreds of other reporters, learned of the events later that morning and hurried over from his apartment. The scene at the Village was dramatic and terrifying, replete with German soldiers, Munich police, Olympic officials, helicopters, bull-horns, and cameras.

"Olympic Village was under siege. Two men lay murdered and nine others were held at gunpoint in imminent peril of their lives. Still," wrote Smith, seething with indignation, "the games went on. Canoeists paddled through their races. Fencers thrust and parried in make-believe duels. Boxers scuffled. Basketball players scampered across the floor like happy children. Walled off in their dream world, appallingly unaware of the realities of life and death, the aging playground directors who conduct this quadrennial muscle dance ruled that a little bloodshed must not be permitted to interrupt play. . . ."

The following day, September 6, Smith sat in the outdoor press section of Olympic Stadium with a packed crowd of eighty thousand and viewed the memorial service for the eleven slain Israeli athletes and six others, after which Brundage announced that "The Games must go on . . ."

"On past performances," wrote Smith, "it must be assumed that in Avery's view Arab-Israeli warfare, hijacking, kidnapping and killing all constitute partisan politics not to be tolerated in the Olympics.

"And anyway, went the bitter joke today, 'These are professional killers; Avery doesn't recognize them.' "

In a retrospective piece, Smith wrote that neither the Games nor the governing heads of the IOC were "in any way responsible for the bloodshed. On the ground of common decency, however, the brass is faulted for blundering on with the frolic while the world stood aghast." He added, "Sometimes, it requires conscious effort to pre-serve a sense of proportion."

Leaving Munich, Smith and Phyllis returned home and went to their new house on Martha's Vineyard for a few weeks. There he found column material as close as his backyard. He wrote about how the squirrels defeated the poor humans' attempts to keep them out of the sunflower seeds. Smith went fishing and bird watching, a pastime of his since childhood. He toured with a group of bird watchers from the local community center. "First stop on the island," wrote Smith, "was a pretty grove of evergreens and oaks around a pond. A pair of yellow-shafted flickers took flight as the jeep pulled in. The [leader of Smith's group] whistled a warbling trill punctuated by a kind of hiss. Somewhere in the tree tops a pine warbler spoke. A chickadee identified himself. A pewee stated his name, rank and serial number."

It was a long way from what Smith called the "anguish" of Munich.

CHAPTER
13

Not long after the Summer Olympics, Smith was interviewed by Jerry Holtzman, a Chicago sportswriter, for his book, *No Cheering in the Press Box,* a collection of reminiscences by older sportswriters. The interview was a fine, wide-ranging discussion of Smith's life and times and thoughts.

"My enthusiasm," Smith told Holtzman, "is self-generating, self-renewing. My life, the way it's been going now, I see very few baseball games in the summer. I'll start with the opening of the season. I'll see the games then, but things like the Kentucky Derby and Preakness get in the way, and lately we've had a home up in Martha's Vineyard, where I like to spend as much of the summer as I can, working from there. By the time the World Series comes along, I may feel that I've had very little baseball for the year. But I find that old enthusiasm renewing itself when I sit there at the playoffs."

About his philosophies, he said, "Unlike the normal pattern, I know I have grown more liberal as I've grown older. I have become more convinced that there is room for improvement in the world. I seem to be finding this a much less pretty world than it seemed when I was younger, and I feel things should be done about it and that sports are part of this world. Maybe I'm sounding too damn profound or maybe I'm taking bows when I shouldn't. I truly don't know. But I do know I am more liberal."

He cited as possible reasons Phyllis, "who is younger and more of today than I was," and his five stepchildren.

In the interview, he also mentioned Howard Cosell, the sportscaster. It was in the context of Smith's "defense mechanism," of perhaps talking too much at parties "to cover shyness. I often hear myself babbling on and wish I'd shut up. . . . I'm not a psychologist, but I do know, for example, that a fellow like Howard Cosell is the braggart that he is because of a massive insecurity. He has to be told every couple minutes how great he is because he's so insecure. And if you don't tell him, he tells you. He can't help this."

Cosell grew up in Brooklyn and avidly read and admired Smith as "the king of drollery, with a magnificent ability to put sports into perspective . . . and a matchless ability with words." Cosell began a law career, but decided to give it up for a career in sports broadcasting. "I was still trying to make my way in broadcasting," he recalled, "and I used Red Smith as my guiding light, as I viewed him as the ultimate journalist in sports." Cosell credits Smith with teaching him a valuable lesson: "To be there, to know the people, to know what's going on."

Smith and Cosell, who lived near each other, became social friends in the early sixties, but began to grow apart in the mid-sixties. "Cosell began criticizing the press, or 'print media,' " recalled Jerry Izenberg. "I remember an argument at Toots Shor's. Howard was abusing the press collectively, and then said to Red, 'Of course, I don't mean you.'

"And Smith said, 'Then you'd better say, "The press" and then list everyone who you don't mean.' "

Smith was not defending all sportswriters but arguing against the sweeping generality of Cosell's remarks. "There are as many incompetents and pricks among sportswriters," said Smith, "as there are among doctors and grocers and shoe salesmen."

For Smith, Cosell's bombastic nature was grating. Once, writing about the horse trainer Sunny Jim Fitzsimmons, Smith said that he had humility—"perhaps the greatest trait of all." Smith appreciated humility in two of his favorite athletes, Joe DiMaggio and Bill Shoemaker, the jockey. The trait of humility is not commonly associated with Cosell. He once asked fight promoter Harry Markson, "How many great sportscasters do you think there are?"

"One less than you think, Howard," said Markson.

"Cosell doesn't broadcast sports; he broadcasts Cosell," Smith once said. Smith believed that Cosell posed as an expert in areas about which he knew relatively little, such as horse racing and boxing. Smith criticized Cosell's histrionics and parodied the announcer's style, such as when, on the day before a fight, he wrote: "Some may consider this a breach of confidence, but as Howard Cosell would say, reportorial honesty compels the disclosure that Joe Frazier is about to defend the heavyweight championship of the world against Terry Daniels. . . ."

Of Cosell's contention that television creates sports stars, Smith wrote, "It doesn't surprise me to see Howard pre-empt God. But I still believe God does the creating and not ABC."

Although the split between the two had become decisive by the 1970's, Smith still had some misgivings about his reference to Cosell when Holtzman's book was published. "I was a little startled to see in print what I said about Howard Cosell and insecurity and so on," Smith would say. "I believe it's true and I undoubtedly said it. Well, if you say it, you stand up, even though it might be a little embarrassing. It wasn't really, but it did seem kind of gossipy."

Flying to Las Vegas for a tennis match not long after that, Smith found himself on the same plane with Cosell and his wife, Emmy.

"Howard lets Emmy sit by herself and she went to sleep," recalled Smith. "And I could see she's angry. He came up and sat with me. Now I got him the whole ride to Las Vegas and there was a head wind; it was an extra hour." Smith believed they were flying over Indianapolis when Cosell brought up the quote. "Look, Howard," Smith recalled saying, "I don't go around telling everybody this. He said, 'Well, you're probably right.' I said, 'I think I am right. But you might as well realize that as long as you and I live, this thing is going to be picked up and quoted again and again. So we might as well get ready for it.' "

Cosell says he "vividly" recalls the conversation. "In effect, Red was apologizing," he said. He added, "And I said to him, 'I think it's not necessary, Red. You have every right to say whatever you think about me. I have the same right to say what I think about you.' " Landing in Las Vegas, they discovered they were both staying at Caesar's Palace, and in adjoining rooms. "He came in for drinks," recalled Cosell, "and he said, 'Here's to Jerry Holtzman.' "

The friendship was gone, however. As years went on Smith would continue to drop an occasional droll but invariably disparaging remark about Cosell's work. Cosell took the slights hard, and he saw faults in his one-time guiding light. He criticized Smith for his many columns on harness racing. "I felt they were inspired by his friendship with Joe Goldstein," said Cosell. "It was an easy way to get a column." In fact, Smith often accepted ideas from publicists and press agents, especially a press agent with a gift for selling a story and telling an anecdote like Goldstein or Sy Presten or Irving Rudd —"Unswerving Irving," as Smith referred to him in print. (Each was representing a client, and Smith understood this, of course, and, unthreatened, took it into humorous account. Once, Presten invited reporters to see Rocky Graziano tap-dance at the Wally Wanger Dancing School in order, wrote Smith, "to avoid publicity for the dancing school.")

Cosell said that as years went on, Smith was losing touch with the sports world as Cosell knew it. "I think many sportswriters write only for themselves and each other, and they are not part of the real world," said Cosell. "I think Smith fell prey to that." Cosell said that Smith had been "locked inside" the sports establishment. Cosell reserved his harshest criticism for a trip in 1979 that Smith took to cover a heavyweight fight in South Africa. Smith traveled with a group of sportswriters, and Cosell charged that Smith and the others were "on the take" from Bob Arum, the boxing promoter.

"I'd never covered a fight in Africa before," Smith later explained. "I've been to all the continents now." And as he did when he covered the A's in Mexico City and visited Trotsky, and as he did when a Japanese submarine was supposed to have shelled the California coast in 1941, Smith would go outside of sports to report on the nearby world.

Smith left for South Africa halfway through the 1979 World Series. On the following evening, Cosell was at the bar of a Baltimore hotel with some members of the press and said Smith's leaving for South Africa at that time was disgraceful. Cosell got into a bitter argument with Pete Axthelm of *Newsweek* over whether Smith was, as Cosell asserted, "in Arum's pocket."

Cosell said that Arum was "the apostle of apartheid" and that Smith's going there gave a sanction or credibility to that segregationist government. Cosell said that Smith in an interview on an NBC television program from South Africa "saw no evidence of censorship. I couldn't believe my ears."

In fact, Smith's comment referred only to how the press was treated. "I'm confident that with the limited time that we have," said Smith, according to the transcript of the NBC program titled *Should It Play in Pretoria?*, "the best we can get is a superficial picture. But everyone I've talked to has answered my questions with every appearance of candor. I have no sense of being intimidated or censored.

"We talked to people in Soweto [the segregated black township outside Pretoria] who've answered our questions in a forthright manner."

Smith also went to Atteridgeville, another black township, and wrote a sympathetic piece about the plight of the family of the long-distance runner Sydney Maree, who was at Villanova University in Pennsylvania. (Smith also felt that Maree was a "victim of apartheid in reverse," since he couldn't run in the Olympics "because the world sports community has ostracized South Africa in hope of persuading the government to abandon its policy of separate and unequal status for blacks. . . .") Maree's family lived in a "house like almost all others in Atteridgeville, a brick box with galvanized iron roof and a front door of sheet metal, sitting cheek by his jowl with identical twins on an unpaved street of flinty red dust. There is a tiny plot of lawn in front, with one green shrub and a miniature triangle of flowers in bloom." In the house, there was no ceiling, "just the galvanized roof." The front room was "immaculate," and in a corner "a glassfront china cabinet held many of Sydney's trophies."

In another column from South Africa, Smith lamented "the painful contrasts that hammer themselves into the visitor's consciousness here. There is wealth and there is poverty in any land. There are slums and swimming pools. Here there is also hopelessness, because racial discrimination is the law." He described the "aching squalor of Soweto." "When a black loses his job," Smith wrote, "when he can't live in a township like Soweto, the Government checks his ethnic origins and dumps him on the tribal chief in his 'homeland.' " A typical homeland, Smith noted from a small airplane taking him around the country, is "a cluster of huts crouched on the bare red plain."

Smith wrote candidly about what he saw, without apparent concern for the Government of South Africa or Arum, "the apostle of apartheid," as Cosell contended. Nor did Arum pay for Smith's trip. *The New York Times* did, according to *The Times*'s accounting department.

Through the years, Smith received numerous letters from readers taking Cosell to task for his reporting and his style. One such letter called for "waivers" to be sought for Cosell, and a list of Cosell's particular offenses as perceived by the letter-writer was included.

"I can't disagree with your appraisal of Howard," Smith wrote back, " but I wouldn't try to get anyone fired. I find it possible to tune him out."

On January 3, 1973, George Steinbrenner and Mike Burke, heading a group of twelve investors who purchased the New York Yankees from CBS, held a news conference. Smith attended and wrote that Steinbrenner had accepted the position of chief executive officer with "a show of class," but credited Burke even more. Smith quoted Mike Burke quoting poetry: "If I may steal a line from Mr. Yeats: 'I balanced all, brought all to mind,' and three or four weeks ago proposed to Steinbrenner the arrangement now agreed upon." Smith added, "Only Mike Burke had the class to quote William Butler Yeats."

Though Steinbrenner had received a modicum of praise from Smith, it would be one of the last times he did. Steinbrenner, whom Smith described as "a collar-and-tie man . . . who listened with arms folded and chin jutting," still felt slightly mistreated in the column. "I majored in English at Williams College," he would say. "I could quote Yeats, too."

In 1974 the federal government found Steinbrenner guilty of having forced employees of his ship-building company in Cleveland to contribute part of their salaries to campaign funds for the reelection of President Nixon, and then of "aiding and abetting obstruction of an investigation." Steinbrenner was convicted of two felonies and fined $1,500. He was able to avoid a jail sentence.

"Steinbrenner wasn't convicted of lying," wrote Smith. "He pleaded guilty to lying and trying to bully employees into lying for him. As Bowie Kuhn put it, 'He caused certain of his employees to make false statements to agents of the Federal Bureau of Investigation and attempted to influence these employees to give false testimony to a Federal grand jury.' "

Kuhn suspended Steinbrenner from baseball for two years. Smith thought this punishment was much too light. Noting that Steinbrenner had tried to conceal illegal campaign donations of $142,000, Smith wrote, "If he wasn't trying to buy favors, then he is generous to a fault, too generous to succeed in baseball." Smith said that baseball had no place for someone like Steinbrenner, though he didn't address the question of why sports should be different from the rest of society. After all, Steinbrenner did pay whatever recompense the courts deemed fair. Nonetheless, Smith remained adamant in his view of Steinbrenner.

(Smith was inconsistent on this point. Sometime later, on another matter, he wrote, "Guys who have, as the cliché goes, 'paid their debt to society' should always be welcome in the ring or in any other jobs they can handle on the square. . . . The question is whether a $320 fine has squared Kallie Knoetze—he had shot a fifteen-year-old black in both legs when he was a constable in Pretoria." Smith thought it had, though the Reverend Jesse Jackson and others disagreed.)

Over the years, Smith continued to write of Steinbrenner, whom he considered "an arrogant, ruthless employer." Once Smith called Steinbrenner "George III"—he was born, in fact, George Michael Steinbrenner III—but the name evoked the rattle-brained English king. Another time Smith published a column in which he called Steinbrenner "the führer," a reference to Steinbrenner's heavy-handed dealings with his players. Joe Vecchione, *The Times* sports editor, believed Smith had gone too far. "I thought that calling Steinbrenner or anyone else 'the führer' had the effect of diminishing Hitler's atrocities," recalled Vecchione. Smith, acknowledging the point, never again used the phrase in that context.

Sportswriter Barney Nagler thought that Smith saw Steinbrenner only "in one-dimensional terms." And Steinbrenner said about Smith, "I don't know in my case that his journalism was balanced. He never asked to sit down with me. It would have been an honor for me to have done it. I respected him in many ways. But he was a human being with faults, as I am. I've got enough dents in my armor for an army."

After Smith underwent a colon operation in 1978, Steinbrenner sent him a note, saying that although they had had their differences, he wished Red a speedy recovery. Smith wrote back, saying he appreciated Steinbrenner's sentiments about his health, but added that the two of them had very different views on things "and that," said Smith, "will never change."

CHAPTER
14

A few years after Frank Graham died, in 1965, Smith began traveling with Jack Murphy, the sports editor and sports columnist for the *San Diego Union.* Murphy was eighteen years younger than Smith but seemed older than his years, perhaps because he was a man of relatively few words, and one of the few pipe-smokers among sportswriters. Like Graham, he was a gentle writer. Smith appreciated Murphy's "nice eye for detail and . . . light touch that [was] always under control." And Murphy, like Graham, had a sense of humor that appealed to Smith. For a *New Yorker* profile of boxer Archie Moore, Murphy asked the light-heavyweight champion, "Does your wife mind kissing you with that beard?"

"No," said Moore, "she's happy to go through a forest to get to the picnic."

Smith and Murphy shared a passion for the outdoors. Tom Callahan, a cub reporter under Murphy in San Diego and later a sports columnist for the *Cincinnati Enquirer,* the *Washington Star* and *Time* magazine, once joined Smith and Murphy on a fishing expedition in Florida. Callahan hated fishing. He recalled:

We'd get up in the morning and it was freezing. This was not my idea of fun, but they loved it. We were with a fourth guy, Sandy Bain. Sandy and I were in one boat, and Jack and Red were in the other, and they were looking into the mango inlets for tarpon. Tarpons are hard to catch because they're bouncing around out there and it's considered a coup if you get a bite. If you do hook one, then you throw it back because you can't eat tarpon. To me, that's not fishing. I said to Sandy, "Let's go find some fish that we can eat." And we did. That night we ate our catch. Red and Jack were so proud of themselves, talking about these bites they got. Well, I got mad. I said, "Who caught all these fish that we're eating tonight?" We had a lot of laughs over that. But Murphy was still rhapsodizing over the fish he almost caught but didn't catch.

The following morning we started driving home. Murphy said, "You know, Red, I dreamt all night long of trying to catch fish."

Red said, "You mean even in your dreams you didn't catch any?"

"Yeah," said Murphy.

"That," said Smith, "is the definition of an honest man."

Callahan first met Smith at the 1972 Kentucky Derby, when Callahan was twenty-five and with the *Cincinnati Enquirer.* Callahan said to Si Burick, veteran sports columnist for the *Dayton Daily News,* "You're going to think this is the most sophomoric thing in the world, but when you get a chance, do you think you could introduce me to Red Smith?"

Burick did, and Smith and Callahan struck up a conversation. Callahan mentioned that this was his first Derby.

"How are you covering it?" asked Smith.

"I wrote about the mint juleps, I guess," said Callahan.

"The best way to cover it," said Smith, "is to go to Lexington because all the people and the pretty scenes are there, and you can wander around." Smith said that only the horses and the hiked menus and the rip-off artists are in Louisville.

About six months later, Callahan received a surprise call from Smith.

"If you're thinking of going to Lexington next spring," said Smith, "you'd better get your reservation in at the Campbell House. Jack and I will be there." Callahan did, and his friendship with Smith developed. As Rice and Graham had once taken in Smith as a traveling companion, so Smith and Murphy took in Callahan.

"Red opened my eyes to many things," recalled Callahan. "He'd point out scenes to me that I was looking at but not seeing. We'd walk around on a horse farm and I'd think there was absolutely nothing to write about, and he'd write about the feeling of the place, the flowers and the smells. And he'd listen to people. I remember he asked Charlie Hatton, the columnist, 'How did Secretariat work this morning?' And Hatton said, 'The trees swayed.' Red loved that."

If Callahan or anyone else said something interesting in conversation, Smith might say, "Mind if I use it?" Callahan turned that around once. "We were in the pressbox at the football playoff between the Dolphins and the Bengals," recalled Callahan. "It was near the end of the game, with the Dolphins leading 34–16, and I said to Red, 'Look at Paul Brown [the Bengals' coach].' Brown was wearing this little brown hat, this brown suit, brown shoes, very tidy, very straight, walking back and forth on the sidelines without any expression or seeming emotion. I said, 'Look at that.' And Red said, 'It's like the homicide inspector viewing the body.' I stole that one."

Sometimes Callahan would give Smith something he wrote and ask for criticism. Once, on a subject on which Callahan had taken a strong stand, Smith said, "You couldn't be more right, but you're writing at the top of your lungs."

In Lexington, Smith, Murphy, and Callahan visited farms in the morning and wrote in the afternoon. Then Smith would call Callahan and Murphy. "The Smith Hilton is open," he would say. And they and their wives, if they were along, would meet in Smith's room for cocktails before dinner.

"Sometimes Jack and Red read the pieces they had written that day," said Callahan. "It was kind of like show-and-tell. They had been talking all day long, and sort of trying out lines, like nightclub comedians. Not funny lines necessarily. Just good lines that would end up in their pieces. I would try to avoid this, and I was sort of mute while walking around, trying to see things they didn't see. I figured that if I used some pretty line that appeared in Red Smith's column that day, everybody's going to assume who stole from whom. And it might be my line."

Sometimes they did share. As Smith's old legs began to protest and made it harder for him to get around, especially in crowds at major events, and with deadline nearing, Callahan and other reporters hurried from the pressbox down to the clubhouses, talked with the athletes, and then hurried back up to write their stories. When Callahan returned, he huddled with Smith and Murphy and shared the information he had gathered. "They'd take it all down," said Callahan. "Red would say, 'That's enough. I'm rich.' And sometimes he'd give me credit. He'd tell someone, 'Tom Callahan wrote me a nice column today,' which of course wasn't true. He led me through numerous columns at the race track. I barely knew which end of the horse eats."

Callahan believed that Smith had few pretensions, but he did have some. One was that he disparaged television. "But he liked to watch *CHiPS* and *Quincy*. He was terribly embarrassed by that. It was taking me into his confidence one day when he said, 'Wait, *Quincy* is on.'"

One night during Super Bowl week in Los Angeles, Smith, Murphy, and Callahan went to a huge party given by a television network. A pre–Super Bowl show had been done live for East Coast audiences and would be seen on tape three hours later on the West Coast. Callahan recalled:

A lot of television celebrities were at the party, and there was this big screen in this big room, and everybody was partying and sort of half-watching the television screen. Sammy Davis, Jr., comes on the screen and sings this song, and Andy Williams jumps over at the commercial break and says, "Great, Sammy, great." Then Williams does his song, and Sammy says, "Great, Andy, great." And Red turns to me, mimicking the bullshit and says, "Life is great, isn't it great, just great!" Then Jack Albertson comes over and starts to talk to us, then says, "Excuse me a second." He goes to the screen and watches himself and then comes back and joins the conversation. He didn't want to see anything else in that show but himself. When he left, Red was breaking up. "Can you imagine studying yourself like that?"

Well, not long after that I'm staying in Red's house in New Canaan, and I'm making a cup of coffee and he's reading his column in the morning paper. He's finished reading it, and now he's reading it again. Now again. You can tell. He's like a man in a confessional. So I went over to him and said, "Remember Sammy?" He knew right away that I was busting his chops, and he laughed. He said, "I guess there's some of that in all of us."

In 1975, Smith was turning seventy years old, and after four years with *The Times* he was continuing to write the way he described Pete Rose playing baseball, with "an almost lascivious enthusiasm."

In one of his pieces, titled "How to Get the City Out of Hock," he ridiculed the mayor of New York, Abe Beame, and other city officials, past and present, who advanced Off-Track Betting as a solution to the city's deep financial problems:

New York City is tapped out like a broken horse player and nobody—not Abe Beame nor the town's smartest bankers nor the best fiscal brains in Albany and Washington—knows what to do about it. This helplessness in high places is mystifying, for there is a simple solution so obvious that it should have occurred to somebody in authority long before this. The city should take over loan-sharking, prostitution and narcotics traffic just as it has taken over gambling. We are assured by all reliable authorities that there is more than enough profit in these fields to make up the $641-million deficit in next year's budget, and in the unlikely event that Mr. Beame still came up short, why, there are other untapped sources of revenue such as labor racketeering and bank robbery.

Prudery should not stand in the way of solvency for the greatest city in the world. A few years ago when there were moral objections to the city's making book on the races, they were hooted down by Honest John Lindsay, the friendly bookie, and his chief sheet-writer, Howard Samuels. Be realistic, they told us, gambling was a biological urge that legislation could not suppress; therefore, was it not desirable that the profits go to support schools, hospitals and deserving politicians rather than the criminal underworld?

Moreover, we were told, illegal gambling provided the treasury from which the underworld financed such activities as loan-sharking, prostitution and dope-pushing. History tells us that organized crime was starved to death in New York starting at 10:52 on Holy Thursday, April 8, 1971, when the Off-Track Betting Corporation opened for business. . . .

Smith pointed out that, despite an expensive advertising campaign for OTB, the city had reaped only about one-fourth of its projected financial goals, while telling the public, in effect, "Bet more! Bet till it hurts. Come on, suckers, don't you want to get rich?"

Smith believed there had to be a better way to solve the money troubles, such as better management by city officials.

This was the lead column in a group of ten Smith columns that *The New York Times* submitted to the Pulitzer Prize Committee. George Vecsey, then a city-side reporter and later a sports columnist for *The Times,* was asked to write the covering letter:

A sports columnist faces a rather special challenge every time he sits down to write. He knows that the vast majority of his readers—no matter how sophisticated in other matters—are conservative about their sports. They want the seasons to roll onward, with a proper mix of good guys and bad guys, victories and defeats, just like it always was. Woe to the Jeremiah who reminds them that, even in sports, the times they are a-changing.

It would be quite easy for Walter W. (Red) Smith to avoid the complexities of modern sports. He could easily dazzle his readers with the gift of language, perfected in half a century of writing.

But at the age of seventy, Red Smith is vitally involved in change. As often as he feels necessary, Red Smith informs his readers about the high finances, the labor disputes, the government involvement in gambling that have sprung up during his renaissance with *The New York Times*. . . .

True to tradition, *The Times* had not told Smith that it was nominating him for the award. There is no separate category for sportswriting among the Pulitzer awards, and Smith's work was submitted for Distinguished Commentary.

In late April 1976, Smith received a call at home from a journalist friend. The friend had unimpeachable information about a subject of interest to Smith. Smith listened, thanked him, then hung up the phone. He turned to Phyllis and said, "Guess who won a Pulitzer Prize?"

The answer, this time, was Red Smith.

When the caller had informed him of the award, Smith said, "Gee, that's nice."

He was, in fact, joyful at having received what many journalists and readers—and Smith himself—considered recognition long overdue. Yet he had strong reservations about the prize, about how recipients were chosen. In any event, he was requested to keep the news a secret until the Committee's official announcement on Monday, May 3.

During the week before the announcement, he and Phyllis went to Kentucky for the Derby and stayed at Campbell House in Lexington with the Murphys and the Callahans. Smith was having a difficult time keeping the news of his prize a secret. He told Murphy, and shortly after Callahan arrived, Smith suggested they take a walk on the grounds of Campbell House.

"I want to tell you something," Smith said to Callahan, "and you can't say anything to anybody, but I've won the Pulitzer Prize."

"Hooray!" said Callahan.

"I'm not supposed to know, and just before it's announced I'm supposed to be summoned to Abe Rosenthal's office and they're going to have a party."

"Great," said Callahan.

"Well, it's not great," said Smith. "I'll tell you how I feel about it because the story is going to come over the wire with me saying, 'Oh, dear diary, how wonderful!' But the Pulitzer Prize doesn't mean anything to me. It's part of being with *The New York Times*. I always said I'd refuse the prize if I won it, but I thought, seventy-year-old crocks who are bitter are boring."

"Smith was just being consistent," Callahan recalled, "because he had told me he had been badly wounded when Arthur Daley won the Pulitzer."

The Derby was held, as is traditional, on the first Saturday in May, which fell on the first day of the month. On Monday, the Pulitzer winners were announced, and Smith was cited for his humor and his humanitarianism. The citation read: "In an area heavy with tradition and routine, Mr. Smith is unique in the erudition, the literary quality, the vitality and freshness of viewpoint he brings to his work and in the sustained quality of his columns."

Smith was characteristically unawed but appreciative in his response. "I wish I'd had time to think up a good epigram," he told United Press International. In the past couple of weeks Smith indeed had had time to think about it, and that may have been the epigram he conceived. He continued to U.P.I., "Of all these trinkets you pin on your playsuit, the Pulitzer is one I've respected. I'll take it and be honored."

To Callahan, he referred to the prize as "a bottle cap." "He had," said Callahan, "won some award early when he was with the *Herald Tribune* and put it on his desk, and Stanley Woodward said to him, 'How long are you going to stare at that bottle cap?'"

Smith had won numerous awards, but the Pulitzer was certainly the most prestigious. Smith was called into Abe Rosenthal's office with Sydney Schanberg, who had won a Pulitzer for his international reporting from Cambodia. They and the top editors of *The Times* celebrated. Rosenthal had several bottles of champagne on ice, Smith recalled, "but I held out for vodka."

During the party, Smith received a phone call. Without introducing himself, the caller said, "You'll refuse it, of course."

Smith laughed. "Not on your life," he said. The caller was Terry Smith. He was in Israel, and only that day had heard his father had won.

"You mean," said Terry, "that all those years of saying how corrupt the Pulitzer is, and now you're going to take it?"

"Precisely," said Smith, laughing above the tinkle of ice cubes in his drink.

Smith became only the second sportswriter to win the Pulitzer for general excellence—Arthur Daley being the other. Numerous articles appeared praising Smith and his nearly fifty years of newspaper writing. "It's about time," wrote Pete Axthelm in *Newsweek*. "Like almost every sportswriter of my generation who had any sense, taste, and larceny in his soul, I didn't just emulate Smith. I stole from him liberally. . . . While other high school sophomores of 1959 were trying out their Hemingway and Fitzgerald sentences, I was marveling at the perceptions of a man who could perfectly capture the day when baseball rookies were sent to the minors—'the saddest day in the year for the passel of young men whose fangs had been honed on major-league sirloins . . . and who had the naive notion that they'd never eat their way through to the other side of the cow.' "

Axthelm added that Smith "is a rare figure who [despite his age] has never stopped belonging to the present."

Frank Deford of *Sports Illustrated* didn't see it quite that way. Deford, like Axthelm, had grown up admiring Smith. In a creative-writing course at Princeton, the professor, British author Kingsley Amis, asked Deford who his favorite writers were. Deford mentioned J. D. Salinger and Tennessee Williams.

"Anyone else?" Amis asked.

"Well," said Deford, "Red Smith."

Amis had never heard of Smith, and Deford explained. A short time later, when Amis was back in England, he wrote an article about his experience in America and, recalled Deford, "devoted much space and many jibes to the typical American boy who had actually cited a sports columnist as a favorite writer."

Deford noted that sportswriting is "still déclassé" even in America, and that's why it took this long for Smith to get the Pulitzer.

"It's petty of me to say this—I must, to make the larger point—but Smith's present work hardly merits an award," wrote Deford, "although he has shown an almost adolescent militancy of late, passionately espousing the players' cause in their continuing struggle with the owners. But on the whole, the words merely hum along now, an old tune, instead of singing, as they once did. I'm happy justice has been served, even twenty-five years late, but what a continuing insult to newspaper sportswriters it is that when the Pulitzer committee deigns to give a sports award—once every blue moon—it makes something of a hash of it."

Deford wasn't the only critic who felt that Smith had slipped. But others who compared Smith's past and present work—side by side—could not support Deford's case. Unless, as Deford did to a degree, one took Smith to task for his "militancy." In fact, that wasn't the sportswriter Deford had grown up with. And Smith meant it that way; his increasing indignation rose from his conscience. But he didn't forsake his wit.

Meanwhile, letters of congratulations poured in to Smith. To another sportswriter, Smith wrote a note dated May 24: "Thanks, my friend. Best thing about the Pulitzer is that it brought notes like yours from guys like you."

One day around that time, Smith saw Seth Abraham, then a special assistant to Commissioner Bowie Kuhn, at Yankee Stadium. Abraham was with another young man, who upon being introduced to Smith, was overwhelmed. "Red Smith!" he cried. "Wow! I can't believe it! I'd give anything to carry your typewriter. I've read you for years. You're the greatest man in the world!" Smith stood and watched the young man as he gushed on. Finally, when the young man was drained, Smith turned to Abraham. "Seth," he said, "your friend needs to be examined."

Smith was having a better time with the award than he let on, perhaps even to himself. He had made a comeback as dramatic as some of the athletic heroes he had written about. He had been virtually written off and forgotten, a faded star wandering in the minor leagues, when he got another chance in the big leagues. Then, at an age when many men are retired, he again burst onto the scene, won the most esteemed prize in his field, and reaped his greatest glory.

Coincidence or not, Smith may have revealed his true feelings in his column that appeared on the day the Pulitzer was announced. The column concerned a springtime visit to Claiborne Farm, in Lexington, to see the great old racehorse Secretariat, now retired, who contentedly roamed in a white-fenced paddock. Smith wrote:

Secretariat pulled up and calmly accepted a handful of grass from a visitor's hand. Cameras clicked, other hands reached out to offer grass or pat his nose. He acknowledged the attention with quiet assurance. He knew perfectly well that he was the attraction, he agreed it was only fair, and he stayed there posing as long as an admirer remained. If he were a singer, it would be said that he was generous with encores.

Art Smith also called with congratulations on the Pulitzer. "It's about time," he told Red. Art was retired and living in a modest apartment in a housing project in Parkchester, the Bronx, with his wife, Patti. Their two children, Pat Smith and Georgia Dullea, were gone from home and both making their way in journalism. Art's call was a welcome one for Red, for he felt warmly toward his brother, and the call meant something else, that Art was not in trouble.

Through the years Red would get a call from Patti or one of the kids telling him that Art had fallen off the wagon again and asking if Red would drive him to the sanitarium in upstate New York and whether he had a few dollars to help Art out. Red dutifully complied.

Pat Smith remembered phoning Red one day in 1960. He said that his father was going to Hazelden, a center for alcoholic dependency in Minnesota, and asked if Red would see him off. "If you're there it will help him and give him strength," Pat recalled saying. "There was a long sigh over the phone, and he said, 'Sure, I'll be down.' "

Red, said Georgia Dullea, "always came through" to help Art and his family, but it was obvious that it was a burden. It was the one sad aspect, the one ripple in the relationship. "I perceived Red as somebody going through a kind of suffering act that I didn't think dignified him," said Pat.

Terry Smith recalled that Red could be very critical of Art. Red said, "Goddammit, can he never straighten out? You don't know how many times we've gone through this process. Why can't he realize how much this hurts the children, hurts Patti, hurts the people around him? It's not fair. He's free to do what he wants to himself, that's bad enough, but he's not hurting only himself."

Art had usually been a carefree, loose-ends person, in contrast to Red, who was consistently more disciplined and goal-oriented. "I don't think my father ever accepted alcoholism as a disease," said Kit Smith Halloran. "I believe he thought, as so many of us have over the years, that it's simply a form of weakness."

Red urged Art "to do something about this—you can if you really try." Art would go on the wagon for a few weeks or a few months, and once, when he was writing for the *Herald Tribune,* he didn't drink for nearly three years.

Art's problem wasn't that he drank a lot, but that he drank at all. "He couldn't drink four beers before he was gone," said Pat Smith. "He always felt angry that he couldn't drink and others—like Red —could, because he loved it so much."

"Art," said Kit, "was the storyteller of my youth. He conned me into believing all the good things in the world. He used to tell me that he was my most beautiful uncle. And it was true. He was also my only uncle. He would take care of me when I was very small in St. Louis. A story from those days was repeated for years. There was a red water lily in a pond, and he said that it was ours, 'the only red water lily in the whole wide world.' When we moved to Stamford there was a pond down the road from us, and it had red water lilies. I was so excited. Art came out and I told him about the red water lilies. He was like a little boy who'd been told there was no Santa Claus. The only red water lily for him was that special one of ours."

Red Smith once wrote that Art, with a dreamer's drive, "would quit a job to see the circus." There is no evidence that he actually did that, but the idea was correct. Art quit the *St. Louis Star-Times* and went looking for gold nuggets in the Yukon. He worked on some twenty newspapers across the country. "He could always get a job," Red wrote, "because he was a hell of a good newspaperman, an enterprising and imaginative reporter whose writing was lively and professional. He used to say he was one of the best bad writers around. A lead comes back to mind, done when he was on rewrite at the [*New York Daily*] *News:* 'The firepower of martinis was effectively demonstrated at the New York Athletic Club last night when a guest sprang across the table and bit off his host's nose.' "

Red enjoyed saying that Art beat him to New York and "had established himself as one of the best rewrite men in the city." Red was proud of Art as a newspaper talent and thought that Art was more of a poet than he was. Red suggested Art to Stanley Woodward at the *Herald Tribune* in 1961, when Woodward needed a rod-and-gun writer.

Art's column on the *Trib* was sometimes excellent, and Red crowed that people asked him, "Where'd that bright young outdoor writer come from?"

On occasion the brothers went fishing together. One year they took a fishing trip to Newfoundland and took gentle jibes at each other in their columns. In one, Red led with, "The fishing editor is out fishing like a mink, coolly leaving it to the poor relations to do the work. . . ." But on the following evening, "the fisherman fished and the fishing editor remained in camp committing aggravated literature."

Art introduced one Red Smith column by writing:

Joe Batts Island, Gander River, Newfoundland, July 29—At precisely 3:45 P.M. the Atlantic salmon with Red Smith's name emblazoned along his silver side came hustling purposefully up Jonitons Pond as if life held no other interest.

Twenty-five minutes later, at four-ten, this was so. The eight-pound beauty lay in the bottom of Heber Torraville's canoe, gasping and dying. Mr. Smith, eyes glazed from the battle, lay back in the bow seat, just gasping.

In such a time and place there is no room for banter. Other fishermen, including this so far skunked adventurer, spoke the ritualistic congratulations, then returned glumly to their work, whipping the wind-ruffled surface of this widening of the Gander River sixteen miles up from salt water.

Mr. Smith returned to camp to gloat.

Now it is evening and he is still gloating and I am damned if I will interview him. As a reporter I have done my job, recording his catch after four catchless days in this wilderness. But I won't listen to the details again, smugly, condescendingly told. You want the details, you'll listen to him yourself. Take it away, mighty fisherman.

And Red, with surprise, with modesty, and with glee, described his uncommon success over a finned "brute" that "to four terrified eyes . . . looked like a world's record tarpon."

Back home, there were times when Art's drinking prevented him from writing his column. Pat or someone else would write it for him. Harold Claassen, who had taken over for Woodward as sports editor of the *Herald Tribune* in 1962, would be patient. It embarrassed Red, Pat Smith recalled. "I'm sure there were times when he was sorry that he had helped my father get the job at the *Trib,*" said Pat.

And the hurt and pain and "fury," said Terry, would return to Red. "It was the closest he could come to cursing someone out." The two, said Terry, "would go at each other."

A sibling rivalry existed to an extent. When Red had a collection of fishing columns published, he sent a copy to Art with the inscription, "Ha, ha!" He meant that he had encroached on the province of the outdoors writer. But they could joke about such things, when times were good for the two of them. "Red might have felt a little guilty about his success when Father was around," said Pat, "but Father never said anything to him that I remember that made him feel that way. My father was aware of Red's success, of course, but he felt he was a success himself, and certainly he was in terms of the rewrite business and city-side journalism."

Art, though, thought Red might have taken on airs on occasion. "He might catch him up on something he'd written, exaggerating something," said Terry. "Pop might have lauded his success over Art now and then. I don't think he spared Art any of that. I don't think he'd ever be obvious, but if he was being asked to go on television or he got an offer to do a monthly column in a magazine, it would come up."

Despite their differences, the brothers continued to see each other, to fish, to vacation together at times, and to share a mutual feeling of warmth and concern. In February 1976, Art came down with pneumonia, then suffered cardiac arrest.

On Sunday, March 6, 1977, Art Smith died from heart failure in St. Vincent's Medical Center. He was seventy-two years old. Red Smith wrote the unbylined obituary in *The Times*, and followed that the next day with a column that told about Art's travels, saying that Art "was light of heart and light of foot and that he drank a lot, too much and too often in the opinion of some editors. Once he landed in New York, however, he stayed put."

Red finished with: "Authorities from Euripides to Shakespeare assure us that the sins of the fathers are visited upon the children, yet Art's father was a sinless man who headed the family business —wholesale produce and retail groceries—in Green Bay, Wisconsin. Nevertheless, he had two sons who became newspapermen and each had a son who became a newspaperman, although Art's son, Patrick, escaped into television. It makes one wonder about sin."

When Pat Smith first read that column, he liked it and thought of framing it. As he reread it, though, he found that some of it made him uncomfortable. He had hoped the column would be warmer, and he wondered, "Why did he have to include some of those negative things, like the drinking?"

Was Red's detachment simply a means of protecting himself from feeling too deeply? Pat wondered. Pat and Red had long had a good relationship, fishing together, talking sports. Red was also supportive —though sometimes critical—of Pat's journalism. But Pat resented some of Red's responses to Art's drinking. Red, Pat thought, didn't have to make it seem so burdensome.

"One night sometime after my father had died, Red and I happened to be having dinner and we had a bunch to drink," recalled Pat, "and toward the end, all this came out. Red didn't say anything. I felt terrible, like, 'Oh, Jesus, why are we going through this? Put it back in hiding.' But I was glad I did it. And he said, 'Let's have a drink at the bar.' I said, 'Sure.' And we had a drink at the bar and talked about Joe Louis or something. But that was his only response. It was probably all he could do, which was to say, 'Okay.' "

CHAPTER
15

A Cincinnati Reds rookie sitting on the dugout bench in Shea Stadium before a ball game in 1979 turned to Tom Seaver, the veteran pitcher, and asked, "Who's that old man?" Seaver looked up and saw a short, white-haired man with a slight paunch, wearing a sport jacket and speaking in a scratchy, slow, and articulate voice to another player.

"That's Red Smith," Seaver said, "but don't let his size or age fool you. He's got Nolan Ryan's fastball and Sandy Koufax's curve. In his league the old guy's the best there is."

Seaver liked Smith, professionally and personally. "His writing wasn't flowery, and he told it straight," Seaver would say. "And anyone who can interest me in fly-fishing in July, during the baseball season, has to be good as far as I'm concerned."

Seaver was returning a compliment. "Tom Seaver," Smith had written, "is Jack Armstrong, All-American Boy in a baseball suit. He is an exceptional athlete who can think and talk as well as he pitches. . . . There are twenty-five teams in the major leagues that could get along famously with Tom Seaver and would deem it a privilege and pleasure. There is one team that cannot, or rather, one man connected with one team who can't. This tells us something about the man."

Smith wrote that in June 1977, during a trying time for Seaver when he was a New York Met. He was battling his boss, M. Donald Grant, the Mets' chairman of the board, in a dispute that made headlines for days.

Baseball players had recently won their struggle for free agency, and Seaver, one of the game's best pitchers, wanted an extension of his contract, in lieu of a renegotiation. Seaver had signed a contract *before* the arbitration victory by the players' union. Grant now had labeled Seaver "an ingrate," saying Seaver's intention was to renege on his contract.

Each man attracted supporters, among them two of the biggest names in New York sports journalism, Red Smith and Dick Young.

Young, a columnist for the *Daily News,* had been a star baseball writer for that paper since the early 1940's. He and Smith had been together on numerous stories and had been friendly rivals. Smith respected Young's aggressiveness in reporting, but often disagreed with Young's viewpoints. Once, disagreeing with Young's stance on an issue, Smith wrote in *Women's Wear Daily* in 1968, "Dick Young, a friend of mine, is a great reporter and a fine writer, quick of perception and usually mature of judgment. Then how did he write himself into that blatant self-contradiction? Well, even Homer sometimes nods."

Yet, as the years progressed, Smith became increasingly disillusioned with Young. He felt Young was often guilty of poor taste (from the use of "gossipy" information to make a point to such language contrivances as "horsepit"). Young, on the other hand, saw Smith as "an essayist," in Young's view a pejorative of sorts for a daily newspaperman. For Young, the ideal newspaperman is one who works quickly, writes concisely, and seeks a scoop. Young, a conservative on many baseball issues, often saw the other side from Smith's increasingly liberal views. The Seaver case dramatized their differences.

Now Smith felt Young went beyond the bounds of reasonable reporting in writing that Seaver's wife had been jealous of Nolan Ryan's wife when both men were pitching with the Mets. Young branded Seaver "arrogant."

Smith then wrote about Grant's "tame columnist" who was "on

a paper of enormous circulation." Readers of the continuing Seaver-Mets saga had no doubt whom he meant. In a column on June 3, 1977, Smith mentioned "M. Donald Grant and his sycophants [who] put Seaver away as a troublemaker. They mistake dignity for arrogance."

In Young's column the following day, he again deplored Seaver's position and added:

And now I expect that two or three other columnists will reply to these observations. If I didn't write a column, there are several guys in this town who wouldn't have anything to write about. They seem to pick up the *Daily News* with their morning coffee, and say let's see what he has come up with now that I can disagree with.

One such is a pitiable shell of a once great writer, reduced to lingering on Connie Mack and Ed Barrow [Smith in his column the day before had mentioned Barrow, a long-time baseball executive who had been dead for twenty-three years] and that's too bad because there are so many good stories today that he can work on.

On June 11, Smith and Barney Nagler were at Belmont Park for the Belmont Stakes. Walking down a long corridor to the pressbox, they saw Dick Young coming from the other direction.

Nagler remembers thinking, "Oh, man, why do I have to be here?"

As they drew closer, Smith said, "Hello, Richard."

"Hi," said Young.

Later, Nagler asked Smith how he could say hello to Young after what Young had written about him.

"It's his point of view," Smith said.

Smith did not respond in his column to Young's unveiled comment about him in the *News*. He was not interested in a vendetta of this sort. But Smith's opinion of Young as a philosopher or a literary critic was not enhanced. Sometime later a reader sent a Young column to Smith. "Just in case you missed Dick Young's latest," said the reader, "I am enclosing same for your examination. I am sure there is a shot for you in there some place. At any rate I wonder if you have a comment."

"No comment," Smith wrote him. "Nothing Dick Young writes merits comment."

A few months later, in the fall of 1977, the two columnists were on opposite sides of another highly controversial issue, but this time the often conservative Young took the more liberal stance and Smith the more reactionary. The issue was women reporters in the locker room.

Smith enjoyed his relationship with women. Both his marriages had been happy ones. "I won the daily double," he said. He had loved and been loved by his mother and sister. He adored and was adored by his daughter and stepdaughters. After overcoming his youthful shyness, he was comfortable in the presence of women and generally amused them with anecdotes and tales, but was also a good listener. He could also be supportive. After his friend Jesse Abramson, the *Herald Tribune* sportswriter, died and his wife, Dorothy, was living alone, Smith occasionally called, and he and Phyllis took her to dinner and a show. Not long after Jesse died, Smith called Dorothy and said, "Goddammit, darling, how are you?" Dorothy broke up laughing. When she used to say something that Jesse disagreed with, he'd begin his rebuttal with, "Goddammit, darling . . ." For a long time, Smith told Dorothy, "I thought your name was Goddammit Darling."

And Marion Roach, a daughter of Jim Roach, former *Times* sports editor, saw an attractively masculine side of Smith. "Red's whole manner was flirtatious," she said, "being so jaunty, alive, filled with life and humor."

But women in sports—or out of sports, for that matter—were invariably, in Smith's typewriter, "dames," "dolls," "peachcakes," or "pieces of fluff." Phyllis and Kit scolded him about being "sexist," and in later years he did improve. Smith occasionally had written about women in sports, from a female weightlifter ("a durable vessel" who operated a bar and found it "unnecessary to employ a bouncer") to female jockeys to the young, conscientious tennis star Chris Evert (who "regards grass with less enthusiasm than some other eighteen-year-olds"). But he did support women fighting for equal pay and equal rights on the playing field, though not with the vehemence he exhibited for such issues as the reserve system.

For the most part, though, his work world was male. He viewed women's involvement in sports with the humor he reserved for most areas of sports. In 1970 he wrote:

It is a confession of negligence to admit that until recently little attention has been paid here to the women's liberation movement or its queen mother, Betty Friedan [he had written "Betsy" in his original copy], who was regarded as just another pretty face. This can't go on, however. The daughters of Eve—to say nothing of some sisters of Lucrezia Borgia and the nieces of Lizzie Borden—have come crowding so insistently into virtually every field of sport that all of us are going to have to stand up and be counted soon. . . .

It should be stated that there is no bias, crotchet, or prejudice against dames around here. Some of my best friends are women, not to mention several relatives.

To be sure, a talent for athletic combat has never struck me as the hallmark of the eternal feminine, and the last doll I admired for her muscular development was Gilda Gray [a shimmy dancer during the 1920's and 1930's]. Still, if the little dears think they'd be happier in the arena than in the kitchen, they'll encounter no barriers here.

Equality was fine, Smith said, but one had to keep a certain sense of balance and propriety to it. The same for language. He rejected the construction "Ms.," and in writing about going fishing with Phyllis, he called her, with humor, a "fisherperson." He said, "Let's have equality in speech, but let's not make the language cumbersome."

During the Yankee-Dodger World Series of 1977, Melissa Ludtke, a young reporter for *Sports Illustrated,* was denied access to the clubhouse at Yankee Stadium. At that point, several locker rooms in various sports had been opened to women reporters, notably in pro hockey and pro basketball. Ludtke and her employer, Time, Inc., brought suit against major league baseball, the Yankees, and the city of New York (which owned Yankee Stadium), claiming that exclusion from the clubhouse had been based solely on her sex, and that it violated Ludtke's right to pursue her profession under the equal-protection and due-process clauses of the Fourteenth Amendment. Commissioner Bowie Kuhn said that women should be kept out of clubhouses to ensure "sexual privacy." He added that the result of having women in a locker room where men undressed "would be to undermine the basic dignity of the game."

In a column shortly after the suit was filed, Smith wrote that Melissa Ludtke would have had a better chance of doing her job in the interview room set aside for the press than she would being "buffeted, elbowed and trampled" in the winning locker room after the last game of the World Series.

"Had she been thus occupied," concluded Smith, "she would have missed the gathering in another room [the interview room] down the hall, where managers of both teams and key players on both sides were present to answer all her questions."

This was the last line of the column as it appeared in *The Times,* but there had been another sentence. And *The Times* news service carried it before it was edited out in New York. The line read, "Still, she might have got to see Reggie in the buff." The sentence ran in numerous out-of-town newspapers. It was an unfortunate line, a demeaning line, and *The Times* sports editor, then a woman named Le Anne Schreiber, along with one of her top editors, Paul Montgomery, excised it.

Smith would later say about the women reporters, "If a girl or woman is a qualified sportswriter, an employed sportswriter, then she should have the same sources that I have. All of that. But there is such a thing as a right to privacy. And there are still laws against indecent exposure, although perhaps we don't realize that today.

"The clubhouse is the ball player's castle and he wants a degree of privacy there."

Smith didn't address the fact that if a woman would have the same sources as men, shouldn't she also have the same access at the same time as men and not be limited in any way? It was also possible—as would happen in the future—that ballplayers could wear a robe or wrap a towel about themselves.

Melissa Ludtke knew Smith and liked him. "I don't think he thought through this issue as much as he thought through other issues," she said. If Smith had thought it through, he would have recalled that many lines he delighted in came not from the mass interview but from an aside in the locker room.

For example, after the sixth and final game of that 1977 World Series, the game in which Reggie Jackson of the Yankees hit three consecutive home runs and each one on the first pitch, Tom Callahan went down to the Yankee Stadium locker rooms seeking quotes. Callahan came back and gave Smith one he loved, the one that ended his column that night. After Jackson hit his third home run, he stepped out of the dugout and acknowledged the cheering crowd by waving his cap. "Not only the customers applauded," wrote Smith. " 'I must admit,' said Steve Garvey, the Dodgers' first baseman, 'when Reggie Jackson hit his third home run and I was sure nobody was listening, I applauded into my glove.' "

The following spring, Jane Leavy of the *Washington Post* found Smith sitting by himself in the visitors' dugout at Yankee Stadium, "the scene of Melissa Ludtke's crime," she would later write in a *Village Voice* article:

My assignment that day required a description of the Yankee clubhouse. My press pass gave me access to the dugout and field but not to the press lounge or clubhouse. "It's your fault," I told Smith, as we sat in the dugout. "Not only can't I get a quote, I can't get a hamburger either."

Red looked stricken. "Don't worry," he said, rising, "I'll do your legwork for you."

Red disappeared through the tunnel that led to the Yankee locker room, stopping briefly to chat with a couple of old-timers named Berra and Howard. Fifteen minutes later, he reappeared on the field. Red Smith, who never takes a note, handed me five pages' worth.

Perhaps Smith stopped to chat with Yogi Berra and Elston Howard not only because he had known them for years, but also because he needed a breather. The long walk up the rising runway was getting difficult for him now.

In late 1977, "a bunch of grapes," as Smith described them, had been found in his bladder. The doctor had a different description. He called it cancer. The doctor, Kaare Nygaard of White Plains, New York, believed that all of it could be removed if Smith was operated on soon. Smith felt optimistic, and entered White Plains Hospital in December. True to the doctor's prognosis, the operation was a success, and Smith was soon on his feet and writing his column again. He grew stronger as the months went on, though at age seventy-two, he found that the operation had taken a toll on his strength.

At the end of 1977, his traditional Yuletide jingle included: ". . . For Billy Turner, Seattle Slew, / Tommy Lasorda and Rod Carew / . . . And—in this season, what the hell—We'll tug the toupee for Howard Cosell. . . ."

Smith concluded with:

> Then greetings, friends, you mentioned here
> And you who didn't rhyme.
> Your health, your wealth, your happiness
> For what is left of time.

Smith was still suffering from shortness of breath and assorted other aches and pains, and was obviously sensing his own mortality.

Perhaps heeding his own words, Smith sought to add "happiness for what is left of time." He planned a trip to Maine. In July 1978, Smith called Bud Leavitt, a friend who was sports editor of the *Bangor* (Maine) *Daily News*, and asked "What's going on up there?"

Leavitt said that in three days he was going on a fishing trip with Ted Williams.

"I'd love to see the big guy again," said Smith.

"Why don't you come along?"

To Leavitt's surprise and delight, Smith said he would.

Williams, when Leavitt told him who was coming, said, "Wonderful."

On July 20 and for the next two days, Smith, in wading boots, joined the group (which included a guide, Roy Curtis) along the banks of the Miramichi River around Blackville, New Brunswick. Williams and Leavitt noticed Smith shaking "more than normal," said Leavitt, and looking frailer than usual. "Ted," said Leavitt, "stayed right by his elbow." But, recalled Williams, "you could tell by the way he handled himself that he had done some fishing before."

Smith wrote a column from Blackville on the fishing expedition:

. . . the Williams party had fished through a long and fruitless day at Swinging Bridge Pool on the Miramichi River, a grand stretch of water that annually produces more salmon than the Fulton Street Market. They had seen a dozen or fifteen fish, a few had rolled under their flys and cocked a snoot in disdain. . . .

[On the second day,] something went thumpity-bump under the [city] guy's fifth rib. He lifted the rod tip slightly, felt resistance and twitched the rod twice to set the hook. "Easy!" Ted Williams shouted. "Slow at first, take it easy, don't hurry." . . . Advice flowed faster than the river. . . . "Easy. He doesn't know he's hooked yet. When he jumps just drop the rod tip a bit don't reel too hard if he wants to run let him go don't touch the line with your left hand you're doing fine easy now rod tip up make sure the reel handle doesn't catch on your clothes. . . ."

The fish jumped once, a twisting blade of silver flinging spray aloft. Then he just lay sullen, finning against the current. The strategy was transparent. Like Ali against Spinks, he would loaf through the early rounds, confident that his opponent would tire. On top of the physical strain, the responsibility of tying into the party's first fish, the nervousness in the presence of such a perfectionist as Williams and the burden of advice seemed enough to wear any angler out.

"He'll run in a minute," Ted said. "Get ready." He waded slowly toward the fish. Ted Williams stands six-feet-three and he weighed 205 pounds when they called him the Splendid Splinter. No splinter now, he is the whole bolt of wood. Anybody who was pitching in the American League between 1939 and 1960 would know exactly how that salmon felt when he saw the man approaching, even without a Louisville Slugger. The fish turned and ran for right field.

The reel was making the sweetest music this side of heaven. "Let him go!" the Master cried. "There's plenty of backing on that line. Come on, you have to follow him down because he's got the current helping him."

The spring of the rod was "having its effect on the angler's wrist, but also on the fish." The salmon slowed and was finally taken when Smith led him into a fellow fisherman's long-handled landing net.

Smith wrote: " 'Eleven pounds,' " Ted crowed, 'maybe twelve. On all counts the finest fish that swims.' Even a horse grazing across the river neighed approval."

Smith—"the city guy"—would be reminded "of Shirley Povich of the *Washington Post.* Shirley is a smallish guy who can't hit a golf ball out of his shadow, but once, with one swing on one hole in one round in his life, he outdrove Sam Snead. Catching that salmon when Ted Williams didn't and Roy Curtis didn't and Bud Leavitt didn't, the city guy knew just how Shirley had felt when his ball came to rest beyond Snead's. His glee was unworthy, and secret."

Because Smith seemed so frail and because of the energy it took to land that salmon—about fifteen minutes of hard work—Williams was concerned and helped him considerably.

Williams and Leavitt correctly perceived that Smith was physically uncertain. He was suffering intestinal discomfort, and in August, after his return from the fishing trip, Smith saw his doctor in White Plains. Smith had thought the problem was his bladder. The bladder was all right, but it was discovered that he had cancer of the colon.

Smith would need immediate surgery, and he entered the hospital September 5. "Although it had been caught early, and everybody was pleased and hopeful, there was still the chance that he might not pull through," recalled Phyllis. "And once in a while he was overcome with sadness at the thought of dying. But he wasn't afraid, and he didn't feel cheated. He just thought that he was going to miss a lot, and that made him melancholy."

But he could still be light and quoted a line of Casey Stengel's: "You gotta remember a lot of guys my age are presently dead."

The operation was successful, but a series of mishaps occurred. Smith's doctor left for a trip to Norway and left Smith in the hands of a team of doctors that Smith's physician had confidence in, but that Smith called "the second string." It seemed that they couldn't get him to heal as quickly as they had anticipated. It depressed him, but he maintained good spirits with visitors. Marion Roach came to see him. He was cheerful, but she wasn't. She recalled: "I told him about a story I was going to do on polo"—she was starting out as a reporter—"and I said I didn't know anything about polo. He said, 'The only thing I know about polo is that in other sports the legs go first. In polo it's always the money that goes first.' I was there to make him feel better, and he wound up making *me* feel better."

Smith remained in the hospital for nearly a month and went home on October 3. Phyllis remembers him sleeping a lot, groaning some, so weak he could hardly come down the stairs for breakfast. "He'd eat a little mouthful of something," she said, "and then he'd collapse on the couch." After three days, he returned to the hospital, stayed there a week, came home for a week, went back into the hospital for three more days, and then, on October 26, was released for the last time. "He didn't fight the sickness," recalled Phyllis. "He let himself be sick. But the moment he was better, he completely forgot about it. It didn't haunt him."

Smith did not write a column for *The Times* for nearly four months. First, because the newspaper was hit by a strike from early August to early November, and then because of his surgery. Finally, on Wednesday, November 22, 1978, his column returned. Smith wrote: "I have been in the shop for a valve and piston job," and during that time "sundry events came to pass that might have elicited comments here." One concerned "a wonderfully uninformed essay about America's sports pages" in *Time* magazine:

Perhaps it's a waste of space to comment on it now. Still, it is difficult to let such rancid prose ("that profusion of purposeful perspiration") go by unmentioned.

The magazine made the valid point that the general level of sportswriting and editing is higher than it was fifty years ago. However, it left the impression that its research into sportswriting of early vintage began and ended with Grantland Rice's 1924 lead about the Four Horsemen of Notre Dame.

"It was not until the 1920s and early 1930s," said *Time,* "the so-called 'Golden Age of Sports,' that such platinum-penned scribblers as Ring Lardner, Damon Runyon, Westbrook Pegler and Heywood Broun brought something resembling literature to the sports pages—and, alas, took it with them when they passed."

Long before the Peglers and Runyons there were perceptive reporters brightening the sports pages with scholarship and wit—stars named Charley Dryden, Hugh E. Keough, Bunk MacBeth, Harry Cross and Hugh Fullerton. If the author of the *Time* piece wasn't around when these men were covering sports, there must be somebody around the shop who is old enough to read in the more recent era of John Lardner, Joe Palmer, Frank Graham, Jimmy Cannon, W. C. Heinz, Dan Parker, John Kieran, Stanley Woodward, Cas Adams and Joe Williams, to mention a few in New York alone.

This was a sequel to a column he wrote before his illness, when he took exception to a *Los Angeles Times* piece by David Shaw, crediting *Sports Illustrated* with injecting "literacy" into sportswriting and crediting Larry Merchant, then sports columnist for the *New York Post,* with leading, Smith wrote, "a trend away from cliché-ridden hero worship and toward 'acerbic, trenchant, iconoclastic reportage.' In fairness to Larry it should be observed that he is not only acerbic, trenchant and iconoclastic in his reportage but also good." Smith continued:

Though there is room for doubt that Larry would admit to peopling the nation with a new breed of sports reporter, he did make a major contribution to journalism. . . . However, with all due esteem and admiration for Larry Merchant, it must be pointed out that about the time he was learning to spell "is," Stanley Woodward was [at work]. . . .

Chances are Shaw never heard of them, but perhaps names like Heywood Broun, Irvin S. Cobb and Percy Hammond have a familiar ring. They won their widest fame outside of sports, but newspapers don't print more informative, witty and delightful copy than Cobb's account of the Dempsey-Carpentier fight, Broun on Jack Sharkey's defeat by Primo Carnera or Hammond's description of the "gladiation" in Benton Harbor, Michigan, where Jack Dempsey flattened Billy Miske.

These were men of learning, grace and professionalism one seldom sees reflected today, even in the *Los Angeles Times.* And even in *Sports Illustrated.* Before that dandy little weekly was a gleam in Henry Luce's eye, Westbrook Pegler and Bill McGeehan were deflating windbags of sports from coast to coast. Hell, Charley Dryden had New York howling with laughter before Henry Luce was a gleam in his father's eye.

Smith thought highly of a number of younger sportswriters and columnists, though he said he didn't "see any Peglers or Lardners or Frank Grahams among them."

Smith was open to a variety of styles. "I always felt," he said, "that if you would assign Shakespeare and Dante and Hemingway and Faulkner to report on the same story, to do, say, 500 words on a particular subject, like a ball game, you'd get five completely different reports. And I don't know. . . . I don't think it would be possible to say which one is the best. You might say you liked one the best. But to say this is the right way to report a ball game? I don't know what's the right way to report a ball game."

Throughout his career, Smith continued to strive to be the best writer he could. He looked back on his own stuff and thought he sometimes "didn't need all those words." "I find myself stopping and knocking out the adjectives and the over-done adverb," he said. He struggled for the exact word, though he didn't always succeed in getting it. "You grope," he said. "I've read about Flaubert rolling on the floor for three days, groping for the right word. I haven't rolled on the floor. I can't afford three days. I'll blow two deadlines if I do."

He had been using a large office typewriter at home for several years when a *Times* editor in 1980 asked if he would be willing to learn to use a video display terminal, a word processor connected to the computer system at *The Times*. The editor expected an old man's recalcitrance to new things. "Okay," said Smith, "if it will cut down on typographical errors in the column."

He made the change with only a little difficulty. On occasion, he might forget to tap the "Save" key before turning off the machine and walking away for a few moments. When he returned and turned the machine on, he realized that he had lost several paragraphs. He got angry, he muttered, but he learned.

I once asked Smith if it got easier to write as he got older. He said no. "Writing well," Smith went on, "always has been and always will be one of the most difficult of human endeavors. And it never gets easier."

"Why not?" I asked.

"I don't know," he said. "I know that—well, how many Mozarts are there in the world at any one time? At the very top in any field —and that includes baseball players and football players and race-horses and writers and artists and musicians and lawyers and brick-layers—on the very top level there aren't many. I bet there are precious few superstars among bricklayers.

"But the best are there because they want to be, or had enough self-respect to do a good job. I found that out one time when Frank Graham and I used to ride the Twentieth Century. We got to know most of the crew—the stewards, the car waiters and all. They were great. And we asked one time how a guy got to be a waiter or one of the crew on the Twentieth Century, which was considered the best railroad in its day. And the answer was that he just excelled and became good enough to get the job.

"I'm not implying that I'm a Mozart of sportswriting, but I am on the top level, and you always try to be there without knowing—with no way of finding out where you really stand. But you try to be as good as you can."

He said he got tired of shuffling his feet and saying, "Aw shucks," when people complimented him on his work. Now, he said, "I simply say thank you." He added, "I know I can do a few things well; I'm good at mixing a martini and I'm good at writing a column."

Often, he said, somebody would come up to him and say, "Oh, you're wonderful. I read everything you write. I wouldn't miss anything you write." And then, Smith said, the guy would also praise "some totally illiterate bum, maybe on the same paper, and here I am blushing and dimpling at his early praise. And then he just absolutely disqualifies himself."

Smith, who was frequently asked about the so called "significance" of writing a sports column, said that his contribution might be "to the gaiety of nations." And, "does everybody have to do something 'significant?' I'll leave 'significance' to the political writers." But he always enjoyed something political writer Scotty Reston of *The New York Times* once told him. "You don't know how important sports are to me," said Reston. "The things I cover have no resolution, no end. To go to a game that lasts sixty minutes or nine innings and there's a winner and a loser, and it's done and finished and a complete thing, that's very important to me."

"Maybe," said Smith, "that's important to us all."

He expounded on that subject in the introduction of his collection *Strawberries in the Wintertime:*

The question of what to do with old newspaper columns isn't quite the same as how to dispose of used razor blades, but the difference is negligible. The axiom that today's news wraps tomorrow's mackerel applies to today's column, no matter how stirring the action, how accomplished the performers or how controversial the issues may have been at the time of the writing. This is especially so in a field like sports where today's defeat makes yesterday's victory meaningless, and the scenes, the action and the characters constantly change.

Then why preserve dead columns for public display, as the remains of Vladimir Ilyich Lenin are displayed half a century after his death? The answer, if there is one, is: Because everything written is part of the record of its time. Everyone who writes reflects the age in which he lives, and this is not less true of the sports reporter than of the dramatist, essayist or historian. Games and the people who play them have had a place in culture. . . .

This book is offered as a partial record of what has gone on around the playing fields in the last several years.

And the angle from which he wrote, he would say, is "from within. From your whole experience. Not necessarily with a particular subject, but your experience in other areas. Out of experience comes your judgment."

One day in the summer of 1979, while Red and Phyllis Smith were on vacation in Martha's Vineyard, Roger Kahn called and asked if he could visit. The Notre Dame alumni magazine had requested him to write a story on Smith.

"When's your deadline?" asked Smith.

Kahn mentioned a target date.

"Maybe you'd better hurry," said Smith. "My contract at *The Times* expires in five weeks and I haven't heard a word about renewal."

"You aren't serious," said Kahn. "Your column is the best thing in *The Times* sports section."

"You aren't the editor of *The Times,*" said Smith.

"Red always sweated out the contract," Phyllis later recalled.

Kahn phoned Abe Rosenthal. "Not renew Red Smith's contract?" said Rosenthal. Kahn remembered Rosenthal's voice getting soft, as though "in shock."

Rosenthal told Kahn, "Do you know what Red means to me personally? I get depressed sometimes editing this paper. But whenever I get down, I say to myself, 'Wait a minute. I hired Red Smith.' "

Rosenthal then phoned Smith. "Red," he said, "we want you forever." Shortly afterward, Smith's contract was renewed.

CHAPTER
16

A few minutes after 6 P.M., a half-hour before deadline, on Tuesday, January 8, 1980, *The New York Times* sports department was busy. Editors seated at the front of the long, large room read the reporters' and wire-service copy for general content; copy readers checked for grammar, punctuation, and errors of fact; phones rang and teletype machines clattered. At a video display terminal, a news assistant named Stephen Jesselli routinely checked a story coming in for the next day's paper. It was Red Smith's column. The normal procedure was simply to check the story for garble and to see that it had been received in full, and then to send it on electronically to the editors. Jesselli skimmed the column, noted the controversial nature of it, and decided he should make a printout on the machine near him. He then brought the hard copy to Le Anne Schreiber, the sports editor, who was seated at her desk.

Schreiber and Smith had a cordial but distant relationship—"Red had a distant relationship with the entire department," she would say, "since he rarely came into the office." Schreiber had been named *The Times*'s sports editor in November of 1978 despite the fact that she had little newspaper experience beyond the nine months she had recently served as assistant sports editor of *The Times*. She had been the editor of *Womansports* magazine, an editor at *Time* magazine, and before that was a teaching fellow in the English Department at Harvard. She was well-read and an excellent writer. Schreiber was named sports editor shortly after *The Times* had been picketed and sued by a group of women for what they contended were discriminatory hiring practices. Though some thought that that may have precipitated Schreiber's elevation, Abe Rosenthal said he chose her for two reasons: one was that a good and unusual idea excited him and that the first woman sports editor of a major metropolitan daily was just that. Second, he felt she was qualified, and he believed it would work. Smith liked her, but was dubious about the appointment. Yet Smith, said Schreiber, "did the most supportive thing he could do. He treated it at face value like it was no big deal."

Now, in the *Times*'s sports department, Schreiber began reading Smith's column with the headline "On Playing in Ivan's Yard." It began:

President Carter has warned that the United States might withdraw from the Moscow Olympics if the Soviet Union's aggression in Afghanistan continues. Some voices have seconded the motion. Saudi Arabia has already pulled out, and sentiment in favor of a boycott will spread as Soviet tanks and troops press on with their bloody work.

It is unthinkable that in the present circumstances we could go play games with Ivan in Ivan's yard. The United States should lead a walkout now, making it clear to the Russians that even if the shooting ends and the invading forces go home, the rape of a neighbor will not be quickly forgotten. With their parades and flags and anthems and the daily count of medals won, the Olympic Games are a carnival of nationalism. The festival is a showcase for the host nation to display its brightest face to the world. It is inconceivable that we should lend our presence to a pageant of Soviet might. . . .

Schreiber got up and, still reading, walked into her office and sat down at her desk. She was troubled by the subject matter; just four days earlier Smith's column had been headlined "Boycott the Moscow Olympics." She was also unhappy with some of the language. Continuing on, she read:

Dispatches from Moscow tell of an "Olympic purge" already under way to present the Communist society as an ideal surpassing even the dazzled view

that Lincoln Steffens got. ("I have been over into the future, and it works.")
To scrub up the capital for an anticipated 300,000 visitors, "undesirables"
will be sent out of the city and contact with foreigners will be discouraged.
Dissidents, drunkards, psychotics and Jews who have applied for emigra-
tion are undesirable. School children will be sent to summer camps. Kevin
Klose, the *Washington Post* correspondent, reports that some teachers are
telling their pupils that American tourists will offer them poisoned chewing
gum.

Unofficial sources, Klose writes, sardonically use the Russian word
chistka or "cleaning" to describe what is going on. It is a word with dread
connotations for Soviets because it is the term used in designating the
Stalinist purges that swept millions to their death in slave labor camps
beginning in the late 1930's. . . .

Smith said that, aside from "the garbage" put out by the Olympic
brass, these are games "for individuals, not nations"; the only argument against withdrawal was that it would penalize American
athletes who had endured a period of four years, more or less, of
training, with dreams fixed on this opportunity for international
competition.

"It would, indeed, be a disappointment, perhaps not their first and
surely not the last they will experience," wrote Smith. "But any
measures taken against Soviet aggression will demand sacrifices from
someone. . . ."

Smith also made reference to a fraternal group:

Chances are the savants who write editorials in *The New York Times* today
weren't even reading the page in 1936, but the paper opposed American
participation in the Nazi Olympics of that year. When the Nazis "deliberately and arrogantly offend against our common humanity," *The Times*
said, "sport does not 'transcend all political and racial considerations.' "

In ancient Greece, wars were suspended when the Olympics rolled
around. It says here the Olympics should be suspended when the caissons
roll.

Schreiber rose and called in her assistant editor, Harold Claassen,
who had been the sports editor of the *Herald Tribune,* and discussed
the column with him. She was particularly disturbed about the reference to Klose's report. Two weeks before, Neil Amdur, a *Times*
sportswriter, had done a piece about the Olympics climate in Moscow and had included information about children being taught that
Americans might give them poisoned gum, and about certain others

being sent away. Amdur's piece was sent to the *Times*'s Moscow correspondent, Craig Whitney. He wired back that "no such things are being said or done here," Schreiber would recall.

She and Claassen decided to cut that particular information and to tell Smith about the cut. Schreiber called, but no one answered Smith's phone. He's *always* home, she thought. But he and Phyllis had gone to the theater that night. Smith, like all the other writers, routinely called the office to answer any possible questions the desk might have about his copy. That night, he didn't call in. He had forgotten. "Well," Schreiber recalled, "I'm sitting with a column with bum information, as I understand it. You can't rewrite it because you can't rewrite Red Smith. So the choice was either holding it on the principle that you don't want false information in *The New York Times* or you close your eyes and say, well, it's Red Smith."

She was also disturbed by the language. "I didn't think it was politically sophisticated rhetoric. It was cold-war 1950's language. It would never have been printed on the Op Ed page. It would have stuck out like a sore thumb, so why is it okay in the sports section?"

But Schreiber's main objection was the information that she deemed false.

Schreiber recalled taking the column to the news department, which is on the third floor of the Times building, one floor below the sports department. She showed the column to Allan Siegal, the news editor.

"We can't print all the material," he told her.

"If we take out the false material," said Schreiber, "there's no column, and we're killing Red's column."

"I can't tell you to do that, either," said Siegal.

Schreiber recalled that she next "snagged Abe"—Abe Rosenthal. "It was a very hasty conversation," recalled Schreiber. It seemed Rosenthal was deeply involved in a late-breaking news story. The essence of the "hasty conversation," apparently, was that Schreiber was the sports editor, and should make the decision; but if she had trouble with the column, she shouldn't run it.

Harold Claassen remembers seeing Schreiber return to the sports department. "It had got a negative verdict down there," he recalled. "The decision had been made." Smith's column would not run. In its place a feature story on Red Holzman, the Knicks' coach, was inserted.

Rosenthal would remember that he hadn't been happy with Smith's column. "Red didn't want us to join the Olympics," he recalled, "and there was a denunciation of the United States government. It was really a highly politicized column. It really wasn't only in relation to the Olympics; it was an attack on our foreign policy, which I didn't think was the place for a sports column. It was just a case of his taking unto himself a role that I didn't think was appropriate to the sports column."

The *Washington Post* reported that a reason for killing the column was that the *Times* executives believed it sounded like a crusade. Arthur Gelb, deputy managing editor, would later deny that. "It's ridiculous—*The Times* is a crusading newspaper," he said. "It's *known* for that."

Though the column was killed in *The New York Times,* it wasn't killed in the *Times* news service. Unbeknownst to Schreiber and other *Times* editors involved, the news service had already electronically sent the column out to its 350 subscribing publications—250 in the United States and 100 more around the world. "They're not supposed to do that until it's been through the whole copy-editing process," recalled Schreiber. "But they had. And now, instead of saying 'hold,' they were told to kill the column. So newspapers all over the world saw 'kill' on a column calling for a boycott. They decided that Red was being censored. When I came into the office the next morning, the phones were ringing."

One of the callers was Red Smith. "He didn't call and say, 'Why in the hell did you?' He asked, 'What's going on?' People had been calling him. And I explained and he was very respectful of my position, although he didn't agree."

Schreiber told him, first, that the part about "press[ing] on with their bloody work" sounded like cold-war rhetoric to her.

"Hell, you could have changed it to charitable work," Smith said.

When she said that the facts were possibly wrong, he said, "They weren't necessary for the column; they could have been excised."

"I thought doing that would have butchered the column," she told him.

Smith received calls from "all the networks, news services and newspapers from all over the country," he would say. "This titillated the curiosity of everybody." When Lee Lescaze, a reporter from the *Washington Post,* called Smith and asked about the events—it was the first time, according to Smith, that he had had a column killed in thirty-five years—Smith said, "I never have questioned the right of an editor to say what can go in his newspaper, but I can disagree with that decision as I do in this case." He said he found the flap "a bloody bore" and added, "I can have my own fights inside the office."

When asked what his future columns would deal with, Smith replied dryly, "I'll write about the infield fly rule."

He also said he couldn't be angry at the paper, "just contemptuous." He retained a sense of gratitude to Rosenthal in particular for having hired him nine years before. "Hell, nobody hires anybody who's sixty-six years old," he said.

The nation's press strongly supported Smith. James Wechsler, political columnist for the *New York Post,* called killing the column "an indignity" to "so eminent a sportswriter as Smith . . ." Mary McGrory, political columnist for the *Washington Post,* wrote, "Let us put aside the merits. Let us pass over the freedom of the press and First Amendment considerations. Let us even turn away from the sad spectacle of editors who were willing to face jail to bring their readers the Pentagon Papers suddenly choking over a legitimate expression of opinion by their best writer. . . . What it comes down to is that *The New York Times* has no right to deprive its readers of anything Red Smith has to say."

Though Smith surely enjoyed such comments, he conceded that, "Everyone likes to kick the big, bad, rich, powerful, celebrated, dignified *New York Times.*" Smith would recall, "They took the heat for about a week. Then an editor called me and said, 'This has gone far enough. Will you rewrite the column?' "

On Tuesday evening, January 15, exactly one week after the boycott column was killed, Le Anne Schreiber began reading Smith's column for the next day's paper: "Last week there was an intramural difference of opinion regarding a column advocating that the United States withdraw from the Moscow Olympics. *The Times* killed the column. Editors felt it was simply a restatement of views I had expressed in a column the previous week. I felt differently. . . ."

Smith went on to restate his boycott position, though "not in the same words because there had been developments in the meantime."

In his follow-up piece, Smith did not mention the information that Schreiber had thought false. The fact that Smith omitted reference to that information disappointed Schreiber. "I thought Red behaved very well throughout, except for that," she said. "To me, the false information was the major issue of the piece not running and Red knew it, but he allowed himself to continue being portrayed as the white knight."

The idea of a boycott wasn't an original one, as Smith had acknowledged in his lead. "But as far as I know, I was the first to come out in favor of the boycott," he said. "NBC, which had purchased television rights to the Games, was terrified at the prospect of a boycott," and it had been calling White House aides to try to learn President Carter's position on it. President Carter soon publicly proposed a boycott and would request, and get, the U.S. Olympic Committee to pull out.

Lloyd Cutler, a White House counsel at the time, said that Carter's staff had considered a boycott some time before as one of about seventeen ways to reduce contacts with the Russians, from ending cultural exchanges to the grain embargo. "But," Cutler told Terry Smith, "your father's column gave the Olympic boycott legitimacy and momentum." Ironically, the furor produced by the killed column brought more attention to the boycott movement than Smith could have mustered if the column had run quietly.

While high officials were debating whether to send a U.S. team to the Summer Olympics, the Winter Olympics in February were getting underway in Lake Placid, New York. And the Russians were coming.

Schreiber wanted Red to go. Smith was reluctant. He had not been a fan of cold-weather sports since his days in St. Louis, though he had covered three other Winter Olympics. Sometimes, recalled Schreiber, Red played the grouch. Once she had asked him to do a column on the Cosmos soccer team after it had astonished New Yorkers by drawing seventy thousand fans to the Meadowlands in New Jersey. Smith bridled. As Schreiber recalled, "He said he had no use for soccer, that it was a foolish game, didn't like any game that involved running up and down the court, kicking or dribbling the ball. But he went and wrote a beautiful piece." After Smith had described the numerous pregame activities, he wrote, "When at last the field was left to the players, the quality of entertainment declined somewhat."

Smith, with some cajoling, went to the Winter Games in Lake Placid, and his first column, noted Schreiber, was "formulaic, in the sense that it was bah-humbug Olympics—the carnival, the hoopla— which was an easy stand to take. It was the curmudgeon role. But after two or three days he was responding with delight to Beth and Eric Heiden. He was suddenly an aficionado of speed-skating, and he was writing with great vibrancy, a fresh eye seeing details that nobody else had seen."

One of his best columns focused on one of the three bars in the press center, in the Lake Placid High School. The column was titled

"Mrs. Whalley's Saloon," because the biggest bar was set up in the room where Mrs. Garth Whalley taught home economics. Smith, just as he had when taking baths in Helsinki and Tokyo during the Olympics, delighted in the offbeat. He got Mrs. Whalley a press pass so she could visit her renovated classroom. Smith wrote: " 'I can't believe it!' she said, standing in the doorway of the grogshop. 'I can't believe it!' The joint was jumping as it never had when she whipped up a blueberry cobbler."

It happened that the story was written on the day the U.S. hockey team beat the Russians in a stunning upset. Smith had told Tom Callahan what he had written, and Callahan said, "I'm sure it's good, Red, but you just took a pass on one of the great sporting events."

"Well," said Smith, "you can't have everybody there." Dave Anderson, the other sports columnist on *The Times* (there were only two since Arthur Daley died in 1974), covered the event along with *Times* reporters Neil Amdur and Gerry Eskenazi.

"I'm content," said Smith.

But it wasn't the same Smith who for so many years had followed Stanley Woodward's suggestion and had gone to the *major* arena to capture the smell of cabbage in the hallways.

Still, "Mrs. Whalley's Saloon" was an excellent column, and Schreiber, too, was content.

One night in Lake Placid, Smith, Callahan, and Jack Murphy went to dinner. Callahan recalled:

Now, Red was never a great driver. I'm sure he thought he was a wonderful driver and loved to drive, but you'd always hear cars screeching on their brakes around him. We were coming back from dinner, with Red driving. We had been drinking, but he wasn't smashed by any means. The Olympic organizers had made all the streets one-way. The street leading to the hotel where Red and Jack were staying was only about 100 yards long and a one-way street the wrong way for us. Red went up it. It seemed like a small sin, but he got pinched. The cop was really surly. And when Red got out of the car, the cop said, "Have you been drinking?"

Red said, "Yeah, I had a drink, but I'm not drunk."

The cop said, "Get in the car."

He put Red in the back seat of the police car, and the two drove off in the snow. It happened so fast it was like Red had been swept away. Murphy ran into the hotel to call for help, to try to pull some strings. I started running down the road after the car. I'm running about a quarter of a mile and it's dark. Then up ahead I see a figure; it's Red, walking up the road. Now, Red's seventy-four years old, and he's wearing a blue snowsuit with a little pointy elf hood that *The Times* provided for all its reporters, and he's trudging up this hill in the snow and breathing hard. He said he had talked his way out of going to the station. He had told him who he was and copped his plea. The cop was agreeable to let him go, but Red was still pissed that he didn't drive him back, just dropped him off. So he and I trekked back to the hotel.

That night, Gerry Eskenazi recalls going into Smith and Murphy's suite and seeing them lying in their twin beds, propped up on pillows, covers to their chins, watching television, and each holding a drink in his hand. The long night had ended blissfully.

Lake Placid was not the only site that seemed uphill for Smith. He was finding it harder to trek around the sports beat. Breathing was becoming more painful for him. He had lost some weight though he still showed a decided belly. Phyllis succeeded in keeping him off Scotch—staying with vodka and tonic—but she didn't have as much luck keeping him away from cigarettes. He stopped smoking on a regular basis, but would borrow cigarettes from friends, instead of buying them himself, reasoning that that wasn't really smoking.

In Martha's Vineyard, he still enjoyed visitors, including his family, and went to cocktail parties or dinners with some of the local residents, including Art Buchwald, Walter Cronkite—with whom he went sailing—and James Cagney. Cagney, Smith wrote, "is famous for many talents, including the ability to do more with a grapefruit than Luther Burbank."

In August, Smith received a phone call from a friend in San Diego, and then called Tom Callahan. "I don't want you to overreact, but Jack [Murphy] has cancer," said Smith. Callahan *was* upset.

"Don't think a thing of it," Smith continued. "I didn't when I had it. We're all going to get dead, but it's too soon for Jack." Jack Murphy was fifty-seven years old.

Six weeks later Murphy was dead.

Smith's doctor urged him not to make the long trip from Martha's Vineyard, where he was vacationing, to San Diego for the funeral. Smith was scheduled to enter White Plains Medical Center in a few weeks. Callahan attended Murphy's funeral. Smith called him in San Diego. "Tom," he said, "be my legs at the service, will you? Take notes."

Smith wrote a column recalling "one of my dearest friends," and said he was writing of Jack Murphy "with something close to physical pain." Smith recalled their times together, their laughs. "Red told me later," said Callahan, "that he didn't cry until he finished writing the column."

Shortly after this, Smith entered the hospital to have fluids drained to try to contain his congestive heart failure. He was released ten days later. But he was far from ready to work. In fact, seeing how difficult it was for him to get around at home, Phyllis mentioned retirement, at least giving up daily writing.

"No, never," he told Phyllis. "If I don't write, I'll die." He talked about the way Grantland Rice "snuffed it" at the typewriter. That, he said, was the way he wanted to go, too.

Le Anne Schreiber called and discreetly suggested he cut back from four columns a week to three. "His reply," she recalled, "was a curt 'no.' "

Phyllis recalled, "He didn't want to cut back, and I decided not to pressure him. I wanted him to do what he wanted to do."

Smith's love for his work, and his competitiveness, kept him at his word processor. So, too, did a certain insecurity, which seemed stronger than his contract fears the previous summer. He said to Kit, "Maybe they won't need me, won't need old crocks anymore. There are good guys coming up." Kit asked who. He hedged, she recalled.

He now wrote, as he often had, about the hypocrisy of college football "scholars" and about the college football factories, which he called "unconscionable." He wrote about Coach Chuck Noll's Pittsburgh Steeler team beating Coach Don Shula's Miami Dolphins in the NFL playoffs. Noll was once an assistant to Shula, and Smith wrote, "How sharper than a serpent's tooth it is to have a thankless employee." And he looked back on the 70's, with the upheaval in baseball about the reserve clause, the boom years of the NFL, the increased revenues for tennis players, golfers, and basketball players. "It has been a gaudy decade," Smith wrote, "a yeasty, uneasy, exciting time of revolt and reform and runaway inflation. In sports, just about the same as in the real world."

He also did a piece about Muhammad Ali. Smith had criticized Ali as a fighter and had always questioned whether he could take a punch. But he was convinced, along with many other doubters, that Ali could withstand punishment after the "Thrilla in Manila"—the bruising 1975 heavyweight title fight against Joe Frazier that Ali won when Frazier couldn't answer the bell for the fifteenth round. "Where interest in the rowdy science had been flagging," Smith wrote, "[Ali] revived it; where interest had been nonexistent, he created it. No other athlete in any sport, not Pele in soccer or Babe Ruth in baseball, ever did more for his game than this man did for boxing."

When Smith wrote a retrospective on the 1970's, he said, "If any single individual dominated the sporting scene in the 1970s, it was Muhammad Ali—it was the 70s that witnessed his second coming. In that decade he attained international stature, raised his purse total past $40 million, twice lost his title and twice regained it. He was almost surely the most widely known athlete of the decade, certainly the loudest and, by his own testimony, the prettiest. On the all-time list of heavyweight champions he ranks somewhere between his own estimate (the greatest) and Primo Carnera (an imposter). He was probably the fastest heavyweight; certainly the biggest draw."

An interview with Ali always turned into a lively column, and Ali was one of the few who could motivate Smith to relate a gag. In a phone conversation set up by a press agent, Ali once told Smith about riding in a harness race, and then grabbing the microphone of the track announcer and telling the crowd how he was going to "destroy" all his opponents in the heavyweight division just as he had Frazier and Liston.

"Still on the microphone," Smith wrote, "[Ali] told a joke: 'What did Abraham Lincoln say after a four-day drunk? Anybody know what Lincoln say after a four-day drunk? He say, "I freed who?"'"

In mid-October of 1980, Smith traveled to the World Series in Philadelphia and Kansas City. At the ball park, Smith still got the "dean treatment," as he called it, which he said he hated. "A lot of people deferred to him," recalled Schreiber, "treated him like a saint." At this time, CBS was preparing a segment for *60 Minutes* on him, and television cameras followed after him.

A major question during the 1980 Series was whether George Brett, the Royals' slugging star, could play game three. He had undergone an operation for hemorrhoids. The operation was a success, and Smith wrote from Kansas City: "A strong unofficial movement was on here tonight to get a Nobel prize for George Brett's proctologist."

One day, Smith had lunch with his old friend and roommate from his St. Louis days, Ollie Olson, who then lived in Kansas City. "I went to his room shortly after he got up in the morning," Olson recalled. "He looked pretty old, I thought. Of course, he was very alert. His mouth with that little half-smile and his mannerisms, the way he talked, were the same. It was his physique that was different.

He had just come out of the bathroom and was shaving, and his arms were thin and he had a little potbelly for the size of him. Physically he didn't look strong."

Smith found it difficult to move from the field to the pressbox. Tom Callahan got him notes on Pete Rose. "I talked him through a Rose column, telling him stuff I had accumulated," said Callahan. "He just took notes as if he were interviewing me. The next day he brought the piece to me and said, 'Read this, will you?' "

Much of it was what Callahan had told him—"but there was so much *him* he had applied to it," recalled Callahan—including personal reminiscences and observations of Rose, whom Smith admired as a professional and a craftsman.

"The Phillies' thirty-nine-year-old millionaire [is] the most devoutly single-minded baseball player on earth," Smith wrote.

"Pete Rose has an almost lascivious love of baseball. He plays with total, intense dedication, relishing every moment. At bat he crowds the plate in a knee-sprung crouch, his tough face regarding the pitcher from the middle of the strike zone. The face looks like a detour on Interstate 95, and it wears the fixed wide-mouthed grin of a cat crouched over a mouse and saying, 'Shall I play with him a little longer or eat him up now?' "

On March 2, 1981, Smith wrote on a subject that gave him none of the pleasure that Rose did. Titan, a New Jersey land company, planned to develop a 954-acre tract in the Catskill Mountains as a recreational facility with a pipeline to carry treated sewage to nearby Roscoe, New York. The sewage would be discharged into the Beaverkill River, "the beloved stream that was the cradle of fly-fishing for trout in America," wrote Smith. He said that this "holy place" is "in imminent danger of becoming a sewer."

The story created consternation, particularly with the Titan Group. The chairman of the company, Robert Frankel, complained in a five-page letter to *The Times*. Frankel said that Smith never got Titan's side of the story, and that he had "misstatements or omissions of fact." In a second column, nine days after his first on the subject, Smith said that Titan's was "a legitimate complaint. On controversial issues it is proper to let each side tell its story. My information in this instance came from individuals and conservation groups opposing the project. I am solely to blame for not inviting Titan to reply."

Though he then printed the other side of the story—Titan contended that its development would be beneficial to the area for a number of reasons—Smith didn't change his opinion. "It is plain," he wrote, "that Titan Group, Inc., with its 330,000 daily gallons [of treated sewage], is the Beaverkill trout's best friend."

Smith chastised himself. He told Sandy Padwe, then deputy sports editor of *The Times*, "The first lesson you learn in journalism is to get the other side."

A month later, in April, Smith made another embarrassing error. He wrote that Mickey Walker, the former welterweight and middleweight boxing champion, had "gone to the great speakeasy in the sky. . . ." But Walker was still very much alive. Smith received numerous calls and letters correcting him. "I could have sworn I remembered Mickey's death," Smith wrote to a New Jersey correspondent. "I remember his being found on a Brooklyn street, unidentified and unconscious. I remember his stay at Jewish Hospital in New York and transfer to a nursing home in Jersey. And I thought I remembered reading of his death—until Ray Arcel [a fight trainer] phoned to tell me Mickey was alive." *The Times* ran a correction the day after the column appeared that Mickey Walker, age seventy-nine, "lives in Marlboro, New Jersey."

There were, to be sure, bright sides to 1981 for Smith. He continued to receive awards, one of them being an honorary degree from Brown University. He attended the Brown ceremony, but he didn't make all of the others, and sometimes he unscrewed the wood from the many plaques he'd been given and used it for firewood. "I appreciate all the salutes and hoorays," he said, "but there comes a time when you don't really feel a pressing need for more, and I've reached that point."

He also achieved one lifelong ambition. He made a pilgrimage to Old Town, Maine. He wrote about the longings of a kid from Green Bay, who, with his friend, Larry Servais, had saved pennies for an Old Town canoe—but never saved enough. "For the first time in his life, the former kid had found himself in Old Town, and had steered directly for the five-story plant where Old Town canoes, kayaks, dinghies, and even rowing shells are built," wrote Smith. "Old Town is a translation of the name the Penobscot tribe of Abenaki Indians had for an ancient settlement on the Penobscot River. To a faithful reader of *Boy's Life* and *The American Boy*, it is pronounced 'Mecca.' " In loving detail, Smith described the tour of the plant by Mike Fraunces and Sandy Christensen. Smith concluded: "In the office archives are records on every boat the company has sold in this century. If replacements are needed, the files will have a description of the necessary parts.

" 'Sometimes it would be cheaper to buy a new canoe than restore an old one,' Mike said, 'but the owner wants the old one.'

" 'It can be a sentimental thing,' said Sandy." There was nothing more Smith needed to add to the column.

In August 1981, Smith and Phyllis left the Vineyard for a week at Saratoga Springs, one of his favorite sporting sites. He delighted in the quaint old town, the small old-time race track, and the feeling of the 100-year-old stable area. "Through the fragrance of wood fires burning under the elms in the stable area behind Saratoga's main track," Smith wrote, "wreaths of morning mist curled up to be burned away by slanting rays of sunshine. Hot-walkers led horses in lazy circles between the barns, while other horses stood relishing the flow of cool water from garden hoses trained on their forelegs. Grooms swathed horses with soapy sponges and rubbed them dry. The rhythmic throbbing of hooves could be heard from the track itself, where horses were working."

That year, when the Pulitzer Prizes were announced, Dave Anderson, with whom Smith had been sharing the "Sports of the Times" column for ten years, won for Distinguished Commentary. *The Times* had asked Smith to write the letter of recommendation for Anderson's columns to the Pulitzer Committee. Smith called to congratulate Anderson and told him, "I now feel I've won one-and-a-half Pulitzers." Smith's letter of recommendation began by quoting Anderson's piece on a news conference called by George Steinbrenner not to fire Dick Howser, the Yankee manager, but to allow him to "voluntarily" resign.

"Steinbrenner," wrote Smith, "fed the guests euphemisms, sandwiches and drinks.

"Dave Anderson accepted none of them. He watched and listened and he wrote a column embodying the perception and healthy skepticism of a great reporter, a faultless ear for dialogue, effective writing and the independence of an editorialist, though he refrained from editorializing. If Steinbrenner came off as pompous, bumbling and not quite truthful, Dave let George display those qualities in his own words. . . ."

Smith and Anderson generally spoke on the phone at the beginning of each week, to check what the other was writing about so they wouldn't overlap. Each did four columns a week—they both wrote for the Sunday and Monday papers; Anderson also wrote for Tuesday and Thursday, Smith for Wednesday and Friday. George Vecsey wrote the Saturday column.

"When I would ask Red what he was going to write for that week," recalled Anderson, "he'd say, 'Gee, I don't even know what I'm going to write for tomorrow. But God is good, God will provide. Something will happen.'"

Anderson left fishing and horseracing, for the most part, to Smith, while Smith left basketball, tennis, and hockey to Anderson. And golf. "Dave," Smith had said, "is a golf degenerate." (Anderson is an avid recreational golfer.)

They split up their mutual interests in baseball and boxing and pro football. There was confusion just once. Smith thought Anderson was writing a column on the Westminster dog show at Madison Square Garden, but Anderson decided to write a hockey column instead. That morning, Smith was having breakfast with a friend, who happened to ask how Smith and Anderson knew what the other was writing.

"No problem," said Smith. "We check with each other, or the office tells us. Like today, I know Dave is writing about the dog show. Here, let me show you."

Smith opened to the sports section and saw the hockey column and no dog column. "I'll be a son of a bitch," he said.

CHAPTER
17

"Grandpa," the fisherman asked, watching his companion crawl under a barbed-wire fence, "did you grow old or were you made old?"

The "fisherman" was Chris Smith, son of Terry and Ann Smith. The "companion" was Red Smith, leading off a column. Grandson and Grandfather were going fishing.

The fisherman had a little plastic rod and a spinning reel with a bobber on the line. He had dug worms out of a compost heap and now he dunked one in Turtle Pond on Ozzie Fischer's farm near Beetleburg Corner here on Martha's Vineyard. He watched the bobber intently, moving his bait here and there beside lily pads. . . .

"Do people who don't have a birthday grow older?" asked the fisherman.

Yes, he was told. There is one way to avoid that but the method isn't recommended.

"Some people don't have a birthday," he said. "They have to pick July." After a silence he added an afterthought. "Or December. I'd pick July."

"It's August now," he was reminded.

"Yes, but there'll be another July."

"Oh, you mean next July. Yes, there are always two—last July and next July." He thought that over and smiled as if the idea pleased him, but he made no comment.

The swans were at the far end of their pond. On the water beside the road were a dozen or more mallards.

. . . The fisherman's companion asked: "How old are you now?"

At first there was no answer. Then, tentatively, the answer came, "Six."

"Oh? When will you be six?"

"Tomorrow." His birthday is in September.

They continued fishing and the companion gave gentle instruction on how to catch a fish. Suddenly, there was something on the line.

"There!" [said the companion.] "Good, now crank. No, I'm afraid you're caught in the weeds. Just keep cranking. No! You have a fish. Keep cranking. See him?"

A pale belly flashed right, left and right again. His lips set, the fisherman reeled furiously. He dragged a nine-inch bullhead onto the bank and stared at it.

"Is that the first fish you ever caught?"

"Yes." The tone was hushed.

"Come on, then. We'll take it home and then I'll skin it so your mother can cook it."

"My mommy will laugh her head off," he said. He was jubilant now.

"I'm crazy about my family," he said. "My mother and father and my sister and my cousin Kim, they'll laugh their head off."

That fishing expedition had taken place in 1977, and now in the summer of 1981, both the fisherman and his companion, out fishing again, were perceptibly older. Both had their birthdays in September; the fisherman would be eleven, his companion seventy-six.

Chris's grandfather Smith was having longer bouts of illness than ever before. But he doggedly worked. Only on a rare occasion would he or Phyllis call *The Times* and say that he had tried but was too sick to write the column today.

Late that summer, Kit and Terry arranged to go to Martha's Vineyard to visit. They had decided to try to get their father to at least cut back on his workload—they knew they couldn't get him to retire. They also knew they would have to approach him delicately.

Before going, Terry thought back on the relationship between him and his father in the late 1970's.

"There was a time there," recalled Terry, "when I suppose I was making a deliberate effort to carve out my own career. We were not in as close touch as we once were."

Some of it was due to Terry's difficulty in adjusting to Phyllis as his stepmother, and some of it was due to his wife, Ann, who expected Red to be a more solicitous grandfather. He forgot birthdays and didn't make as great an effort to see their children as she thought he should. Smith had acknowledged some of that. Once, talking with Jane Gross, then a sportswriter with *The Times,* he said that he couldn't relate to his grandchildren when they were very small. And only when he could converse with them did he grow more responsive.

As for Kit, she and her family lived farther away. But when her father was with her four children, as with Terry's two children, they enjoyed his company, his stories, his word games, his taking them fishing. Once, Red sent Kit and her family a regulation-size trampoline for their backyard. "For all the birthdays I missed," he wrote.

But Terry and Red had both been busy. "He was on his beat, and I was on mine," Terry recalled. And they communicated less frequently. It wasn't until the winter of 1980 that they drew closer again. Terry had been having lunch in midtown with his cousin, Pat, when Pat said, "Terry, you know the old man's not feeling well. Who knows how much longer he'll hang on. Why don't you go up to see him?" Terry did.

At about this time, Dick Schaap did a profile of the Smiths, father and son, for the ABC-TV Sunday-night news and captured the affection father and son had for each other. In that segment, Red and Terry, then a White House correspondent, illustrated the similarities and differences in their work. "On the whole," said Terry, "the people he covers are better paid and probably more honest." And about Terry, Red said, "That's my boy—he's way beyond me—he's so far outstripped me that I—I rejoice. . . ."

Terry said later: "He seemed to think I had gone to a world that was beyond him—of foreign affairs, world politics, and so forth. It may have been a reflection of spending his life in sports. But he wanted to stay in that world. He knew it, and it held the broadest possible latitude for him to write."

Red took great pride in Terry's doing so well so early. By thirty, Terry had become an outstanding journalist with *The New York Times.* It had taken Red "a helluva lot longer" to make what he considered "the big time."

On a summer evening in 1981, after arriving in Martha's Vineyard, Terry and Kit drove with Red to a quiet stretch of sand to watch the sun set into Buzzards Bay. They climbed up a small rise of sand; Terry had purposely looked for such a place of easy access to the beach. It was getting cooler, and Red wore a print sweater but strolled barefoot in the sand. They had stopped off to buy beer, and the store had only two cans left, so they shared the two beers as they sat on a log.

The conversation rambled until Kit mentioned Red's cutting back the number of columns a week. Red refused. "I need to feel room to be lousy once a week," he said.

"But you don't have to produce perfection every week," countered Terry.

"But I have a better chance at it if I have more columns to do," Red said.

"You don't need a chance to be rotten," said Kit.

They were getting nowhere with that line of argument.

Kit and Terry mentioned the possibility of poor health one day preventing him from continuing. Since he received no pension from *The Times,* being an independent contractor, they asked how his finances were.

"If you stopped writing and didn't write again," asked Terry, "would you have enough to live on? Can you live without the money from *The Times*?" Red had received regular raises at *The Times* with each new contract and was now up to sixty thousand dollars a year.

"Yes," he said.

"Then it's not money that's making the difference," said Terry. "You don't have to work for financial reasons."

Red said that was so. But they insisted on going point-by-point through his finances.

They knew he was never careful with money matters, from personal finances to business. The Internal Revenue Service often audited him, apparently finding it hard to believe that he was a writer. And when filling out his expense acount, Smith was always general —he called that exercise "plot and character."

He told Kit and Terry of a small annuity, savings of about one hundred thousand dollars, a moderate income from stocks (his "Wolf of Wall Street" stockbroker had made a modest comeback for Smith since the financial beating of '71), and social security. He had also paid in full for the houses in New Canaan and in Chilmark on Martha's Vineyard.

"Maybe that wasn't the most sensible thing to do, to pay up the mortgage; you lose a tax deduction," said Kit.

"You don't really expect me to do anything sensible about money, do you?"

They laughed. They felt a breeze pick up. The sun had gone down, and it was feeling colder. The three rose and, in the twilight, left the beach.

Though failing to get their father to lessen his workload, let alone retire, Kit and Terry were relieved that he had enough to live on should he have to quit working or if *The Times* did not renew his contract. His contract was ending in about six weeks, and he had heard nothing from the paper. "It's an accountant's job to contact me about it, and they often just don't catch it," he told Kit and Terry. But, as usual, he was concerned. His financial foundation was not insubstantial, but neither was it great for one who had worked hard for more than half a century and had achieved the highest stature in his profession. But his attitude toward money remained the same.

"It seemed to Pop," recalled Terry, "that he had a lot of money compared to what he had made all those years in Philadelphia and St. Louis, when he was so desperate that it just seemed like there was no end to it. He never saved much. He never built up any kind of pension. Yet there was a kind of pride in being oblivious to money. I think it was the reaction of somebody who hadn't had an extra nickel for years. Once he got a pretty good salary, he just relished it, luxuriated in it, and spent it."

His regular raises at *The Times* had been unsolicited. "I've been perfectly satisfied," he said. "I make far more money than I ever dreamed of making in the newspaper business. If you're looking for money, you don't go into the newspaper business in the first place."

Earlier that summer, Samantha Stevenson called to request an interview with Smith for *Playboy* magazine. "They are very thorough interviews," she told him. "Have you ever read *Playboy*?"

"To tell the truth, I never read anything in *Playboy*," he said. "I just look at the naked women."

He asked how long she would need, and Stevenson said fifteen hours, which would be stretched over a period of three days. He said he was very tired and that it was too much time and would take too much out of him. She persisted, and he finally consented. When she arrived on Martha's Vineyard in July, Smith had forgotten that he had said yes. His memory, too, was very tired. He didn't ask her to leave, but went ahead with the interview and enjoyed it, losing none of his wit. One day Stevenson brought him a box of candy. Smith ate several pieces and then said to her, "Please, help yourself to your candy."

They sat in his living room, generally with Phyllis and their dog, Putois, nearby. It likely was the most extensive interview Smith ever submitted to, and when finished, it would add up to 550 pages of transcription. The questions ranged from Babe Ruth to "How do you go about being romantic?" ("I'm in love with my wife, simple as that") to "In your heart, do you know if there is a place called heaven?" ("No," said Smith. "I've been told there was since I was a little boy. Do I believe it? I don't disbelieve it. I would like to, yes, believe it.") He went on:

I question whether any person, unless it's a totally devout person with absolutely profound faith, is free of doubt about what happens. You know, the veil through which we could not see. That's Omar. There was the veil through which we could not see, there was the door to which there was no key. Some little talk of thee and me, there was no more of thee and me.

We all wonder what happens beyond the veil. I do. I do not now fear it. Whether I knew, whether I would fear it if I was going through that door and was aware that I was, I don't know.

One time when I was having something called a congestive heart attack, I was in such poor shape I wasn't aware of what was happening. I can remember the evening, I can remember my difficult, labored breathing. But I don't remember any sensation that, "Whoops, this may be it, and here I go and am I afraid or not." No such thoughts. So it's quite possible that nature is kind to us often that way. Many people slip into a coma before they go.

Smith mentioned Wilson Mizner, a raconteur and wit. "When he was dying, they asked him if he wanted to see a priest and he said, 'I want a priest, a Protestant minister and a rabbi along to hedge my bets.' He slipped into a coma, and when he came out, a clergyman of some denomination was sitting next to his bed and Mizner said, 'Why should I talk to you? I was just talking to your boss.' That's a bit more than I can manage."

At the Vineyard that summer Smith also began selecting columns of fond farewells he had written over the years. The idea for the book came from Alfred (Pat) Knopf, Jr., whose father had published Smith's first two collections some thirty years before. It was also Pat

Knopf, while working at the *Herald Tribune* in the late 1940's, who had suggested the earlier collections to his father.

Smith found it somewhat depressing to go back and read the accounts of so many dead people he liked so much. He missed his friends, and he also believed he was spending too much time in the past. But he dutifully edited the columns, with help from Phyllis. She pointed out to him that he was overly fond of the word "flabbergasted." He was surprised at how frequently he used the word and ran a black pencil through many of them. In the foreword to the 1974 collection, *Strawberries in the Wintertime,* Smith wrote, "However many and grievous the faults may be, the reader should know that they would be worse if it were not for the firm editorial hand of Phyllis W. Smith. Make that read mailed editorial fist." Phyllis later noted the acknowledgement with a wry smile. But with both collections, she said, "I hardly did anything. Hardly anything had to be done."

In his writing, Smith still sought strength through simplicity, unlike an author whose novel on baseball Smith reviewed. He's a "young man," wrote Smith "dedicated to the ruthless stamping out of the simple declarative sentence."

Smith continued to work at "the art of rejection," as he called it. That is, editing as one writes. The poet Donald Hall noted about Smith that he could allow "one word to leap forth and do the work of hundreds." Years earlier, Smith had realized that the writer couldn't tell everything, that he had to leave something to the reader's imagination. He believed in Hemingway's "iceberg theory," in which "seven-eighths" of the story is submerged. But if the writer is deft enough to use the significant details, the one-eighth that is above the surface is sufficient and wholly satisfying for the reader. Smith told a story about such esthetic instruction in regard to not revealing everything. As a young reporter in St. Louis, he interviewed Miss Ann Corio. As he would later recall in print, "What, I asked the many-splendored queen of the strippers, was the secret of undressing artistically? 'Always keep your pants on,' she said, 'it brings the boys back hoping next time you'll take them off.'"

Smith considered whether he was over the hill, or, as he said, "if I've lost the hop on my fast ball." He said he would quit if someone he respected—"like Terry"—told him he had lost it. He felt, however, that he had not. "The music is still there," he said. "I still enjoy it. You get gaited to a column as a trotter in a race."

As for not getting around as much as he once did, a rule he had always strenuously adhered to, he now found qualification: "As you get older, you don't always have to be there, no matter what anybody says. Because you have built up a knowledge and an instinct and, whatever, but it takes a number of years before you can build that up. But," he added, "you must go everywhere you can."

Later that summer, Marion Roach brought her mother, Allene, widow of Smith's friend Jim Roach, to the Vineyard and they stayed with the Smiths. Allene Roach was suffering from an unknown ailment—later diagnosed as Alzheimer's disease—that involved loss of memory. Red and Phyllis were very concerned and very patient with her. Sitting on the porch Red recalled to Allene the days when she and Jim and Red and Kay and others traveled by train to the Kentucky Derby and the World Series. Marion would recall Red sneaking a smoke from her cigarettes and coughing a harsh cough that, she said, "made you wince." She noticed his hands trembling. He and Marion walked along the beach and threw a boomerang. She was twenty-five years old, with long red hair and long legs. She was a strong swimmer, and Red said, "I want to see you swim." He sat on the beach and watched her. When she started back, he called, "Swim more. I like to see you swim."

That night, Red watched himself on a rerun of the *60 Minutes* show. Morley Safer noted that when Smith came into a locker room at the World Series, the young writers moved aside to let him get close to the player being interviewed.

"No," Smith said to the television set, "we're all working; I don't get preferential treatment."

Marion remembers that he sat cross-legged, like a boy, and for the most part seemed transfixed by the segment. He was both the philosopher and the curmudgeon. When asked about Howard Cosell, Smith said, "I've tried very hard to like Howard—and I've failed." He said George Steinbrenner is "frequently tasteless." When asked about making a contribution to society through sports, he said, "Hell, I set out to make a living, not to make a contribution. But maybe, like anybody else who writes for the papers, I make some small contribution to—to what? The gaiety of the nations?" When Smith commented about baseball that "ninety feet between bases represented man's closest approach to perfection," he added, in the living room, "I think I've said that one too many times. I'd better knock that off."

That summer, there had been another baseball players' strike, a strike that Smith lamented particularly for the recalcitrance of the owners. When the strike ended, Smith wrote that both the owners and the players suffered through "the long, hot empty summer." Yet baseball, he added, "like the Winged Victory . . . can be mutilated but it will survive."

Readers wrote him in response to his columns. The letters, sent to *The Times*, had been forwarded in a package to the Vineyard. He wrote his replies in shaky but still wide-looped longhand at the bottom of a letter or on the back of it and returned them in a package to Fern Turkowitz, an assistant in the sports department. She typed the replies and sent them off.

One unusual letter came in response to a Smith column that had begun, "Jacques Barzun wrote—and if he isn't sick of rereading it, he has a strong stomach—that 'whoever wants to know the heart and mind of America had better learn baseball.' "

In response, Barzun, the noted scholar and author, wrote about his oft-quoted line:

Dear Red Smith,
I *am* sick of rereading it and my stomach is a shambles (from *scamnum*, the Latin for a butcher's bloody stall).
But that's nothing to the stall the owners have put up and which in your unique judicial prose you have shown for what it is. You ought to be on the bench—or else chair the negotiations. But I see I'm cluttering up this note with too much furniture.
All good wishes. . . .

Smith replied:

Remember What's His Name:
"Ah, yes, I wrote the Purple Cow;
I'm sorry that I wrote it.
But this I'll tell you here and now:
I'll kill you if you quote it."

A travel magazine asked Smith to write an article about "great horse races." He was a month tardy in his response when a second letter arrived, enclosing the first. "On rereading your letter," Smith wrote, "I realized you never mentioned money, pelf, loot or swag."

A reader complained about the large amount of money some ballplayers made: ". . . If not for their ability to play ball, they would be nothing but blue collar workers. . . ." Smith wrote back: "If Beethoven couldn't compose music, what would he have done?"

An eighteen-year-old high-school student asked Smith if he had "a particular saying, quotation, or advice that has inspired you in your life or career?" The letter writer also said he would be "honored and thrilled" to get a handwritten reply. Smith answered: "No, I have no magic formula, and if I wrote a letter in longhand you couldn't read it."

Someone sent Smith, an alumnus of a Catholic university, a short story and asked for his comments. He replied: "I'm afraid your story is a mistake. It would almost surely offend non-Catholics and, I'm afraid, many Catholics as well. The notion that the Catholic school's team is composed of the good guys and the opposition the bad guys is acceptable to nobody."

Someone asked Smith his opinion of a new play about the late Casey Stengel. Smith wrote: "Until I see the play I won't know a thing. Maybe not then."

A young man asked Smith his advice about going to graduate school in journalism or taking a job in journalism. Smith wrote: "If you can get a job, the hell with journalism school."

A young journalist from a small town in Pennsylvania said his sports editor referred to him as "a budding Red Smith." Smith: "I humbly salute any budding Red Smith, having ceased to bud."

A priest wrote: "Granted that the passing years exact their toll, but surely they have not devastated your mind to the extent that you no longer realize that in the [he quoted from a recent Smith column] 'seven-year stretch from 1944 through 1950, he [Earl Blaik] built what may have been the finest undergraduate team' there was with a war going on. Even muscled zombies knew it was better to go to the Military Academy than to be sent overseas to face bullets. . . ." Smith: "Dear Monsignor, What I liked best about your letter was your charity toward 'muscled zombies.' "

Someone complained about a Smith column favoring gun control: "Your suggestion that target competition should be carried out with dart guns is about as sensible as the replacement of professional football players with a giant electronic game in order to reduce violence on the playing field." Smith: "I'm not sure you have not found a desirable substitute for pro football."

A reader suggested a book Smith might write: "Thanks for the suggestion but I'd rather commit adultery than do a book."

Sam Brightman, who had worked with Smith in St. Louis, wrote from Washington: "Dear Red, Some of our children were eating with us when we watched *60 Minutes* this Sunday, and the consensus was that you were less shifty-eyed than most of those interviewed on that program. . . ." Smith: "TV has little to recommend it, but it does put a guy in touch with long-lost friends."

Joe Brieg, a Notre Dame classmate, wrote and said Smith was not right about boxing, which Brieg felt should be "outlawed from civilized society." Smith: "Where else but in boxing would a guy named Lew Diamond be known as the Honest Brakeman because he had never stolen a boxcar?"

A letter from George F. Howlett, a dentist in Green Bay and a high-school classmate, mentioned that he had retired. Smith: "Happy retirement. I still scuffle for our daily pheasant-under-glass."

Then there was a letter from Roger Lowenstein, on the staff of the *Wall Street Journal:* ". . . You bring fistfuls of good reading and sheer delight to this reporter and sports fan every week." Smith: "You're a kind man and I thank you. Can't say more, though wish I could."

CHAPTER
18

The 1981 World Series between the Dodgers and the Yankees opened in Yankee Stadium on Tuesday night, October 20. Many of the writers there had not seen Smith in several months, since he had been away for most of the summer and hadn't traveled to many events because of poor health. Despite the bright red sweater he wore under a tan corduroy jacket, Smith looked wan. He was fleshy under the chin, and his nose was reddish, the mark of a lifetime of long nights. His blue, rheumy eyes looked large behind thick glasses. His hair was snow-white and a little shaggy, curling around the ears. In the press dining room, he sat at a table with a drink, his hand trembling when he raised the glass to his lips. Around the table sat several reporters, and Smith as usual was the focal point, relating anecdotes in his raspy, almost squeaky voice. When he made a subtle witticism, he would pause, with his characteristic "But, uh—" waiting a beat for listeners to respond to the line. I came over and said hello. It was the first time I had seen him since I joined *The Times* seven months earlier. I asked if he had received the birthday card I sent him—Smith's birthday was one month before. Smith said, "Yes,

I'm surprised anybody remembered." He immediately went on to another subject. I was surprised by Red's abruptness. I didn't know the reason for it. Was it me—had I offended him in some way? Or was it him?

Later, in the press working room, I was trying to get my video display terminal to function. I was new at it, and while punching various keys, I said to no one in particular, "Can anyone get this thing to work?" Behind me came a familiar voice. "I don't know much about these things, but I've been using one for a little while." It was Smith. He fiddled a few minutes and the machine suddenly began to hum electronically.

"Well, Red," I said, "after all these years I still need you." Smith smiled. He seemed pleased.

But Smith's temper did seem shorter now. At a bar one night an obnoxious man was drinking nearby, and Smith, recalled Phyllis, "got really huffy, told the guy off. The guy tried to make up afterward, but Red wouldn't let him. That was surprising; he'd usually let a guy apologize. He said, 'I'm getting to be a nasty old curmudgeon in my old age.' "

Phyllis and Terry urged Smith not to fly to Los Angeles for the middle games of the Series. Travel had become so difficult for him. But he insisted. (His last sentence to the Pulitzer Committee about Anderson had been, ". . . He works tirelessly, realizing that the only way to keep a sports column fresh and timely is to be there.")

Smith was now seeking desperately to be there.

Once, when asked what it's like being old in America, he said, "Being old in America is for other people." He said he was "not so good on stairs" as he used to be, and running was out of the question. "Never was enthusiastic about it," he said. "But I can still wade a trout stream." But when he walked in the woods with Phyllis, she recalled he had to stop every few hundred yards. "It frustrated him, made him angry," she said. But he felt he could still cover a Series. He had told the *Playboy* interviewer Samantha Stevenson that he was still learning and growing. He felt he hadn't hardened into conservatism. "I still think of myself," he told her, with a half-smile, "as a young sportswriter again. Quite a dewy-eyed child."

At the Series, Dave Anderson noticed Smith had lost the spring in his step. "He used to zip along," recalled Anderson. Now sometimes he would stop and put down his portable video display terminal and catch his breath. Another writer would come along and, without saying anything, just pick it up and carry it for a while.

Smith didn't protest and thanked him, though it was obvious Smith felt self-conscious.

"It was a tricky thing at the Series," recalled Anderson, "because I didn't want to make him feel like I was hovering around him and yet we all were." The handful of *Times* writers decided that Jane Gross, a *Times* baseball writer, should stay close to him. "He seemed more willing to accept help and concern from me," she would say, "and he was doggedly putting up a macho front for the men."

On the night after the second game, the reporters were to catch a charter flight to Los Angeles leaving at 2:30 A.M. At the curb outside Yankee Stadium, the driver of the press bus was about to close the doors and pull out for the airport. Jane Gross was aware that Smith wasn't on the bus. She had last seen him in the pressbox around midnight finishing his column. She asked the driver to wait, then went looking for Smith. She found him slowly making his way around the building with his computer and suitcase.

At Dodger Stadium the next evening, Smith was jammed into the auxiliary pressbox, instead of being seated in the main press area. "He never complained," recalled Gross. "He just squeezed in happy as a clam. He was staying out of the postgame clubhouse crush, and Dave was working very hard to divide up the column ideas so that Red was not tempted to abuse himself physically."

Instead, he happily abused George Steinbrenner in print. Smith wrote that the Yankees had performed "dreadfully at times."

The key hitters left crowds on the bases. . . . Meanwhile, George III's mastery of the manly art of self-defense continued to hold top billing over children's games. The Yankee owner's proficiency with his maulies was self-confessed. Some hours after the Yankees had suffered their third straight defeat in the earthly paradise of Chavez Ravine, falling behind three games to two, in a Series they had led, two to none, George III called a news conference Sunday night to describe his adventure in an elevator in Los Angeles's Wilshire Hyatt Hotel.

He wore a bump on his head, a fat lip and a bandage on his left hand, but he claimed a knockout victory over two strangers who, he said, had accosted him in the elevator. By his account the strangers spoke ill of New York and its baseball team, and when George III responded, one of them skulled him with a beer bottle. He said he had dropped one with a left hook, removing several teeth, then disposed of the other and left both on the floor of the elevator. In the encounter, he may have broken his hand.

The clear implication was that George III hits better than his subjects.

Smith relished this tale of derring-do, and continued: "After George III had delivered his account of the battle, efforts were made to identify the adversaries or find witnesses. They failed."

Back in New York, after the sixth and final game of the Series, Smith went to the pressroom and drank until two in the morning with a group of reporters, including David Kindred, sports columnist for the *Washington Post*. "He looked tired," Kindred recalled. "And before they closed the room, I remember that he lifted his glass and said, 'To tomorrow's column.'"

After the series, Smith returned home and for the rest of the fall rarely ventured from New Canaan. One time, he went into Manhattan and stayed to see a basketball game at Madison Square Garden. Red Holzman, coach of the Knicks, knew that Smith disliked basketball, and was surprised to see him there. "Hey, Red," said Holzman, "did you do something wrong?"

That night in the press room Smith spoke about what happens to old guys who retire. He told a story about Gene Tunney, the former heavyweight champion who read Shakespeare. Tunney and Smith had once been to a dinner party, and Tunney, drinking heavily, recited something in a mumble that others were unable to understand. Smith did, since Tunney had once sent him a letter with that quotation. Smith now quoted it from memory:

> Time hath, my lord, a wallet at his back,
> Wherein he puts alms for oblivion,
> A great-siz'd monster of ingratitudes.
> Those scraps are good deeds past, which are devour'd
> As fast as they are made, forgot as soon
> As done. Perseverance, dear my lord,
> Keeps honor bright. To have done is to hang
> Quite out of fashion, like a rusty mail
> In monumental mock'ry.

In November and early December Smith stayed home near the fireplace, though not like a rusty mail. He still worked, but with great difficulty. "It was a true act of will," recalled Terry. It was an act of will because writing was so integral to his life—it was not only what he did best, but he was still able to express his feelings, still able to touch people emotionally and intellectually. In mid-December he went into the hospital for ten days for a heart checkup. After he returned home in late December, Terry called. He asked to have lunch and said he'd come out. No, Smith insisted, he would come in. The next day, he drove into Manhattan and Pat Smith joined them. Terry recalls walking to the restaurant from the parking lot with his father. "It was cold but he soon warmed up in the restaurant and began telling stories," said Terry. "It was a long, happy lunch for the three of us and ended about three. I walked him back to the parking lot. He was winded from the cold and he seemed very frail."

Smith found it harder than ever to work. He missed some column days. And his columns often ran shorter than the usual nine hundred or one thousand words—even as short as five hundred words. When he spoke on the phone, Joe Vecchione recalled his voice had a gasping quality and was "sometimes a little incoherent." Smith wrote a column dealing with ESPN, the cable sports network. It was a good column, funny, well-constructed, but it had an error. Smith wrote that the network had planned to televise races on Sunday. It wasn't so. *The Times* had to run a correction.

Terry Smith talked with Vecchione. Both felt it would be less of a strain if Red wrote one less column a week. They agreed that Terry should again try to talk his father into it.

Phyllis doubted he would go for it. "It was almost as though, if he let go of his work, any part of his work, there wouldn't be anything left of him," Phyllis recalled. When Terry called and suggested that Red do one less column, he said, "I'd rather go to the dentist."

On New Year's weekend, Smith covered the plethora of football bowl games from home. The language of the television announcers assaulted his ears. The men who spoke of "picking up the blitz" also said, "And he's swarmed under on the twenty." Smith wrote, "Can a man swarm? Be swarmed?

"Anybody around football who talked like normal people would be out of work in a week."

He added: "Pursuing the dial to bowl games around the clock is a good deal like staring at the Equatorial sun from horizon to horizon. It induces headache, causes the vision to blur and does not sweeten the disposition."

Smith's health was deteriorating rapidly. The seventy-foot walk from his house to his office in the barn was an effort. His doctor told him to rest. Terry called and again brought up the idea of his cutting back, and to Terry's surprise his father agreed. "I guess you're right," said Red. "I won't fight you on that anymore."

Terry recalled, "Then, after talking with his doctor, I raised the ante. I told him that, tired as he was, he shouldn't go to the Super Bowl next week in Detroit. 'Watch it on television,' I said, 'like millions of other Americans, and write your column based on what you see.'

"*Now* I had gone too far. 'Nothing doing,' he said. His voice suddenly got stronger and louder. 'I'm going to the Super Bowl on January 24, *then* a month after that, I'm going to Florida for spring training!' We adjourned the argument."

During these talks, the conversation often turned to dying, but not for very long, recalled Terry. "He always turned to living and what a kick it was." Red said, "I can't complain about dying, not after the life I've had. I've had a very good run. I've always done what I wanted, and I've loved it. My life has been strawberries in the wintertime, and you can't ask for more than that."

On Sunday afternoon, January 10, 1982, Smith, sitting in the window of his barn office and facing his snow-covered yard, began his first column in his new three-a-week schedule. He began to tap the keys on the video display terminal, watching the white letters appear on the small black screen as he typed. When he would finish, he would dial a number at *The Times,* get a buzzing signal, and insert the phone in the coupler on top of the terminal. Then, barring human or mechanical mishaps, the column would be received in the computer system in New York in about five minutes.

Arthur Pincus, the editor on the weekend, had earlier called Smith as usual and asked what he was planning to write for Monday's paper, in order to get a photo to accompany the column and to consider where the column might be placed in the section.

"He said he was writing about writing less," recalled Pincus. "I was naturally concerned." It was out of the ordinary and Pincus decided to call Vecchione to let him know. "Joe and I discussed it," recalled Pincus, "and we thought it might be wonderful. I remember the time I called Red and he said he was going to write about a ringneck pheasant he saw on the Merritt Parkway, and I thought, 'What!' But I didn't say anything to him, and I remember reading the piece when it came in. I took it around to people saying, 'You've got to read this. This is great!' "

Pincus had spoken to Smith at about one in the afternoon. Hours went by and Pincus did not hear from Smith again. About six o'clock, dark now, about a half hour from deadline, Pincus decided he'd better call Smith.

Red said he had written the column and filed. But he didn't get it in. "Maybe it didn't transmit," he said. "Could you check?" I checked. It hadn't come in.

I asked him to file again, and he said he would. He sounded tired. He filed again, and most of it got wiped out. It disappeared, but somehow he was able to transmit part of it. I called the systems people to see if they could help him get the rest. I don't know why, but I remember feeling that I had to help him, help him more than I normally would. Some people in the office said, "Let's go without." I said, "No, we're not going without it. We're going to get it in the paper no matter what happens. We'll close the paper late." . . . We could easily have gone without it. And now I was talking to him, and there was a resigned quality in his voice. He said, "Aw, hell, go with what you have." He had only about 300 words, and that wouldn't be enough. I asked him if he had written it out on paper. He said, "No, but I can reconstruct it." I asked, "Can you reconstruct it in twenty minutes or so?" He said yes. I said, "All right, reconstruct it and then call me back and read it to me. I'll take it over the phone."

I guess he wrote it out longhand, or maybe typed it out on a typewriter. But he reconstructed it, because what actually got in the paper was about 650 or 700 words and that was only about 300 words fewer than the normal column.

He called me and began to read it to me. His voice was very old and shaky. He was obviously either in pain or just so tired that he couldn't really function. He finished and I said, "Is that it? Do you want more? If you want to put in more, I'll stay with you." He said, "No, that's enough." I said, "Are you okay?" He said, "Arthur, I'm about two vodka and tonics away from being okay."

It made me laugh, but I was probably crying a little at the same time. I remember rushing it over to the desk to get it through and get it into the paper, never really having a sense of what he had written because I was concerned with getting it in. I had no clear sense then of what he was dictating.

The column appeared on page three of SportsMonday, with the headline Smith had written, "Writing Less—and Better?" It read:

Up to now, the pieces under my byline have run on Sunday, Monday, Wednesday and Friday. Starting this week, it will be Sunday, Monday and Thursday—three columns instead of four. We shall have to wait and see whether the quality improves.

Visiting our freshman daughter (freshwoman or freshperson would be preferred by feminists though heaven knows she was fresh) we sat chatting with perhaps a dozen of her classmates. Somehow my job got into the discussion. A lovely blonde was appalled.

"A theme a day!" she murmured.

The figure was not altogether accurate. At the time it was six themes a week. It had been seven and when it dropped to six that looked like roller coaster's end. However, it finally went to five, to three and back to four, where it has remained for years.

First time I ever encountered John S. Knight, the publisher, we were bellying up to Marje Everett's bar at Arlington Park. He did not acknowledge the introduction. Instead, he said: "Nobody can write six good columns a week. Why don't you write three? Want me to fix it up?"

"Look, Mr. Knight," I said. "Suppose I wrote three stinkers. I wouldn't have the rest of the week to recover." One of the beauties of this job is that there's always tomorrow. Tomorrow things will be better.

Now that the quota is back to three, will things be better day after tomorrow?

The comely college freshman wasn't told of the years when a daily column meant seven a week. Between those jousts with the mother tongue, there was always a fight or football match or ball game or horse race that had to be covered after the column was done. I loved it.

The seven-a-week routine was in Philadelphia, which reminds me of the late heavyweight champion, Sonny Liston. Before his second bout with Muhammad Ali was run out of Boston, Liston trained in a motel in Dedham.

I was chatting about old Philadelphia days with the trainer, Willie Reddish, remembered from his time as a heavyweight boxer in Philadelphia.

"Oh," Willie said apropos of some event in the past, "were you there then?"

"Willie," I said, "I did ten years hard time in Philadelphia."

There had been no sign that Liston was listening, but at this he swung around. "Hard?" he said. "No good time?"

From that moment on, Sonny and I were buddies, though it wasn't easy accepting him as a sterling citizen of lofty moral standards.

On this job two questions are inevitably asked: "Of all those you have met, who was the best athlete?" and "Which one did you like best?"

Both questions are unanswerable but on either count Bill Shoemaker, the jockey, would have to stand high.

This little guy weighed ninety-six pounds as an apprentice rider thirty-two years ago. He still weighs ninety-six pounds and he will beat your pants off at golf, tennis and any other game where you're foolish enough to challenge him.

There were, of course, many others, not necessarily great. Indeed, there was a longish period when my rapport with some who were less than great made me nervous. Maybe I was stuck on bad ballplayers, I told myself. I told myself not to worry.

Some day there would be another Joe DiMaggio.

When the column appeared, it caused some talk at *The Times*. What was Red saying? What was the purpose of the column? Why write it? Some didn't like it at all. Others liked it very much. It was a kind of summation of Smith's life and times, of his humor, his insights and his character—a looking back as he embarked on yet another turn in his long life. Arthur Pincus noted that this "tough little rooster," as he called Smith, chose a ninety-six-pound athlete, Shoemaker, "this little guy," as Smith called him, as perhaps the athlete he most admired. The other was the smooth, quiet, confident, dignified DiMaggio. Both men were strong, physically and mentally, elegant and doughty, detached and yet passionate in their approach to their work, humble in their acceptance of applause—the traits Smith most admired.

The night Smith wrote "Writing Less" he went to bed early, after the two vodka and tonics he so thirsted for while battling through that column.

On Monday, he was so weak he could hardly move about the house. Tuesday was the same. Phyllis called *The Times* sports desk to say he wouldn't have a column for Wednesday. His breathing became so labored that Phyllis called their doctor in New Canaan. He suggested they call an ambulance to have him taken to Stamford Hospital. Smith said no, he didn't want to go in an ambulance. Phyllis would drive him there. She was upstairs struggling to get Red out of his pajamas and into street clothes when the doorbell rang.

Earlier in the morning, a water pipe had broken and the basement had been flooded. Phyllis called a plumber. He now appeared.

"It seemed like everything was breaking down at once," recalled Phyllis. "I asked Red if he could dress himself while I let the plumber in and took him downstairs. He said he could. When I came back up, I saw he had put some clothes on, but he was taking them off to put his pajamas back on. Then he laughed at himself when he realized what he was doing, poor man."

Red tried to call the office, Phyllis recalled, "and he kept getting the wrong number. He wanted to let them know he had to go to the hospital and he wasn't going to write. But they knew that already."

At Stamford Hospital, Smith was quickly hooked up to life-saving oxygen devices and put under sedation. He looked in great pain. Terry and Kit were called that night and told that the situation was grave. Terry was on a skiing trip in Sun Valley, Idaho. On Thursday morning he flew to Stamford. Kit flew in from Wisconsin and arrived in late afternoon. A blizzard had begun raging in the East, and Terry, encountering airline delays, didn't get to the hospital until midnight, arriving by police escort. He was allowed to go to his father's room.

"He was literally gasping for air," recalled Terry. "He had an oxygen mask over his face and he was taking in deep drafts of air."

There was congestive heart failure and his kidneys were malfunctioning. Terry asked the doctor about hooking his father to a dialysis machine to try to alleviate the kidney problem. "All his systems were collapsing," recalled Terry. "I don't know if he was alert, but his eyes were open and doctors say that in a state like that people know quite a bit about what's going on around them. I spent a few hours with him in the night, talking to him. I said to him, 'Pop, I love you. I'm proud of you. I'm proud to be your son, and I'm proud of the way you lived your life.' "

At about 5:30 in the morning, just as dawn was breaking, Terry and Kit drove back to New Canaan to get some sleep.

Around noon on Friday, January 15, 1982, Phyllis was sitting with Red in the white hospital room. She was holding his hand. "He raised his eyes and he looked at me, right into my eyes," she said. "He looked at me so hard."

Then Red Smith's eyes closed for the last time.

CHAPTER
19

January 20, 1982, was a cold, windy day in Manhattan. Snow from the recent heavy storm still lined the curbs as some 500 mourners bundled in overcoats climbed the steps of St. Patrick's, the twin-spired Gothic cathedral on Fifth Avenue, to attend the memorial Mass for Walter Wellesley (Red) Smith. From the world of sports, they included Penny Rindquist, owner of Secretariat; Pete Rozelle; Wellington Mara, owner of the New York Giants; Sonny Werblin, president of Madison Square Garden; Tom Seaver; and Monte Irvin, the former star baseball player who was representing baseball commissioner Kuhn's office. Numerous journalists and friends, such as Walter Cronkite, Shirley Povich, Robert Daley, Roger Angell, and Bill Heinz, were there. At the altar glimmering with candles, priests went through their rituals. Soon, there were Bible readings by Red's daughter, Kit, by her son, Michael Halloran, and by Patrick Smith, Art's son. There were recollections of Red by Terry; by Jenifer Weiss, Phyllis's daughter; and by Dave Anderson and Tom Seaver.

The celebrant was the Reverend John Quinn, who began by introducing a quote from Smith: "Dying is no big deal. The least of us will manage that. Living is the trick." And Red had performed the trick very well—not perfectly, to be sure, but very well. He had been happy with his friends, his two families, and his work. He had traveled widely, met a fascinating variety of people, and brought millions to see and feel and understand some of the most important —or at least intriguing—events of this century. He had pursued and lived "the deep romance of journalism," as he said he sought when he left Green Bay for Notre Dame, and Notre Dame for Milwaukee, more than half a century earlier..

Robert Merrill, the renowned baritone of the Metropolitan Opera, sang *Ave Maria.*

Tom Callahan, the sports editor of *Time* magazine, had come to the cathedral early, well before the Mass. He saw Merrill there. Merrill, who would not be using a microphone, sang a few notes at various places at the front of the church, testing where the acoustics were best.

It reminded Callahan of a night in Yankee Stadium when Merrill had sung the national anthem, and shortly after, he, Callahan, and Smith happened to be going up together in the Stadium elevator.

"Fine rendition this evening," Smith said.

"Sang the shit out of it, didn't I?" said Merrill.

And Red, remembered Callahan, "broke up."

The afternoon before, under overcast skies, the ashes of Red Smith were buried in the Long Ridge Cemetery in Stamford, Connecticut, beside Kay. Another space beside Red is reserved for Phyllis. Many newspapers and magazines across the country ran warm editorials, and each of the three network's nightly news shows devoted time to Red Smith and his fifty-four and a half years in the newspaper business. The annual stakes race in May at Belmont Park, the Edgemere Handicap, would be renamed the Red Smith Handicap, and funds would be raised to provide a Red Smith Writing Scholarship for journalism students at Notre Dame.

Red Smith had loved to sit around with friends and tell stories until two in the morning. He loved to party, and he loved to drink. "For most of his life," said Terry, "he had a genuine hollow leg. It was astonishing the amount he could drink and still function, and function very well." Shortly after Smith died, Terry was discussing with the doctor the various ailments—mainly kidney failure and congestive heart failure—that finally killed him. Terry recalled, "I said, 'By the way, Doctor, how was his liver?' He shook his head and said, 'Perfect.' "

Shortly after Smith's death, two collections of his columns would be published, *The Red Smith Reader* and *To Absent Friends*. The first would sell about 25,000 in hardcover and the other about 10,000, and each would be reissued in paperback, selling better than any of his books in his lifetime.

On the morning before the burial, Terry and his son, Chris, then eleven years old, went to New Canaan to collect some of Red's effects that Phyllis wanted them to have. Terry and Chris browsed about the house and then in Red's barn office. Chris noticed the video display terminal and sat down at it. He asked his father how it worked. Terry turned it on. "It's almost like a typewriter," Terry said. "You just hit the keys, then you punch the SAVE button, and then you turn it off."

Chris had never typed, and had no knowledge of computers. After a while, Terry left, but Chris stayed at the machine, struggling with the keys. After a short period, he turned off the machine, put out the lights in the barn office, and closed the door behind him. Nobody touched the machine until a few months later, when Howard Angione, systems editor of *The Times,* received the machine back in his office and, checking it out, discovered something in the memory bank. He made a printout and sent it to Terry. It read:

```
RED SMITH WAS THE BEST
I LOVED MY GADDAD SO MUCH
THAT I CRIED AND CRIED
I HAD TO LEAN TO LIVE
WITH IT HE TOOK ME FISHING
IT WAS THE FIST TIME I CAUT
A FISH WEN HE DIAD PEOPLE
TOLD ME THAT HE WAS A GRAET
SSPORTS RITER
I LOVED HIM
SO MUCH THAT
I BROKE IN TERS
HE
WASTHEGRAET
```

Among the reviews for *To Absent Friends* and *The Red Smith Reader,* Wilfrid Sheed's was perhaps the most hard-edged. In the *New York Review of Books,* Sheed, reviewing both books, wrote that even when Smith was writing about non-sports or "sub-athletic" subjects—from Trotsky to the baseball labor relations—"his method remained blessedly the same. All those chortling evenings had not produced the razor mind that some of his fans wanted and celebrated (in fact Red's logic could wobble all over the place, puffed along by his sentiments) but they had produced a wonderful cartoonist in words who could skewer the guilty parties in a dispute even if he couldn't quite skewer the issues. . . ." Sheed added that, though Smith "had a sure sense of the essay form," it was his "phrasing" that made him famous. "Without them," said Sheed, "Red Smith was (to use one of his favorites) just another working stiff."

In *The New York Times Book Review,* Donald Hall, a poet who had written a book about baseball, reviewed the two posthumous Smith collections. Smith, he wrote, practiced "the literary form of the sports column—in his hands something like the sonnet." Hall had his criticisms, particularly with *To Absent Friends.* "A generous and affectionate man," wrote Hall, "he is given to eulogy (the word 'great' uses itself up fast) and sometimes the sentimental distortion; we learn soon enough that the word 'guy,' as in 'class guy,' signals disorder among the sincerity neurons. [Smith didn't necessarily disagree with this. While choosing the columns for *To Absent Friends,* he said one day to his daughter, Kit, "You know, I could get awfully repetitious."] Sometimes we suffer the portentous coda—the sportswriter's devil—as in a column about Red Rolfe, which ends with the brief graph:

" 'Class was something Red had no trouble recognizing. He saw it every morning when he shaved.' "

Despite this, wrote Hall, Smith was never pompous or self-important, and was funny enough "for laughter." He added: "Within the pastoral of the sporting world, general human concerns become isolated and magnified—success and failure, youth, aging and death —so if we have moral ideas in our heads, we have a scene to which we can apply them. . . . [Smith was] on occasion a fierce moralist." Hall added:

Maybe moral ideas become *most* useful in the ethics of decency in prose style. Smith is a writer before he is a sportsman. . . . It seems to me that honest sportswriting helps to keep prose alive. For a culture survives not only through its high-art embodiments; we study beauty less from paintings at the Metropolitan than from daily encounters with an honestly designed beer bottle. It is commonplace to observe that the best newspaper writing occurs in the sports pages, that editorials bore, news stories deaden, features inflate, reviews pontificate. But sports pages do remain lively, play with words (when Mr. and Mrs. Zatopek won gold medals at the 1952 Olympics, Smith called his column "Czech and Double Czech") and seek out figures of speech.

Metaphor is a way of thinking available to everyone, which has nothing to do with elitist education. . . . Shakespeare could talk no other way, and the pit had no trouble following him. . . . So the sports column—as Red Smith did it—becomes a wildlife refuge for metaphor and all liveliness, where language lives and breathes. . . .

I still have columns of Red Smith's that I saved from the 1950's. The pages have yellowed, and when you pick one up, little pieces of paper flake off and drop in your lap. The prose is graceful and literate, the wit irreverent, the humor warm, the insights often penetrating.

Red had his faults. Sometimes, by his own admission, he overwrote, sometimes he was too generous to friends—excusing Connie Mack's racism, for example. He said he had "tried not to exaggerate the glory of athletes. I'd rather, if I could, preserve a sense of proportion, to write about them as excellent ballplayers, first-rate players. But I'm sure I have contributed to false values—as Stanley Woodward said, 'Godding up those ballplayers.' " Sometimes he didn't see the breadth of certain issues (like women in the locker room). Away from work, he sometimes might have been self-involved to a degree that rankled and frustrated those close to him. In later years, racked with illness, he grew crotchety.

But he was also a man who never ceased to grow. He struggled always to improve his writing. Unlike some others, he did not find it confining to remain in sportswriting and did not seek so-called wider horizons, from political reporting to novel-writing. He felt what he could do well was enough and worthy, and he loved it.

When in his sixties, at a time when most men become hardened in their view—"conservative" is the word most often applied—he was able to expand, to become "more liberal."

He mastered detachment, but detachment did not mean withdrawal. He still infused his work with the delight he perceived for the ever-changing "newness" of each day's game. He said his enthusiasm was "self-generating." His was a colorful, variegated world of unusual characters and places and events. He possessed the genius to place the reader into the scene where, through his words, one could experience the emotion and drama and pathos and joy integral to the story he was weaving.

Primary to the success of Red Smith was his integrity: When you read Smith, you knew you were getting an honest and accurate account of the goings-on. He was a writer, with all the power and poetry and steady good sense of the fine writer, but he was perhaps a reporter first.

In a letter to me once, he wrote that in being a newspaperman, "the essential thing is to report the facts; if there's time for good writing as well, that's frosting on the cake." Smith made his reputation with the "frosting." That's what set him apart and elevated him to a position as one of the best writers of his time. Yet he always understood that he was writing for newspapers and that his primary responsibility was to get the facts right.

"The reporter," he once said, "has one of the toughest jobs in the world—getting as near the truth as possible is a terribly tough job." From the *Milwaukee Sentinel* in 1927, where he began his professional career, to *The New York Times* in 1982, he sought to get "as near the truth as possible."

"I respect a good reporter," he said, "and I'd like to be called that."

On January 16, 1983, one year and one night after Red Smith died, some 250 people—including friends, colleagues, and a few Smith family members—attended a Red Smith Pipe Night at the Players Club on Gramercy Park South in Manhattan. Smith had been a member of the Players Club, which is housed in an old wood-beamed mansion once owned by renowned nineteenth-century actor Edwin Booth. Booth had bequeathed his home to actors and their ilk who, at the turn of the century, were generally not considered worthy of membership in other places. Writers, often of humble origins, were included in that pejorative category, and one of the early members of the club was Mark Twain, whose cue now hangs above the fireplace and beside the pool table in the basement.

The Red Smith Pipe Night, a dressy but low-key affair, featured reminiscences of Red Smith and readings of Red Smith's work. Jack Whitaker, the sports announcer, served as master of ceremonies and recalled closing the tent at Saratoga with Smith late one convivial night a few years earlier. Frank Ryan, the former pro quarterback and then athletic director of Yale, recalled Smith, as did the actor

Alfred Drake and the former mayor of New York, John Lindsay. Enos Slaughter, a bright red bow tie nestled under his chin, remembered Red Smith the reporter from the 1940's.

Whitaker then said that he had a tape recording of Smith speaking less than two years before at a dinner in his honor at the National Arts Club. The lights were dimmed, the audience grew quiet, and on a screen at the front of the dining hall appeared a silhouette of Smith at his typewriter.

And then Smith's words, slightly scratchy, a combination of the recorder and the man, were heard in the room. Smith said:

This is a peculiar business we work in. I have to tell you a little about what it's like. There was a sportswriter in Cincinnati years ago named Bill Phelon. He was a bachelor and a lot of people considered him eccentric because he shared his apartment in Cincinnati with a five-foot alligator. And he had a pet squirrel that he carried around the National League circuit in his topcoat pocket.

Bill Phelon loved baseball, and he was kind to animals, and above all he loved Havana. The city of Havana. As soon as the World Series was over, he would go to Havana, join up with his friend Pepe Conte, who was a sportswriter in Havana at the time, and spend as long a time there as his bankroll and the patience of his paper would allow.

And eventually the inevitable happened. Bill Phelon died. And in obedience to directions in his will, he was cremated and his ashes shipped to Pepe Conte. Pepe got a letter and a little package. And in the package was a small urn. The letter said, "Hello Pepe, this is Bill." Bill asked that Pepe rent a small plane and scatter his ashes over Morro Castle.

Pepe was deeply grieved by the loss of a friend and he took the little jug under his arm and went down to El Floridita, one of the places they had frequented, and there were a few hangers-on sitting around the joint, and Pepe put the urn up on the bar and he said to the guys, "Remember Bill Phelon?" Sure, they all remembered Bill Phelon. Pepe said, "This is to Bill Phelon. Have a drink on Bill Phelon." So they all had a drink on Bill Phelon, and Pepe tucked the jug under his arm and went on to Sloppy Joe's.

Went through the same routine. "You guys remember Bill Phelon?" "Sure." "Drink to Bill Phelon." He went on to the Plaza Bar, maybe the Angleterre, I don't know. All the spots that were favorites of Bill's and Pepe's. But somewhere on his appointed rounds, Pepe achieved a state of incandescence and he mislaid Bill Phelon.

Bill was undoubtedly swept out the next morning with the cigar butts and the empty bottles. And I tell this story to make it clear that sportswriters lead glamorous lives and come to unexpected ends. And I thank you.

SELECTED BIBLIOGRAPHY

Books

Allen, Frederick Lewis. *Only Yesterday.* New York: Perennial, 1964.
——. *Since Yesterday.* New York: Perennial, 1972.
Angell, Roger. *Late Innings.* New York: Ballantine, 1982.
Barber, Red. *1947—When All Hell Broke Loose.* New York: Double-day, 1982.
Berkow, Ira. *Beyond the Dream.* Foreword by Red Smith. New York: Atheneum, 1975.
Broeg, Robert. *The Pilot Light and the Gashouse Gang.* St. Louis: Bethany Press, 1980.
Brown, Leonard, and Porter G. Perrin. *A Quarto of Modern Literature,* 4th edition. New York: Scribner's, 1957.
Cannon, Jimmy. *Nobody Asked Me, But . . . The World of Jimmy Cannon.* Edited by Jack Cannon and Tom Cannon. New York: Holt, Rinehart and Winston, 1978.
——. *Who Struck John?* New York: Dial, 1956.
Clark, Tom. *The World of Damon Runyon.* New York: Harper & Row, 1978.
Considine, Bob. *Toots.* New York: Meredith Press, 1969.
Daley, Arthur. *Sports of the Times: The Arthur Daley Years.* Edited by James Tuite. New York: Quadrangle, 1975.
Foley, Betsy. *Green Bay: Gateway to the Great Waterway.* Woodland Hills, Ca.: Windsor, 1983.
Graham, Frank, Jr. *A Farewell to Heroes.* New York: Viking, 1981.
Heinz, W.C. *American Mirror.* Foreword by Red Smith. New York: Doubleday, 1982.
Hemingway, Ernest. *Across the River and Into the Trees.* New York: Scribner's, 1950.
Holtzman, Jerome, ed. *No Cheering in the Press Box.* New York: Holt, Rinehart and Winston, 1974.
Lipsyte, Robert. *Sportsworld.* New York: Quadrangle, 1975.
Morris, William and Mary. *Harper Dictionary of Contemporary Usage.* New York: Harper & Row, 1975.

Palmer, Joe H. *This Was Racing*. Edited by Red Smith. New York: Barnes, 1953.

Powers, Ron. *Supertube: The Rise of Television Sports*. New York: Coward–McCann, 1984.

Primm, James Neal. *Lion of the Valley, St. Louis, Missouri*. Boulder, Co.: Pruett, 1981.

Reichler, Joseph L., ed. *The Baseball Encyclopedia*. New York: Macmillan, 1982.

Rice, Grantland. *The Tumult and the Shouting*. New York: Dell, 1954.

Rowan, Carl, with Jackie Robinson. *Wait Till Next Year: The Story of Jackie Robinson*. New York: Random House, 1960.

Rudolph, Jack. *Green Bay: A Pictorial History*. Norfolk, Va.: The Donning Co., 1983.

Runyon, Damon. *Short Takes*. New York: McGraw-Hill, 1946.

Russell, Fred. *Bury Me in an Old Press Box*. New York: Barnes, 1957.

Silverman, Al, ed. *Best from Sport*. New York: Sport Magazine Library, 1961.

Smith, Red. *The Best of Red Smith*. New York: Franklin Watts, 1963.

————. *Out of the Red*. New York: Knopf, 1950.

————. *Press Box: Red Smith's Favorite Sports Stories*. New York: Norton, 1976.

————. *Red Smith on Fishing*. New York: Doubleday, 1963.

————. *The Red Smith Reader*. New York: Random House, 1982.

————. *Red Smith's Sports Annual, 1961*. New York: Crown, 1961.

————. *Strawberries in the Wintertime*. New York: Quadrangle, 1974.

————. *To Absent Friends*. New York: Atheneum, 1982.

————. *Views of Sport*. New York: Knopf, 1954.

Smith, Red, ed. *The Saturday Evening Post Sports Stories*. New York: Pocket Books, 1949.

Smith, Red, and Richard Mark Fishel. *Terry and Bunky Play Football*. New York: Putnam's, 1945.

Torinus, John B. *The Packer Legend: An Inside Look*. Neshkoro, Wis.: Laranmark, 1982.

Tygiel, Jules. *Jackie Robinson and His Legacy*. New York: Oxford, 1983.

Walker, Stanley. *City Editor*. New York: Blue Ribbon Books, 1940.

Woodward, Stanley. *Paper Tiger.* New York: Atheneum, 1964.

————. *Sports Page.* New York: Simon and Schuster, 1949.

Woodward, Stanley, with Frank Graham, Jr. *Sportswriter.* Foreword by Red Smith. New York: Doubleday, 1967.

Yardley, Jonathan. *Ring.* New York: Random House, 1977.

Selected Articles

Deford, Frank. "Viewpoint." *Sports Illustrated,* June 7, 1976.

Einstein, Charles. "The Case for the Red Smith Irregulars." *Harper's,* March 1955.

Grant, James. "Just a Newspaper Stiff." *The American Spectator,* November 1977.

Green, Lloyd. "At 140 pounds, Red is Tops in Sports." *Chicago Sun-Times,* November 7, 1950.

Hall, Donald. "First a Writer, Then a Sportsman." *The New York Times Book Review,* July 18, 1982.

Hewitt, Bill, as told to Red Smith. "Don't Send My Boy to Halas." *The Saturday Evening Post,* October 21, 1944.

Kahn, Roger. "Red Smith of the Press Box." *Newsweek,* April 21, 1958.

Kern, John L. "Red Smith in the Final Innings." *Writer's Digest,* June 1982.

Leavy, Jane. "Red, He Juggled for Us." *The Village Voice,* November 20, 1978.

Mailer, Norman. "Ten Thousand Words a Minute." *Esquire,* February 1963.

Newsweek. "One was the Brightest." August 27, 1956.

Newsweek. "Smith the Bleeder." October 10, 1949.

Novak, Ralph. "Sportswriter Red Smith Goes to the Head of the Class." *People,* February 3, 1975.

O'Neil, Paul. "The Gifted Mr. 'Red' Smith." *Life,* January 9, 1956.

Sheed, Wilfrid. "Reds." *The New York Review of Books,* September 23, 1982.

Smith, Art. "My Brother's a Sports Writer." *Sign,* June 1959.

Smith, Red. "Green Bay, Wisconsin." *Lincoln-Mercury Times,* January–February 1953.

————. "Mucha Trucha." *Outdoor Life,* April 1953.

————. "My Press-Box Memoirs." *Esquire,* October 1975.

————. "Out of the Fleabag." *Elks,* March 1946.

Time. "Red from Green Bay." May 15, 1950.

INDEX

Catalog

If you are interested in a list of fine Paperback
books, covering a wide range of subjects
and interests, send your name and address,
requesting your free catalog, to:

McGraw-Hill Paperbacks
1221 Avenue of Americas
New York, N.Y. 10020